Kurt Hahn

From the German edition by
H. Röhrs

English edition edited by
H. Röhrs and H. Tunstall-Behrens

Preface by H.R.H. The Duke of Edinburgh

Routledge & Kegan Paul   London

Original German edition first published by
Quelle Meyer, Heidelberg, 1966, as
Bildung als Wagnis und Bewährung: Eine
Darstellung des Lebenswerkes von Kurt Hahn
Editor Hermann Röhrs

English edition with additional material
first published 1970
by Routledge & Kegan Paul Ltd
Broadway House, 68–74 Carter Lane
London E.C.4
Printed in Great Britain
by Western Printing Services Ltd, Bristol
© *this edition Routledge & Kegan Paul 1970*
No part of this book may be reproduced
in any form without permission from the
publisher, except for the quotation of
brief passages in criticism
ISBN 0 7100 6885 9

Contents

List of Illustrations

Preface

His Royal Highness The Duke of Edinburgh

Salem is an immense Cistercian monastery in the south of Germany. How it came into the possession of the ruling family of Baden is a longish story in which Napoleon played a part.

Salem first came into my life when in 1931 my second sister Theodora married Berthold only son of Prince Max of Baden who figures quite prominently in this book.

The Baden family lived in what was called the 'Prelaten Quartier' or 'Abbot's Quarters' at the east end while the school occupied the monks' quarters in the rest of the main building as well as several other buildings which together formed the monastery complex.

I first became aware of Hahn's existence while staying with my sister and brother-in-law on holiday. Oddly enough one of the senior boys at Salem at that time was a Prince George of Hanover, later to marry my youngest sister Sophia and later still to become Headmaster of Salem during the critical period of reconstruction after the war.

As the Founder Headmaster as well as a man with distinctive mannerisms and a considerable reputation his name inspired awe and respect. However I was then a small boy at a very conventional English preparatory school and the sight of his large figure, head bowed and covered by a very wide-brimmed grey felt hat with a handkerchief clenched in his teeth, rather naturally struck me as a little funny.

Not long after, I left Cheam a year earlier than usual and went to one of Salem's preparatory schools at Spetzgart on the lake of Constance. Hahn had left by then and as the struggle between the staff and the Nazis developed so the whole structure of the school began to disintegrate. After two terms at Spetzgart I moved to Salem as a junior. I did a little work and played a bit of hockey but discipline and organization were breaking down. Nazi flags started to appear and a number of senior boys joined the Hitler Jugend. Some stuck out against the Nazi takeover and one senior boy in particular, who was responsible for us juniors, so displeased these thugs that they caught him one night and shaved his head. I lent him my Cheam 2nd XI cricket cap and I hope he has got it still.

The next term I moved on to Gordonstoun where in company with some twenty other boys we found ourselves starting a new school. The rest of the story is fully described in this book.

I don't pretend for a moment that I was conscious at this time of all Hahn's theories and methods in education, but looking back I realize that the whole basis and foundation of Gordonstoun was coloured and influenced for Hahn and those of the boys who had been at Salem by our experience of Nazi Germany. I realize now that it was probably the dreadful mass hysteria of the Germans of those days which made Hahn so aware of the need to encourage boys to develop as responsible individuals; strong enough in mind and character to reject the standards of the mob and to resist the temptation to run with the herd.

Foreword

Sir Robert Birley

I shall not attempt in this short Foreword to write an account of the life of Kurt Hahn. The very varied contributions in this book tell of this. I shall try rather to express what seems to me to have been his most important contributions to European education, and also something of what he has meant to me during my life as a school-master.

There is an obvious division in his life, before and after his being forced to leave Germany when Hitler and the Nazis came to power and his coming to this country. But the same principles inspired him throughout. Perhaps for an Englishman they can be seen most clearly if one looks back at the German scene. The sharp contrasts make them stand out. But it is a mistake to think that the moral collapse in German society in the 1930s was merely an isolated German phenomenon. It was a manifestation in an extreme form of a diseased condition in Western civilization as a whole, and it is something with which we are familiar today. Kurt Hahn's reaction to this is therefore very relevant to us now. The most obvious symp-tom of the spiritual disease of our civilization is the widespread feel-ing among men that they have lost control of their own destinies. The determining movements are too large for them to influence; in particular, the organization of industry—and it makes very little difference whether it is under private or national control—is their inexorable master. What Hitler seemed to offer the Germans above all else, both individually and as a nation, was the faith that they could control their own destinies. Even the violent nationalism of his movement was largely an expression of this.

I should say that there were two main elements in the education provided under Kurt Hahn at the school of Salem in South Germany. The first was the insistence on personal responsibility—a responsibility not only for others at the school, but also for those living outside it. This was Hahn's answer to that sensation of helplessness, of surrender, which gave Hitler his opportunity. In the Outward Bound schools in this country and the school of Gordonstoun we can find an insistence on the same educational principle. It may be seen very clearly in the training of boys in rescue work at sea and on the mountains.

But there was a second element quite as important. It was most impressively expressed in an address Kurt Hahn gave in Hamburg on 16 February 1933. (The significance of the date, seventeen days after the Nazis gained power, will be obvious.) It began with a study of the Fascist state and educational ideals, and an account of Fascism which seems to make inevitable the uncomfortable statement which is to be found in the address, that, if one looked at the educational principles of the Italian youth organizations, 'you find that you might be quoting the whole Salem Certificate of Maturity with its capacity to endure hardships, to face dangers, a talent for organization, prudence, a fighting spirit, presence of mind, success in dealing with unexpected difficulties'—and then come the words, 'Only one item is and must be missing: The power of carrying out what is recognized to be just'. And a little later, '*Sacro egoismo*, sacred egoism. There is also sacred lying, sacred killing, sacred perjury, sacred breaking of promises.'

To speak in this way of Fascist principles at that moment was indeed courageous, but Kurt Hahn went on to turn to his own country, and it was with continual references to the state of things in Germany that he gave his reasons why Salem rejected Fascist education. Among these was to be found this one: 'We need to be able to feel that as a people we are just and kindly. On this consciousness depends our inner strength.'

A sense of responsibility for others and a refusal to surrender this responsibility; a belief that in kindness and a love of justice lay strength: it is not surprising that already before 30 January 1933 Kurt Hahn had made clear his own position and that of his school.

On 23 August 1932 Hitler sent a telegram of congratulation to two Nazi storm-troopers who had been convicted of the murder of a Communist, whom they had trampled to death in the presence of his mother—the famous Beuthen, or Potempa, murder. In a circular letter to all members of the Salem Association, the Old Boys of the school, Kurt Hahn, referring to this telegram, showed that the parting of the ways had come: 'It is a question now in Germany of its Christian morality, its reputation, its soldierly honour: Salem cannot remain neutral. I call on all members of the Salem Association who are active in the SA or the SS to terminate their allegiance either to Hitler or to Salem.'

Working in Germany after the war and knowing of Kurt Hahn's action on this occasion, this message of his was constantly in my mind. To secure the adoption of the principle expressed in it seemed to be the essential task for German educators. And we in this country should realize the courage that lay behind it. It was a very solitary action. Perhaps I may quote words I wrote about it in an address given in December 1947: 'Salem was a school of considerable renown, but its Association had no standing comparable with that of certain societies connected with the German universities, the famous *Altherrenverbände*. If one of these societies of past university students had taken such a step, the effect in Germany would have been profound. As far as I know, such action was never even contemplated.'

I have dwelt on these happenings of what may seem to some as far-off days in a foreign country because I think they should be known in this country, and because I believe that Kurt Hahn's contribution to British education is implicit in the stand he made then. In recent years, however, he has gone further, for the conception of the Atlantic Colleges shows an appreciation that one of the main educational tasks of the future will be to bring together young men and women of different nationalities.

I myself came to know Kurt Hahn first when I was a young assistant master. He had recently come to England after being imprisoned by the Nazis. Since then we have had many conversations. Quite often I have disagreed with him. Sometimes I have felt an English discomfort at hearing moral principles expressed so earnestly. I have felt at times that he takes boys almost too seriously, so that there is some danger that they may become too self-conscious. Perhaps he has sometimes forgotten that it is healthy that some of a boy's time should be such as was expressed by Polixenes to Queen Hermione about his boyhood friendship with Leontes in *The Winter's Tale*:

> We were, fair queen,
> Two lads that thought there was no more behind,
> But such a day tomorrow as today,
> And to be boy eternal.

But I cannot recollect that I have ever had a conversation with him after which I have not found some idea or point of view or even a phrase left stirring in my mind. One of these I recall especially vividly; in fact, it has been with me ever since. It is, I think, an idea which is of special value in education today when it seems in the nature of things that so many of our pupils are destined to be rebels. 'Whenever you have to deal with a boy', he said to me once, 'who is a rebel, remember that you must not fail at some time or other to get him to face the question, Are you going to be a fighter or a quarreller?'

This book is a tribute to a great educator, one who has shown much originality and caused many to think deeply about education; but whose strength lies mainly in his determination that certain simple ideals should be put into action, above all that there must be no surrender of responsibility and no denial of the overriding claims of kindness and justice.

Acknowledgments

H. Tunstall-Behrens is indebted to Dr Röhrs, the editor of the German version of this book, which was published for Dr Hahn's eightieth birthday. A selection has been made from this volume, and much revision carried out to bring the various subjects up to date. New chapters were introduced in order to present a book more oriented to the interests of a much wider and English-speaking public.

Tom Price's contribution, given as the Edmund Rich Memorial Lecture, 1966, is included by kind permission of the Royal Society of Arts.

Editor's Note

The authors in this symposium are writing independently and express their own opinions. Readers who had hoped to find here a consistent assessment of Dr Kurt Hahn's life's work must wait for a biographer and even for a later generation to judge him. This book cannot pretend either to be a complete account of his many activities, but a selection rather. Hahn's connection with the foundation of the International School in Ibadan, Nigeria, for instance, or the co-educational boarding school at Box Hill, Surrey, both of which were established by former senior masters at Gordonstoun, could not be followed through for lack of space, and this applies to the story of the Trevelyan Scholarships at Oxford and Cambridge, a pioneer attempt to select scholars for their character and practical achievements beside their academic ability, a scheme which has fallen in abeyance since the first edition of this book. Hahn has been active in many human projects. One with which he associated and worked for was the successful persuasion of the many public and official life-saving institutions, both in Europe and the New World, to accept the mouth-to-mouth method of artificial respiration. This too has been outside the scope of this book, but the bibliography, with the careful notes of the author, is perhaps the best indication of Hahn's copious thought and action.

While acknowledging these limitations, however, this book can claim to be the first attempt under one title to present the panorama of a remarkable life's work. The record of the several fields in education where his influence has been decisive may be familiar to some, but it has not probably been appreciated hitherto in this country that Hahn had a career in politics behind him before he ever put his hand to education, and that in a sense he never ceased to be the active philosopher politician.

It may be helpful to those who come fresh to the subject to have a time chart of events relevant to Hahn's career, so that the various chapters have some context.

Time Chart

Some events associated with Kurt Hahn

Hilary Tunstall-Behrens

GERMANY

1886   Born a German of Jewish parents.
        Educated Wilhelmsgymnasium, Berlin; Universities of
        Berlin, Heidelberg, Freiburg, Göttingen, and
        Christchurch, Oxford.

1910   Publishes a novel on an educational theme.

Politics

1914   Political career: acted in a freelance capacity, closely
        connected with the German Foreign Office. Advises
        against torpedoing of civilian ships. Private Secretary to
        Prince Max of Baden, the last Imperial Chancellor of
        Germany after the war. Prince Max resigns and Hahn
        later edits his memoirs.

1919   At Versailles as Private Secretary to Dr Carl Melchior, a
        delegate.

Salem School

1920–33 Headmaster of Salem School in Germany, near Lake
        Constance (a co-educational public boarding school,
        founded by Prince Max).

Reinhardt, Privy Councillor in the Prussian Ministry of Education, was the first Director of Studies. Hahn himself taught history and politics.

1921   Attempted assassination by political enemies.

Late 20s Plans to introduce his educational ideas in Germany on a wider basis (a race against Hitler) were unsuccessful.

The Nazis

1932   After the Beuthen (Potempa) murder, Hahn published a telegram to all the Old Salemers, challenging them to break with Hitler. He followed this up with open criticism of the Nazis in public speeches and the Press.

1933   Hahn taken into custody.
He is released, due to the intervention, amongst others, of Ramsay MacDonald, and escaped to England.

GREAT BRITAIN

Influence

In England Hahn was in close touch with Barrington-Ward, later Editor of *The Times*, when he sought to expose Hitler's ruthless nature and the concentration camps. During the war he was at one point invited to give his views on German soldiers' training and its bearing for the British to the Adjutant General, Sir Ronald Adams, personally.
He sought in vain to persuade the British to appeal to the resistance movement in Germany and bring about a negotiated peace. He was outspoken against atomic warfare after Hiroshima. He travelled in Germany after the war hoping to influence the reconstruction of the German educational system.

Gordonstoun

1934–53 Headmaster and founder of Gordonstoun School,

Morayshire, for boys. Prince Philip was educated at the
school, and later, under Robert Chew's Headmastership,
Prince Charles was also at Gordonstoun. The ideas
which ultimately gave birth to Outward Bound and the
Duke of Edinburgh Award grew from Gordonstoun
activities: schooner voyages, Finland sledge expedition,
King George VI playing field, Moray badge, County
Badge and public services, such as Coastguards, Fire
Service, etc. (The fact that teams from Salem School
won the Schools Athletic Cup at the White City in
1935, 1936 and 1937, had aroused an interest in
Gordonstoun's methods of training.)

1938   Hahn becomes a naturalized British subject.

1940   Gordonstoun moves to Wales for the duration of the
       war, returning in 1945.

1941   First Outward Bound Courses run in Aberdovey, Wales,
       the brain-child of Hahn and Lawrence Holt of the Blue
       Funnel Line.

1945   Salem, which had been taken over by the Nazis towards
       the end of the war, was reopened.
       Hahn, brought up in the Jewish faith, but already for
       some years a Christian by conviction, becomes a member
       of the Church of England.

1946   The Outward Bound Trust is formed, Chairman, Sir
       Spencer Summers, M.P.

International Scene

1949   Anavryta, the Greek Gordonstoun, was founded in close
       association with Hahn, as were also the following
       schools in the post-war period: Luisenlund in
       Schleswig-Holstein; Battisborough in Devon; Rannoch
       in Perthshire; Box Hill in Surrey; Dunrobin in
       Sutherland; and the International School in Ibadan,
       Nigeria.

1951   The first Outward Bound courses are run in Germany

for the young crews of the sailing barques *Pamir* and
Passat. (See separate Table for the growth of the
Outward Bound movement all over the world.)

1953   Hahn is made an Honorary Doctor of Law by Edinburgh
University.

1956   The County Badge is planned on a national scale and,
with Royal sponsorship and Sir John Hunt as the first
Director, the Duke of Edinburgh Award Scheme gets
underway.

1962   The first International Atlantic College at St Donat's
Castle, Wales, for sixth-formers is started. Now under
the Chairmanship of Lord Mountbatten and renamed
the United World College of the Atlantic, it is planned
to make other foundations abroad. Atlantic College has
pioneered the sixth-form college in Britain and is
seeking to obtain a wide acceptance of an international
qualification for university entrance in Europe and the
New World.

1964   Hahn is awarded the C.B.E.

1966   Hahn's eightieth birthday.

Further Honorary degrees

1956   Hon. D.Phil., Göttingen.
1961   Hon. D.Phil., Tübingen.
1966   Hon. D.Phil., Berlin.

Further Decoration

1961   Grosses Verdienstkreuz des Verdienstordens der
Bundesrepublik Deutschland.
1962   Freiherr-vom-Stein Prize, Hamburg.
1968   Foneme-Prize, Milan.

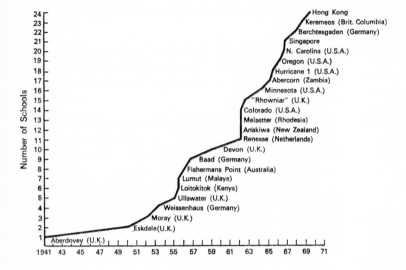

Number of Schools

Hong Kong
Keremeos (Brit. Columbia)
Berchtesgaden (Germany)
Singapore
N. Carolina (U.S.A.)
Oregon (U.S.A.)
Hurricane 1 (U.S.A.)
Abercorn (Zambia)
Minnesota (U.S.A.)
"Rhowniar" (U.K.)
Colorado (U.S.A.)
Melsetter (Rhodesia)
Ańakiwa (New Zealand)
Renesse (Netherlands)
Devon (U.K.)
Baad (Germany)
Fishermans Point (Australia)
Lumut (Malaya)
Loitokitok (Kenya)
Ullswater (U.K.)
Weissenhaus (Germany)
Moray (U.K.)
Eskdale (U.K.)
Aberdovey (U.K.)

1941 43 45 47 49 51 53 55 57 59 61 63 65 67 69 71

Hahn

Donald McLachlan

It was in 1934 that I first came into Kurt Hahn's orbit. He was then forty-eight, in his prime of energy, creative activity and topicality as a teacher. He had arrived less than a year before, an exile from Germany, released from prison and enabled to leave the country thanks only to the personal intervention of Ramsay MacDonald. The long persecution by the Nazis of his school at Salem had begun, and a new sister foundation was forming in an old mansion in Moray-shire. Now its headmaster was engaged in the first of his extra-ordinary explorations of British society, in search of disciples and supporters and benefactors. Thirty years later, he was still doing for Atlantic College in Wales what he was then doing for Gordonstoun in Scotland; and the Outward Bound schools, the Duke of Edin-burgh's Award, and the Salem-type foundations in the United States, Greece and Africa were planned or in full operation. As Golo Mann says later in this volume, Hahn may have failed in politics, but he was a man who got important things done with the energy and cunning of an accomplished politician.

For my part, I had recently joined the foreign sub-editors' room of *The Times* with nothing to distinguish me from my colleagues except recent knowledge of Germany and a brief experience of teaching at Winchester. One day I was sent for by the Assistant Editor, Robin Barrington-Ward, who said he wanted me to do some-thing for him as a personal favour. 'Do you know Kurt Hahn?' he asked. I had heard from German friends about Salem and his troubles with the Nazis, but no more than that. 'Kurt is an old friend,' said B.-W. 'Our friendship goes back to Oxford in pre-war days. I love him dearly and want to help him; but he is a most determined enthusiast and I cannot give him in this office the time and thought he will expect. Will you look after him for me?' The invitation to become intermediary—even buffer—between one's editor and his friend offers opportunities that no young journalist will sensibly refuse. 'What would it involve?' I asked. 'Keeping in touch with Gordonstoun,' B.-W. replied. Discussing Hahn's educational and political ideas with him, helping with any writing that he wanted to do, ensuring that nothing in his plans of public interest was missed by *The Times*.

I accepted at once. After my own Winchester experiences, I was curious to know what Hahn thought of public schools; and it was obvious that he would have much of value to say about Germany. Our first meeting was at Brown's Hotel, in one of those great sitting-rooms where he worked and gave audience. I was immediately enmeshed in what I can only describe as the Hahn cause. I use the word with hesitation, for it has a German flavour; but any attempt to describe his work and ideas should have that flavour. Although it is thirty years since he became a British subject and twenty years since he joined the Church of England, his ways of thinking, his English style, his view of history, even his appearance, remain noticeably German—reflecting a liberal pre-war culture which is little known in this country. German, too, is the feeling he communicates of ideas on the march, of a play of politics and education in which he is active. For his allocutions—'talk' is an insufficient word—are not the sermons of a preacher, but the explanations of a producer, interpreting character and plot—indeed, life itself—to the players, in the drama of school and family.

It was not to be expected that such characteristics would make easier Hahn's progress as a British headmaster and educational thinker, even though Gordonstoun was from the first conceived and presented as an international school. Many liberal persons knew of him as one who had challenged the Nazis in Germany and would continue his defiance from Scotland; but others thought they saw strong Nazi influence (or a traditional Prussianism) in his preaching to boys of self-confidence and self-mastery, to be achieved by such disciplines as athletic training and sea and mountain rescue work.

Enthusiasm as the tonic for listless adolescents; team-work to harness the individual; dedication in service to the community—these
were ideas well known, as they thought, to our own traditional
advocates of cricket, cadet corps and the prefect system in the
boarding house. But they sounded quite different, even somewhat
sinister, in the eloquent parable language of Hahn with echoes of the
Bible, of Plato's *Republic*, of the sayings of his remarkable Jewish
grandmother and of the philosophy of Edwardian Oxford. And when
Hahn asked his British audiences: 'What happens in adolescence to
your children who in the nursery are so self-confident and happy?',
they resented the question, because it disturbed complacency. However, this very suspicion and opposition from older schoolmasters
and parents was an additional reason for some of the young to
be interested, and even enthusiastic. They felt, as I did, that this
prophet from Germany had flung open the windows of classrooms
and dormitories and pointed to the mountains and the sea, where the
human spirit could learn its limitations and, with practice, master
them.

It is understandable that some of Hahn's ideas should have become
associated with Nazi methods in the minds of people of the left who
could not distinguish between the Salem and Hitler Youth concep-
tions of discipline—which were, in fact, worlds apart. Yet, only the
year before his arrival, he had sent to all old boys who were members
of the Salem Union a circular letter about the Potempa murder for
which the Nazis never forgave him. Some storm-troopers in Silesia
had trampled to death a young Communist in front of his mother.
They were condemned to death by the civil court and Hitler sent a
telegram demanding not their reprieve but their release. 'Your freedom,' he declared, 'is our honour.' Hahn in his letter said:

> Hitler's telegram has brought on a crisis which goes beyond
> politics. Our soldiers' honour, our Christian civilisation, our
> good name are at stake. Salem cannot remain neutral: I ask
> everyone of you who are members of the Salem Union and of a
> S.A. or S.S. to break with Hitler or with Salem.

Perhaps the friendship of *The Times*, in the earliest days of exile,
helped gradually to overcome public misunderstanding. Certainly
the paper was kind to the projects that he launched in the next seven
years: the County Badge scheme, the first draft of Outward Bound,

the reform of infantry training and the plea for more enlightened physical education in schools. Nothing did more to get Gordonstoun widely talked about than the success of the Salem athletics team in the public schools sports of those days. For three years at the White City they won the trophy and for two years they were runners-up. Admittedly, the standards in other schools were low; but the achievement of a small school with few special talents to draw on required some explaining away. Those who inquired closely discovered that the school's best athletic successes were with children of sub-normal health, of frail physique, with sensitive and timid natures. The secret was patient, daily self-training.

A visit to Gordonstoun in those days (1935) made a puzzling impression. I recall wondering how the boys there, so various in their abilities and backgrounds, would get through their examinations with what seemed a scratch staff. The music and the riding were well looked after, and Hahn himself was specially proud of the teaching of mathematics through navigation by an officer of the Merchant Navy and of the boys' activities with the Morayshire coastguard. One heard about the Headmaster's eloquent teaching of history, which paid much attention to the Treaty of Versailles (Hahn had been at the Peace Conference as a young attaché) and to the politics of ancient and modern times. One felt, too, the influence of the monastic disciplines, and the vocabulary of the *Republic* would suddenly spurt into a breakfast-table conversation. Not knowing of Hahn's long search for health in the Scottish countryside years before, I was surprised that he felt so deeply at home in Moray.

It quickly became clear that his expectations of *The Times* and of his old friend went beyond Gordonstoun and education. Barrington-Ward was deeply interested in Germany and was convinced that the Versailles Treaty and French post-war policy were largely to blame for the Nazi hold on the majority of Germans. With this diagnosis Hahn at first agreed. He tried to believe that 'Hitler was only the condoner of cruelties' and that he wanted nothing more than to right the wrongs inflicted on his country. Where they differed as the years of appeasement passed was in their estimates of Hitler's ability and willingness, to restrain the passions he had unleashed. B.-W. remained hopeful until the Nazi occupation of Prague; Hahn ceased to hope long before Munich.

Years later Hahn, who was never afraid to change his mind and who would say, like Churchill, that he would rather be right than consistent, thought better of the treaty, and was prepared to admit that there was an evil drive in the Nazi movement which should not be attributed solely to the injustices and frustrations of defeat, and which nothing would appease.

It is, however, reasonable to see in Hahn's ardent advice one of the main influences holding Barrington-Ward, and therefore *The Times*, to a belief in a decent, Christian stratum of the German people on which resistance to Hitler could be built with encouragement from outside. From his work between 1915 and 1917 with the German Foreign Office and General Staff, advising them on political warfare against Britain, he knew the ways of thinking of the Army, the Churches and the Civil Service. Just as he had then turned his knowledge of the British ruling class to Germany's advantage, so he now wished to turn his knowledge of the German ruling class to Britain's advantage. In both cases, as Golo Mann insists, the objective was not a patriotic victory, but a reconciling peace; and Hahn may well have felt that his access to influential circles through B.-W. could be as valuable as had once been his access to Ludendorff through Colonel von Haeften.

Although Hahn used his influence to make known the horrible facts coming out of the concentration camps, he did not, as I remember, care to work publicly with the people in Britain who were most prominent in speaking and writing against Germany. He was tenderly sensitive to the embarrassments of a refugee's position; he knew the errors to which exiled politicians are prone. As allies he preferred the gentlemen of England, to her people; not because he was a snob, but because he knew that his own kind of German would listen to them. To the Left Wing Book Club he preferred the English Liberal—the more like his beloved Prince Max of Baden the better. I recall how Hahn, once satisfied that a British visitor knew about that remarkable statesman, would illustrate point after point from the practice and philosophy of his Salem patron. I have, too, a vivid memory of his tone and expression when he presented me at Brown's with the English translation of the Prince's *Memoirs*: it was like a sacrament. Indeed, Hahn at his most solemn and deliberate, eyes intently cast down, bending from his great height and awaiting with folded hands the effective moment to speak, sometimes has the mien of a priest. At such a moment it is hard to believe that the same man used to be seen until quite recently running round Green Park after dusk to keep himself fit.

Change of work and travel interrupted my liaison work; but others have remarked how quickly and easily friendship with this man can be resumed where it left off, even after years of silence. Perhaps because he has no small talk; he enquires earnestly and with considerate memory about one's family, comments on one's apparent tiredness or freshness—and then the dialogue is resumed where it left off and we are back into the world of politics, education and character. I enjoyed more than anything helping Hahn from time to time with speeches and articles. He was less confident than he is now of his English idiom in writing; yet even then I sometimes felt it would be philistine to correct his natural elegance of style in the name of correctness. He would listen intently while one explained why 'slothful' was perhaps slightly archaic, or that 'holy wrath' was a locution probably unheard by the British public since the time of Carlyle. Sometimes the correction was not accepted and we were presented with some memorable phrase, which was to stay in the language.

Advice was also sometimes offered to him, though seldom sought, about the anecdotes of which he had a vast stockpile. Told in the wrong place and at the wrong moment, his stories of Scottish shepherds and tinkers and other simple people with something to teach of truth and beauty, could sound a little corny. Yet I must say that I have never seen anyone smile at them in Hahn's presence. The point is made in such a gentle and intoning voice, with such a modest inclination of the head, and with such a glint of amusement in the eye, that one might be listening to Kurt the eldest son, telling his younger brothers stories by the Wannsee Lake in far-off days. How is this talk, the vital part of his technique of influencing and persuading people, to be defined? It is only slightly didactic, and direct exhortation is, in my experience, unusual. It is a form of preaching, but not in the manner of the pulpit. It is argumentative, but fair and never quarrelsome. Where a logician would set a trap or turn a flank, Hahn tells a story. I would describe it as intimate rhetoric, with something of Dr Johnson in its confidence and something of Socrates in its invitation to join in the search for truth. Rationalist psychologists may disdain his analysis of the souls of the young; businessmen at first distrust what they think is the jargon of impractical idealism. But one has only to hear Hahn analysing a problem of discipline with a Salem master, or considering the tactics of a campaign with his supporters (and Prince Philip in the chair) to concede that the rhetorician is capable of the closest down-to-earth reasoning. In 1917 a friend of Prince Max wrote to him praising in Hahn the quality of *realpolitische Idealität*—the pursuit of high-flying ideas by methods which will get results.

Of the telling of parables and the coining of phrases I take a few examples from an address given at Maidstone in 1962 to an audience of people interested in the service that youth can give and the educational value of the experience. Hahn referred scornfully to those who say that all is well with the young and that whatever is wrong is the fault of adults. They form, he said, 'the trade union of the peace-of-mind preservers'. 'I know parents,' he continued, 'who negotiate with their children as if they were a foreign power.' For that, he warned the laughing parents in the audience, children were not always grateful. 'I had a boy,' said Hahn, 'who was never contradicted in his lifetime by his parents. I inquired one day about his St Bernard dog. He replied, 'I am very worried about the dog. It is with my parents and, as you know, they have not much educational talent.' With this kind of story, delivered with the most charming smile and revealing a confident intimacy with the young, the prophetic figure would win the audience to his side.

Then follows the diagnosis, in essence unchanged over forty years: 'The young to-day are surrounded by tempting declines—declines which affect the adult world—the decline of fitness, due to modern methods of moving about; decline of memory and imagination, due to the confused restlessness of modern life; decline of skill and care, due to the weakened tradition of craftsmanship; decline of self-discipline, due to stimulants and tranquillizers. Worst of all, the 'decline in compassion', due to the 'unseemly haste with which modern life is conducted'. Then to illustrate the decline in compassion, Hahn told a story from the shattered Berlin of 1945. He had been taken by an American friend to see the refugees from the Russians arriving at the Lehrter Station. This friend had rescued many such Germans at the risk of his life. As they watched the heart-rending sight of homeless, sick and bereaved, the young American sergeant in the driver's seat of their jeep went on listening to the jazz programme from the radio. He was a kindly-looking man, but he looked surprised when he was told angrily to switch it off. 'What then was wrong with him?' asked Hahn. 'He had a dispersed mind, which he could not assemble even before the majesty of death.'

Then he asked his audience the question that has made him most unpopular among his superficial critics: 'What is it that is done to our children that their puberty should deform them? They have the joy of movement; they have an enterprising curiosity; they are ready for sensible self-denial; they dream ahead, and they have a faithful memory, and, above all, great compassion.' He regarded it as his mission in life to 'unseat the dogma that the loss is inevitable'. 'The guardian angels of adolescence' must be the healthy passions: the zest for exploration and research; the love of music and painting; the passion for building; active sympathy for the needs of your neighbour; the love, particularly in girls, for protecting the weak. The satisfying of such passions, he would stress, required stern self-discipline. 'The well-meaning educator who flatters and humours the young not only does a disservice to the community, but also damages the individual by depriving him of opportunities of self-discovery.'

Just before and during the Second World War, when Hahn was dealing with such departments as the War Office, the Political Warfare Executive and the Ministry of Education, he would take care to consult his friends about the kind of language and presentation most likely to assist his cause. In attention to detail and persistence in contact-following he was a masterly conspirator. In the late summer of 1940 Hahn was making progress with his campaign in Whitehall for a system of training in agility, fieldcraft, stamina and self-confidence which would make the British infantryman in a few months the equal of the young Germans who had begun their preparation for war years earlier in the Hitler Youth. He was offered an interview with the Director of Military Training in Whitehall, and was advised to present his proposals in the simplest and briefest form. Discovering that his old link-man with *The Times* was at Southern Command Headquarters, Hahn had me sent for through the War Office and given two days' leave to visit London as his adviser. As this was the time when the German invasion of Kent and Sussex was expected daily, if not hourly, my Colonel was understandably inquisitive about what business in London with Herr Hahn

1   Kurt Hahn receiving the Honorary Doctorate of Law at
Edinburgh University from his ex-pupil the Duke of Edinburgh,
1953

2 Kurt Hahn

could possibly be more important than my duties at Wilton House with General Auchinleck.

I was fetched by car, so that Hahn could explain on the way up to London the nature of the conspiracy and the tactics to be employed. We worked out a brief statement of the advantages which the young German soldier was believed to have over the British, and an outline of the remedy which the experiences of Gordonstoun had shown to be possible. If the General was impressed, then we would offer to return the following day with a detailed training scheme to be discussed with his advisers.

So it worked out. The Major-General—he was most unfortunately killed in a motor accident not long afterwards—was charmed by his visitor, understood at once the advice that Hahn had to offer, and asked for the detailed memorandum that was suggested. My role was to interrupt when Hahn became too eloquent, to restate one or two propositions in the simplest possible manner, and to offer reasons for thinking that the Germans would not attempt invasion, and that there was therefore time to carry out fundamental changes in battle-training and preliminary conditioning of men. When we came away, not unsuccessful, Hahn found it difficult to understand why I chuckled again and again at the picture of an ex-German headmaster and a mere Lieutenant on the General List explaining to this high officer how soldiers should be trained. He thought it wonderful and characteristic of Britain at war that such a meeting should be possible. So did I!

From 1940 right through to the failure of the conspiracy of July 1944 against Hitler there were unsuccessful efforts by Hahn to give political substance and moral appeal to British propaganda to Germany. He believed that a British statement of war aims which gave promise of a reasonable peace might cause in all ranks of German society a split which would widen and deepen as Hitler found his difficulties increasing. It is still a matter of argument whether this analysis was right so early in the war, when the Nazis were basking in success. But the particular Germans to whom Hahn thought he could look for action against Hitler were of little interest to the men then in charge of British political warfare against the enemy. Although the authority for their work lay with the Foreign Office, the planning and writing for the B.B.C. and other media was done for the most part by men of left-wing views—men like Richard Crossman,

Patrick Gordon Walker and Hugh Green—and others under *émigré* influence, who chose as their audience and potential allies the workers of industrial Germany. The non-party, idealistic, Christian appeal to churchmen, generals, civil servants, professional men and academics which Hahn favoured was not yet within the imaginative grasp of British propagandists. If it were to be attempted at all, it would have to be made by individuals and groups who would be reported indirectly to Germany through neutral newspapers and wireless.

There was a further fundamental difficulty. When Hahn began pressing his views on Whitehall through friends he did not perhaps understand how impossible victory for Britain then seemed. True, everyone rejected the idea of defeat; but hardly anyone could see how the *Wehrmacht* was to be beaten. The mere mention of peace terms in those days smacked of defeatism. For Hahn's ideas to work it was necessary to have a British peace party whose motives and courage would be above reproach or suspicion. That did not exist, because the quarter from which its inspiration might have come—the radical, humanitarian, internationalist left—was committed to winning an ideological war against Fascism. Their object was not an honourable peace with Germany and Italy, but the destruction of the Nazis and their doctrines. Hahn, the liberal Jew, who had suffered at Hitler's hands ten years before, was too moderate for them.

Hahn has on occasion said that he was prevented from putting his views personally to Churchill because it was feared that he would convert the Prime Minister to his vision of a Christian resistance in Germany checking Hitler in full course. It may be true that men like Brendan Bracken kept him out, but my own view is that such an interview might have been for Hahn a disaster. Whatever Churchill's record showed of magnanimity in action and sentiment, he was in no such mood in 1940-1. The men closest to him—Beaverbrook, Lindemann, Bracken—would not have understood, let alone accepted, what the Headmaster of Gordonstoun was cunningly aiming at. They knew nothing of Hahn's brilliant record as a political warfare expert in the First World War. Later, when the Soviet Union was forced to become Britain's ally, and the United States was forced by Japan to follow suit, the time had passed for the exclusive and subversive Anglo-German dialogue which Hahn believed he could bring about with Churchill's help. The British no longer had control of their own policy; any public initiative towards peace terms in 1943-4 would have roused the bitterest suspicion in Moscow.

During the last three years of the war I lost touch with Gordonstoun and its Headmaster, then carrying on precariously and enthusiastically in Wales. But once Germany had surrendered, I heard of his return to an exhausted, shattered and disillusioned Germany to breathe on the embers of Salem. After twelve years of struggle, the Nazis had prevailed and imposed their will; the school narrowly escaped becoming in 1945 a *Trotzburg*—a point of backs-to-the-wall resistance to the French advance. Men and women of the staff survived, and they returned to show that the spirit of the place was not dead. Indeed, it may be said to have been freshened by the conspiracy of July 1944 against Hitler, in which old boys were prominent. Those were days of incredible activity by the Headmaster, then approaching his sixties, moving between Baden, Scotland, Wales and London. He found time to speak out firmly against Hiroshima, protesting against total war, quoting Franck, the American physicist, in condemnation of atomic weapons and Plato and Thucydides against the indiscriminate slaughter of an enemy.

Hahn had been distressed and alarmed at the steady brutalization of the Allied conduct of the war, which he claimed was happening: the hushing-up of the Katyn murders of Polish officers, the bombing of Dresden and Hamburg, the behaviour of the Russians as they advanced through Eastern Europe, the failure to offer hope to the German people. Henceforth he would return again and again to the deep error of casting away the moral advantages that we had had over the Nazis when the war began, and the effect of these events on the young. Hahn was to admire the spirit of the Aldermaston marchers while criticizing their logic.

However, peace under the nuclear deterrent brought fresh opportunities to the teacher, even if he found himself—as in 1919—without success on the edge of politics. The school was able to return home to Gordonstoun. His ideas found readier acceptance in the hopeful atmosphere of post-war reconstruction. His British disciples were quick to understand and put into practice the international features of his teaching. Outward Bound schools were to spring up abroad; Gordonstoun and Salem were imitated and adapted in the United States and Greece. The formation in 1949 of the North Atlantic

Treaty Organization gave currency to a new idea: of the permanent association of the United States and Canada with a Europe that would move towards unity. The Atlantic idea became a major theme of Hahn's thinking and speaking. His advocacy of sixth-form and university requirements which would be uniform for Atlantic countries opened the way to genuine international education at the secondary stage. Hahn had powerful and devoted backing for his projects from men in industry, notably Spencer Summers in the steel industry and Lawrence Holt in shipping. They not only contributed money and spoke up for the claims of the young, but also sent their apprentices and recruits to courses.

For the wider public the most significant proof of Hahn's progress must have been the emergence in a position of unique influence at the Queen's side of his old pupil, the Duke of Edinburgh, who had been sent to Gordonstoun before the war from Salem where he had laughed at the saluting antics of the Nazis. From the Duke in 1954 came the initiative which revived the old Gordonstoun scheme of the County Badge (to be awarded for self-training in fitness, rescue and other achievements of the individual boy) and turned it into the nation-wide Duke of Edinburgh's Award. The idea was tried out for three years in 1956, was successful in quarters where such ideas had been previously ignored or resisted, and after ten years awards were being competed for by more than 100,000 youngsters. Hahn was concerned, too, in founding the Trevelyan Scholarships at Oxford and Cambridge, to be awarded to those who showed, as well as intellectual quality, a capacity for decision, dealing with people and setting oneself an aim and achieving it. He had shown his readiness to admit intellectual and artistic as well as physical effort into the category of adventure. One may doubt whether any individual episode of his experience with British boys has given more pleasure than the expedition of the Trevelyan scholar who traced the marches of Marlborough from the Low Countries to the Danube carrying on his back the same weight of equipment as an eighteenth-century grenadier.

Anyone who tries to sum up briefly what Hahn has contributed to the British education tradition is defeated by the versatility of the man. For first-class powers of initiative, persuasion, preaching, conspiring, thinking and writing to go together is unusual. Even more unusual is it for a refugee and exile to bring these qualities to bear so successfully on the country which has sheltered him. That this should have been achieved by a German and a Jew in a period of such hostile and confused relations between Britain and Germany is—in spite of Hahn's exceptional experience of Oxford and Scotland —astonishing. The public sign of this success—although Hahn is the last man to claim it—was the royal decision that Prince Charles should attend the school which had educated Prince Philip. True, the Prince was not under his personal direction, but certainly under the influence of methods and men chosen by him.

How much their power depends on their creator's personal advocacy is uncertain and an important question, hard to answer. So far his following have shown flexibility: there have been modifications, developments, rejections of some of his ideas in the light of British and other non-German experience. But the essential message to parents and teachers remains: self-mastery achieved through adventure and experiment which tests mind and body; compassion learned through the opportunity and ability to help others in distress. One has only to ask the ordinary head of a secondary school for boys or girls what is being done to endow pupils with self-mastery and compassion to see how revolutionary is Hahn's challenge to conventional practice in the classroom and the home. Even those who have disagreed violently with him, pointed out fallacies in his thinking, disputed the adequacy of his psychology of the young, questioned his respect for solid academic achievement—even they have had to take notice of some of the trends which the Gordonstoun influence has set in motion. In the ideas themselves there is no great originality, Hahn himself acknowledges his debt to Germans like Lietz and to the long line of British experimental and radical headmasters. The originality lies in the man, in his combination of qualities, and in the experience of life and politics that he has brought to the work of teaching and founding schools—experience which guarded him from the danger of becoming a crank.

Family and Tradition

Lola Landau-Wegner

When dealing with distinguished personalities, we are inclined to trace the sources of their inheritance and to investigate the character and talents of their ancestors. For that character is composed of a unique blend of the various hereditary features of their predecessors, sometimes far remote, and thus it forms a newly creative personality. So too in the case of Kurt Hahn, the pioneer of a new education, the spiritual heritage of his forbears makes itself felt in this way. His code of ethics, his passionate will to implement his ideas in practice, the magnetic influence he exerts on youth—all these traits have their roots in certain characteristics possessed by his forefathers. But, on the other hand, they have found in him, a child of his time and a man moulded by German landscape and culture, unique and original expression.

Kurt's father, Oskar Hahn, possessed the qualities of the born leader: authority and a gift for organization. He had inherited these features from his father, Albert Hahn, the founder of the tube-rolling mill in the Rhineland. Being a product of his age, Albert Hahn was a pioneer in business life. His rise from modest beginnings to become the owner of an enterprise worth millions of marks seems like a success story straight out of a fairly tale. Born in Breslau in 1824 as the son of a merchant, Albert Hahn entered his father's business at the early age of fourteen. But his desire to be independent drove the young man out of this narrow sphere of activity into the thriving town of Berlin. In 1851 Albert Hahn arrived in the capital on a goods waggon with a few thalers in his pocket, and founded a general store, together with a friend who put up the small amount of capital required. Unremitting hard work and business instinct soon attracted a new partner and fresh capital, and a few years later Albert Hahn took the decisive step of turning the firm over to the manufacture of textile material. At the same time he became an agent for a British gas-pipe factory, which at that time was a completely new departure. For until then only hand-wrought pipes a few feet long had been known in Germany. Sales of this product were so successful that the firm was able to open a tube-rolling mill of its own in Upper Silesia. In 1873 there followed the building of a new rolling mill in Düsseldorf-Oberbilk. In this way the foundations of the industrial enterprise were laid.

There are some men who have a special gift for grasping a unique opportunity for self-advancement: Albert Hahn was one of them. But besides this he possessed tough powers of perseverance. When his partner left the firm, for years he bore single-handed the burden of both firms, the textile factory and the rolling mill. Later he took his two sons, Georg and Oskar Hahn, and a few loyal employees into partnership. The tube business expanded and spread beyond the borders of Germany. Branches were opened in Moscow and, later in Oderberg, Austria.

This vital man remained hard at work until a ripe old age, and it was only in 1896 that he turned the firm into a joint-stock company.

Albert Hahn's life is the story of a tremendously successful career. But he was more than a careerist. His character combined intelligence with a frank and engaging disposition, an acute knowledge of human nature with humanity and kindness. He was extremely popular both with his colleagues and his subordinates. He also showed a great deal of public spirit, was a commercial judge for many years and took a particular interest in the extension of social insurance. He was appointed a councillor of commerce. But all the outward honours bestowed on him and the wealth he acquired left the core of his being unchanged—that is, his creative desire for fruitful activity.

His younger son, Oskar Hahn, Kurt's father, was by no means only his father's heir. He carried on the development of the firm; he was a merchant on a large scale and a man of the world. His work frequently took him on long journeys abroad, to Tsarist Russia and to England, where he took a particular liking to the country and its people. It was probably this love of England which persuaded him to send Kurt to study at an Oxford college; and English education decisively influenced the future educationist.

Oskar Hahn was a gentleman in the best sense of the word, being chivalrous, broad-minded and generous and possessing a sense of humour. He took particular pleasure in nature and in country life; and it was no coincidence that he built his summer residence, Wannsee, in English country-house style, with broad green lawns, a rose-garden, a cricket ground and tennis courts, stables and orchards.

The lady of the household, Charlotte, brought to this enchanting home her own special atmosphere, one of buoyant and detached artistic serenity. The house was always open to the numerous guests, who, when drawn into this peculiar ambience, were carried away from the world of every day as though entranced.

For the younger children, Kurt and his two younger brothers, Franz and Rudolf, Wannsee became the summer paradise where they romped about with their friends. Boating on the lake, roaming through the woods exploring, a life lived in the midst of Nature left their stamp upon the years of the Hahn brothers' youth. School cares were forgotten, and when the school-bags were flung into the corner at midday the real business of life would begin at Wannsee.

Being the eldest, Kurt became a kind of tutor to the troop of children while still only a youth himself. Often, on hot afternoons, he would gather the children in the white pavilion and read to them. He always chose what he read with great care; usually a heroic figure played the central part. His voice and the questions he put to his audience made so deep an impression that the children listened with bated breath. Kurt's inborn talent as an educator also found expression in urging them to excel at sport. He often went on long hikes with the younger children over rough country, through thickets and across swampy ground. Although he was perhaps not yet conscious of it at the time, this leadership already contained the germ of his educational principle: the toughening of youth and the gaining of experience in the framework of a community.

The first essays in education were soon to become deadly serious when Kurt's father succumbed to a heart disease while still in the prime of life. His death and the destruction of a happy marriage brought dark days to the home. His widow was left with Kurt, who had not yet finished his studies, and two sons not yet of age.

The Landau family on Kurt's maternal grandfather's side represented an aristocracy of the spirit; with its tradition of religious learning and teaching, it consciously cultivated family pride, and maintained that it could trace back its genealogical ancestry over about 180 generations to King David on the basis of a family tree—a claim which seems almost legendary.

The family's most distinguished representative is Jecheskiel Landau, Chief Rabbi of Prague, whose writings on the Talmud literature made him famous in his time; and even today they are taught at academies of Jewish studies. This man, a teacher and a model of religious piety, who lived in Prague in the age of Maria Theresa, exerted an influence far beyond his immediate circle. Thus, as the representative of his flock, he successfully prevented the expulsion of the Jews from Prague, which was planned by the Austrian Government at that time.

One of the family possesses a picture of him, the portrait of an old man bearing the words 'Grand Rabby, professeur de Prague', that gives us a clear notion of his personality. Dressed in a black robe trimmed with fur, his hand resting on the book containing his writings, his bearing is expressive of dignity and sovereign calm. The gaze is penetrating and stern—a gaze which even from the picture casts its spell on the observer and holds him captive.

Instinctively we ask: does not a straight line connect this ancestor, though he belongs to an utterly different age and intellectual climate, with Kurt Hahn's character? His ethical demands—namely, self-control and self-education on the part of youth—are a repetition of the crystalline hardness of that predecessor. Indeed, Hahn's personality repeats his sternness; and it provokes him to anger at what is low and base. That saying of Kurt Hahn's that there must be a 'holy wrath'—the wrath needed to condemn and not to tolerate any sickly weakness—has its roots in that same mental attitude of his ancestor. Sometimes when Kurt Hahn spoke of this 'holy wrath', his glance had a magical power to transform men. But since it was far removed from the rigid dogma of the past and set right in the midst of the modern world, this wrath acted as a spur to new and positive ideas.

In the Landau family, the refined blood of the scholar mingled with coarser, more down-to-earth components. The women brought in elements of the secular and temporal world into that sphere of the Book and of Bible study.

Indeed, we meet this practical ability and worldly wisdom again in the personality of Anschulka Landau, Stanislaus's wife and Kurt Hahn's grandmother, who played a particularly important part in the latter's youth. (She was the daughter of a prosperous family of Warsaw merchants who had already been assimilated into Polish society and felt Poland to be their home—indeed, so deeply that some of Anschulka's brothers took part in the Polish national uprising against Russia in 1848 and had later to emigrate for this reason.)

Young Anschulka witnessed this drama only as an onlooker. But later, as an attractive seventeen-year-old girl, she carried out her own domestic rebellion. For she decided to marry 'for love', which was unusual in her time. Her choice fell on young Stanislaus Landau, one of those sensitive, scholarly personalities who had been marked out for a career as a merchant and whose pecuniary circumstances in no sense matched the riches of his intellect. But despite her parents' warnings, Anschulka married her chosen husband and persuaded him to emigrate to Germany soon afterwards. They settled in Breslau. Seven sons and a single daughter, Charlotte, were born of the marriage; Charlotte, the youngest child, became the mother of Kurt Hahn. Their modest dwelling in Breslau was dominated by Anschulka's energy and zest. She aimed to give her children the best possible educational opportunities. Her efforts were rewarded. All her sons rose to occupy respected positions. The eldest, Leopold Landau, who invented a new operating method, became Professor of Gynaecology at Berlin University. The daughter, conspicuous for her beauty and charm, married the industrialist Oskar Hahn at the age of eighteen.

After the death of her husband, Anschulka went to live in her daughter's home; and thus out of their daily contacts with each other arose that special relationship between Kurt Hahn and his grandmother.

'Isn't she an absolute spring of vitality!' Kurt would often say. Yes, she was a veritable spring of worldly wisdom, a true character, and still full of youthful vitality at an advanced age. She was the patriarchal centre of the family, which sought her advice when taking important decisions.

Young Kurt Hahn discovered 'his Anschulka' with his special gift for making people unbosom themselves to him. Nobody knew as well as he did how to make her tell stories, to elicit from her graphic descriptions and observations, and to extract from her as though by magic her droll and yet so wise sayings, many of which he noted down in a book in which he recorded memories for later on. Sometimes Kurt Hahn asked staggering questions, such as: 'Anschulka, which of your children is the best?' Anschulka replied in one of her vivid sayings: 'A mother is like a shopkeeper—she has various kinds of goods.'

Many of her pronouncements revealed her rare knowledge of human nature. She could invariably summon up stubborn energy to gain acceptance for what she had decided was right. It was impossible to refuse her anything, so charmingly did she produce her requests. Even in extreme old age she still lived in the present and followed the political events of the day with lively interest.

We recognize some of her qualities in the person of Kurt Hahn—an instinctive flair for sizing up human beings at once, a lively nature sparkling with vitality, originality, a gift of repartee and the ability to act with lightning speed.

Kurt Hahn needed to take only one step from this, his grandmother's domain, to set foot in his modern world, to enter the atmosphere of his parents' house, which was a centre for social gatherings in the life of the cultural metropolis of Berlin. Attracted by the generous hospitality of the host, Oskar Hahn the industrialist, and his beautiful and highly educated wife Charlotte, eminent scholars, politicians and artists met here. It was more than a salon in fine surroundings. This home radiated human warmth; it was receptive to a broad, liberal view of human affairs. Often during conversations at table, sparks would fly which kindled a fervour of enthusiasm for some idea. Sometimes when men met here, their meeting led on to fruitful co-operation. Like the whole intellectual climate of this pre-1914 Berlin, the atmosphere prevailing in Hahn's parents' home was at once German and cosmopolitan.

The beauty and harmony of this home, the happy mutual affection of his parents, respect and dignity even in their daily dealings with one another, reverence and loving care for his old mother—all these features of the household remained stamped upon Kurt Hahn's memory. It was not disciplinary warnings but his parents' example that formed his personality and continued to exercise a profound effect on him.

After his father's death, Kurt became the tutor of his youngest brother, who was then still a child. He watched over the boy at work and at play and shaped his character. This was a preparatory exercise for his future mission.

Later this brotherly guardianship developed into an unusually close friendship between the two grown-up men. Kurt Hahn informed his brother of his designs and ambitious plans; Rudolf Hahn not only took the liveliest interest in these, he also became, with his sense of realities and practical experience of life, an irreplaceable adviser for Kurt. Active ties of friendship also linked Kurt with his second brother, Franz, and when Franz fell victim to a skiing accident Kurt ever afterwards kept alive the memory of this admirable man, who was a kind of pioneer in business life.

From his early youth up, Kurt Hahn was a man who gave, but also a man who listened and received. He derived the sources of his moral strength from his mother. Goethe's concept of the '*schöne Seele*', the beautiful soul, fitted this woman of rare quality. Her striking physical beauty mirrored the splendour of her soul. She had lustrous deep blue eyes and dark hair. Charlotte Hahn was a woman with faith in the world. She believed in the innate goodness of man, and, since she was not merely an idealistic dreamer, but wanted to make her mark on human affairs, she was convinced that the good in every man could be awakened and developed. She felt within her a burning desire to influence people, and she did not hesitate to intervene in others' vital affairs.

All the while she worked incessantly to improve her culture. She had married at eighteen when she was still only half grown up. She became a mother at nineteen. She constantly strove to continue her education. She applied herself to the study of philosophic works and books on education and psychology. She loved music and was an accomplished pianist. Her way of influencing people was itself an art, and possessed the magical power of charming people over to embrace the good. She had a spellbinding influence on her children, one stronger than all the rules of discipline then current.

Kurt was the living image of her, and her relationship with him was like that of an elder sister or a best friend. They understood one another without needing to speak; and many suggestions of Charlotte Hahn's later crystallized into educational theories in Kurt's mind.

Thus strangely did the threads of his spiritual inheritance entwine to form the tissue of an inspired and highly gifted personality. The will to realize ethical principles, authority, impassioned vivacity, originality and a gift of leadership formed the personality of the creative educationist.

Salem School 1919–33: Foundation and Expansion

[An abridged version of the chapter which appeared in the German edition of this book]

Marina Ewald

During the First World War, Kurt Hahn joined the Foreign Press Centre of the German Foreign Office and became Private Secretary to Prince Max of Baden. Thus it was in the field of politics, not of education, that he was first active, although from early youth and in his student days at Göttingen and then Oxford he had reflected on and studied the principles and the effectiveness of education. He read the classics, and many of his ideas developed from Plato. He admired the British public schools of the Victorian era which overtly fostered a sense of public duty in their pupils, and thought the prefect system gave a calculated system of self-government. Here was a very real contribution towards the democratic education of the nation as a whole which could, he believed, be adapted to the German boarding schools, and could, if systematized, have an important effect on post-war Germany. From England too and from the Greeks he saw the value of a healthy balance of athletic and sporting activity with academic training.

When Prince Max resigned from the Office of German Chancellor he had failed to achieve his political aims, and many of his hopes had been disappointed. In Prince Max Kurt Hahn had an ally in his educational aims: their hope was that the rising generation might take their civic responsibilities more seriously than their predecessors. Prince Max made a wing of his castle, Schloss Salem, available for a school. He made his son the first pupil, and became the school's first patron. Their educational aim was to awaken in the pupils a sense of duty as citizens. A great believer in the effectiveness of habit and practical experience in guiding behaviour, Kurt Hahn tried to bring about in them a greater readiness to serve the country, having served their fellow men, first of all, at school.

A nucleus of staff who were also pledged to his ideas, gathered at Salem, which was originally a Cistercian abbey, with its church, its cloister and cells. Old traditions played their part in moulding the school. The official opening took place on 21 April 1920 in the former library of the Abbey. There were twenty pupils, boys and girls, eight of them boarders, the rest living locally; from the first there was a mixture of social classes and backgrounds.

For the nation as a whole it was a time of austerity, reflected in the meagre material equipment of the school. Since there was only one lamp, everybody in the evenings pursued his work in one splendid room, formerly the decorated, baroque apartment of the Abbot.

Karl Reinhardt, Privy Councillor in the Prussian Ministry of Education, was the first Director of Studies. He had helped to save classics in secondary education by creating the 'reformed grammar schools'. Now he was delighted to keep the promise he had made to the young student Kurt Hahn before the war, to come to teach at his school, if he were to start one.

Hahn continued to work for Prince Max, ordering and editing his political papers, and contributing topical political articles and comment. This double activity of schoolmastering and being absorbed in public affairs Hahn saw not as a conflict, as it kept the pupils in direct, personal touch with current affairs. The children were aware of this and it influenced them, just as a similar atmosphere in their homes would have done.

When Kurt Hahn taught in the school, his subjects were usually the history of the First World War or English, or both at the same time. During his classes, as on every other occasion, he had an exhilarating effect on the pupils. He encouraged them to take sides and pretend they themselves were the prominent men in history under discussion having to decide how to achieve the desired end. In this way he revealed history and literature as the result of actions taken rightly or wrongly, and thus aroused in his listeners a regard for the champions of law, justice and humanity, particularly when they were the weaker side.

Equally, the Headmaster was deeply concerned for the children's general good health. The run outside before breakfast, drinking milk at meals, the mid-morning break for athletic training and the rest after lunch were practical realizations of this concern. Having a shower after taking physical exercise, reporting illness, the loose-fitting pullover and shorts, rules against smoking or cycling uphill, which could strain the heart, were aimed at teaching the children to care for their physical well-being. A practical diagram to see that these rules became habit was the 'training plan' kept by each pupil, the various items being checked off by him or herself every evening, with a plus or a minus in the appropriate columns.

Points	Mon.	Tues.	Wed.	Thurs.	Fri.	Sat.
One warm wash						
Two cold showers						
30 skips						
High jump						
Running						
Throwing the javelin						
No eating between meals						
Report illness						
Rope-climbing						
Account book						
Duty						

The plan was not checked by anyone else. On demand, a pupil had to produce it and discuss it with his housemaster, but it was mainly of private concern, and was considered a privilege and a trust.

New pupils, on arrival at the school, would wear their own clothes, and only after a certain time, when they had settled down, would they be given their uniform as an outward sign that they were now members of the school community. Thereafter the uniform could be taken away if basic decent social behaviour was infringed—for instance, in cases of untruthfulness or cruelty.

Receiving the uniform was occasion for congratulations. The

3   Kurt Hahn in 1944, talking to Jeremy Chance, an
ex-guardian of Gordonstoun, who is paying a visit to the school
at its wartime home in Wales, having won a commission in the
R.N.V.R.

4 Kurt Hahn in 1962

wearer was under obligation not to cheat or copy in school. From this obligation grew a long tradition of honesty at Salem, the more remarkable when seen in the light of the accepted degree of cheating in schools and examinations at that time in Germany. It was Professor Baumann, co-founder of Salem, who, when correcting tests and finding that children had copied cheerfully from one another as usual, had cancelled sports for the rest of the term. The school was deeply upset. Diplomatically they tried to persuade Hahn, the sports enthusiast, to reduce the punishment. Before he gave them hope, however, they had solemnly presented Herr Baumann with a box containing the ashes of all the exercise books in which they had cheated. From this time onwards, teachers could safely leave the classroom when a test was in progress.

During a Final Examination, taken externally in Constance, one girl sat staring despondently at her mathematics paper. The supervisor, noting this, took pity on her and gave her a hint—enough for her to solve the problem. But having done so, she immediately realized what had happened, got up from her place and told the supervisor, 'Without your help I could not have answered the question. Will you please tell all the others what you told me.' Some time later the supervisor asked the Director of Studies if he could offer an explanation for this girl's unusual behaviour. The reply was: 'That is Salem.'

The day's routine had a firm programme. As the provision of food was essential in those difficult times directly after the war and as there were few employees, two afternoons a week were spent working on the farm and performing other tasks necessary to the running of the school. Naturally, some duties were more attractive than others: caring for animals, mowing the dewy grass at dawn and haymaking were sought after; weeding was not so popular. There was a great deal to be done, and every pupil had a special duty to perform every day. Whether in games, athletics, or any other activities, they accepted the duties allotted to them, just as they accepted their academic work. Each one practised running, jumping, throwing the javelin, worked in the garden, went on an expedition in the surrounding countryside and took over duties and responsibilities as part of the daily round. The special duty became the most important item on the training plan and paved the way for the more responsible offices in the self-governing community.

The training plan was seen to be a preliminary step towards self-government. 'To acquire the habit of checking one's own behaviour was considered a prerequisite to checking other people's.'

The training plan was received as the next step after the presentation of the uniform, and until that time the dormitory room leader would ask the new boy or girl the points of the plan and fill it in for them.

To understand the early days of Salem it is essential to appreciate that the day's programme did not separate children and adults. They lived, worked and spent their free time together. The adults thus heard almost everything that the children talked about; they knew what they did and knew their feelings. Any deviation from the Salem idea of gentlemanly behaviour could therefore be checked immediately. There was no room for hushing up, and the children knew that their motives were seen through. Thus it was relatively easy to use the training plan to accustom the children to be precise in their statements. After a few terms, it very rarely happened that anyone holding a training plan tried to conceal or gloss over his failures, whatever they might be. Thus the foundation was laid for successful self-discipline. Individual points could be added to the general ones in the training plan, provided that they were neither abstract nor equivocal. It is not a difficult step from registering an omission on the training plan to frankly confessing guilt when some misdemeanour is discovered and the wrongdoer sought. All the children owned up, and they would have thought it unfair to allow suspicion to fall on others or to let others take the punishment alone when they were also incriminated.

Self-government implies that boys and girls are entrusted with serious duties and responsibilities which, if neglected, would soon lead to a breakdown in the working of the school. The full burden of such office was not too heavy as the bearer was responsible to his house-master who was easily available to give advice.

Salem's constitution reflects Kurt Hahn's attitude to government in the political sense. Being a democrat of the British type, he attached importance to traditional practice in the democratic state. The Colour Bearers (prefects) are not, therefore elected by the mass of the pupils, but they as a body elect their own new members when necessary. In other words, one must have proved one's ability to assume responsibility in order to have the right to vote or to raise one's voice. The Headmaster is the chairman of the Colour Bearers' meeting; the vice-chairman is the 'Guardian' (head boy or girl). He or she is not elected, but is appointed by the Headmaster. Only a few staff belong to the Colour Bearers.

The Colour Bearers may be compared to knights of an order rather than to a parliament, but their assembly also deliberates and passes laws. Its most important concern is to ensure that Salem's laws are respected and observed, particularly the unwritten laws which represent the general spirit underlying the formulated laws.

In Salem's early days Kurt Hahn was still a member of the Jewish community; for him the brotherly love and responsibility to one's neighbour which he strove to realize was expressed in the words of the Prophet Ezekiel:

> When I say unto the wicked, Thou shalt surely die, and thou givest him not warning, nor speakest to warn the wicked from his wicked way, to save his life; the same wicked man shall die in his iniquity; but his blood will I require at thine hand.

By this he meant that he expected everyone at Salem to feel himself responsible for his neighbour.

The Colour Bearers represent the school both inside and outside the school boundaries: they exact more of themselves than of others. On Sundays they each go for a solitary walk lasting two hours. They wear a little purple stripe sewn on to the school uniform. From time to time there were protests against this badge. Hahn insisted upon it, however, convinced that young people require some outward sign to remind them of the obligations they have undertaken. Prince Max's son and a girl pupil were the first pupils to wear the colours.

Colour Bearers need the courage of their convictions. Their personal influence is all they have to help them assert their authority; they are granted no privileges, and must continually prove their worth as leaders of the school community. Should anything happen in the presence of a Colour Bearer which required punishment then he alone would be punished.

Meanwhile, the number of pupils had so increased that they were no longer all occupied in the same place at any one time and so the individual Colour Bearers could no longer be held responsible for everything that happened. Accordingly 'helpers' (senior prefects) are entrusted with particular aspects of school life, studies, games, cultural activities, the girls' and boys' houses and the health and safety of the juniors. Room-leaders, not necessarily Colour Bearers, are answerable to the helpers of their house for the conduct of their room.

Demotion was a serious punishment, and losing colours was keenly felt. However, with these means of dealing with offences, expulsion could be avoided, and rehabilitation was possible.

The joint activity of boys and girls in the running of the school was an important adjunct to the success of co-education in Salem.

Disciplinary offences were punished as a matter of routine without further ado. But if, in Kurt Hahn's eyes, not only human rules and regulations but the ten commandments had been transgressed, then the child's future and the well-being of the school community were at stake and Kurt Hahn was in a state of great agitation. The whole school was kept in suspense. He made the offender see reason, often after a violent argument, and did not rest until all the implications of such an offence had been understood by everyone, both pupils and teachers. Not infrequently the whole school had to wait and stand in silence for half an hour or more until he was ready to give details of the offence, elucidate the facts, proclaim the punishment and give the reasons for it. Anger and indignation, however, were expended on the deed and not the doer. As soon as he had atoned for his offence, the wrongdoer was held to have started afresh. Anyone who alluded to the incident afterwards aroused Kurt Hahn's wrath anew, which was vented on teachers and children alike.

Each offence and the punishment inflicted were posted on the notice-board. This nipped rumours in the bud. Hahn was a specialist in the campaign against rumours. His light blue eyes twinkled mischievously when he had succeeded in unravelling the inaccuracies which had originated a rumour. 'On my tombstone', he used to say, 'will be inscribed the words: "Here lies Kurt Hahn. He scotched a rumour every day".'

The degree to which headmaster and staff were concerned about the moral and physical welfare of the pupils is well illustrated by two reminiscences about Hahn and Reinhardt.

Anthony, the son of the innkeeper, was taking his first public examination in Constance as an external candidate; it must have been the intermediate examination (*Sekundareife*). Kurt Hahn cycled with him to the station in order to revise English words and phrases with him up to the very last minute. Reinhardt saw the unsatisfactory report of a pupil living on a farm some distance away. He did not send the boy's report by post, but went on foot to the farm, delivering the report personally in order to dispel the father's anger and prevent the storm bursting over the boy's head.

Two afternoons a week were given to field games. Hockey was the main team game—it was Hahn's speciality. He played on the wing in the first eleven. Professionalism was not approved; there were only two games a week and no practising was allowed between. There was intentionally no professional coach. Hahn was concerned lest a passion for games were to stifle other interests. The school's success in athletics and hockey was due to good general physical condition and real enthusiasm. Other schools in Germany had little sport on the curriculum, and there were no schoolboy teams against which to compete, so Salem played matches against various men's clubs where play was sometimes rough, but the school had to keep their tempers and observe fair sportsmanship. The following day a match was reported in detail on the main notice-board, for all the school to see. The boys awaited the Headmaster's criticisms eagerly, yet not without some trepidation. It was always succinct and witty and made clear his views of the aims of such games: to encourage concerted action rather than the brilliant individual performance. For Hahn hockey was also an educative force to correct in his pupils exaggerated traits of self-satisfaction and the use of brute force as a last resort. Everyone had to learn to be modest in success and prepared to carry on in defeat with renewed effort and exertion.

In 1932 a Salem Hockey and Athletics Team made a tour of England, competing successfully with various public schools. This trip led to a regular exchange of visits between English schools and Salem, which were often coupled with a production of a play by Salem pupils. The culmination of the school's sporting success was winning the Challenge Cup of the Public Schools Athletics Competition at the White City in 1935, 1936, and 1937.

Saturday afternoons were devoted to 'guilds'. Hahn wanted each child to have the opportunity of doing something creative and of pursuing his or her own favourite interests thereby finding contentment and a sense of fulfilment. In this way young people would discover themselves, their gifts and perhaps their vocation. He was convinced that the flagging energy of adolescents would be avoided if the natural treasure of childhood could be preserved unimpaired—namely, a thirst for knowledge, compassion and the gift of wonder. During the years of puberty particularly, he sought for every pupil a hobby to which they were passionately devoted and which could help keep these gifts alive. Amongst these mixed activities, of which there was a free choice, were practical crafts of various kinds. There were guilds for the library and editing the school magazine, music and painting, drama and natural science. The staff were often members of these groups making their contribution under the chairmanship of an elected boy or girl leader. In the past Hahn had seen that important issues were all too frequently jeopardized by personal prestige. He therefore encouraged free co-operation by members of a guild regardless of age or status.

Music and the school plays profited particularly by boys and girls being together. On Sunday evenings the orchestra and choir performed at school chapel, which took place in the monks' former summer refectory, and this also served as the German Evangelical Church for the village of Salem. The music, which was usually a devotional choral work with orchestra was followed at the end by the whole congregation singing a hymn. Special occasions were concluded, and still are, with the school hymn, the Netherlands' hymn of thanksgiving, *Wir treten zum beten*, which ends, 'O Lord, make us free'.

Kurt Hahn took an active and often a leading part in staging the plays. He regarded the Salem stage as a formative influence on both players and spectators. In the very early days after the first world war, the 'Rütli' scene from *William Tell* and the play *Cathleen ni Houlihan* about Irish independence were performed several times. Later on Greek tragedies and Shakespeare's greatest tragedies were produced. Expanding their personality to grow into their stage roles left a lasting mark on the young amateur actors. On such occasions they surpassed their ordinary selves and the school as a community would rise to a climax that left everyone loath to return to normal routine.

Girls in particular came into their own in the plays. Sexually, boys and girls were not expected to take much interest in each other, or come into physical contact. Even ragging and fighting among the boys was taboo, although if there really was a case for a fight, a fair boxing match was staged in private with staff or Colour Bearers supervising, care being taken to avoid all semblance of professionalism. But in the upper forms good friendships often developed, also between boys and girls.

Hahn's attitude to girls was peculiar to him. On the one hand he held them responsible for the tone of the school and even for callousness by other pupils of which they had been in complete ignorance. On the other hand he was capable of ignoring them completely. But he was readily forgiven and girls felt they represented Salem in the front line.

Friendships were extended outside the class and age group during artistic activities and in the various guilds. A mixing of juniors and seniors was encouraged here too, so that a genuine spirit of comradeship grew throughout the school.

Duty to the school and to one's fellows did not come to an end with the final examination. The candidates' lessons stopped after the examinations, but they continued their duties as helpers, captains, and so on until the end of term. When they left they received not only the Government-awarded School Leaving Certificate, the 'Abitur', but also a 'Final Report to Parents' issued by Salem, containing information on the pupil's attainments in all spheres of Salem life. Here is a copy of the Report:

FINAL REPORT TO PARENTS

Public Spirit
Sense of Justice
Ability to state facts precisely
Ability to follow out what he/she believes to be the right course in
    the face of
  Discomforts
  Hardships
  Dangers
  Mockery
  Boredom
  Scepticism
  Impulses of the moment
Ability to plan
Imagination
Ability to organize
  Shown in the disposition of work

In the direction of younger boys/girls
Ability to deal with the unexpected
Degree of Mental concentration
    Where the task in question interests him/her
    Where it does not
Conscientiousness
    In everyday affairs
    In tasks with which he/she is specially entrusted
Manners
Standard reached in studies:
    German   Natural Science
    Modern Languages   Mathematics
    History
Practical Work (Handicraft, etc.)
Art Work (Music, Drawing, etc.)
Physical Exercises
    Fighting spirit
    Endurance
    Reaction time

In 1924 the first public examinations were taken and all eight candidates were successful. *Geheimrat* Reinhardt did not live to see this day, having died in 1923. He was succeeded by *Geheimrat* Wilhelm Schmidle, a scientist and for many years headmaster of schools in Baden. Soon he became a true friend of Salem, Prince Max and, above all, Kurt Hahn. His strong independent personality also helped to mould the Salem of his time (1923–30). Under his direction, the laboratories were established in 1929 and this made it possible for Salem to become a State-recognized school and receive the right to conduct the final school examinations at Salem.

At the time of the first final examinations numbers had increased to about eighty boarders. Although the number of boarders had thus multiplied tenfold in four years, the pupils who had been awarded the colours continued to set the tone in the school without encountering any organized opposition. Salem's ideals were generally acclaimed by the newcomers too. In the shortest possible time they ceased to be spectators and actively joined in the Salem community.

Attacks from without helped to consolidate Salem. As early as 1921 Prince Max of Baden and Kurt Hahn were the objects of violent plots. Communists intended to kidnap Prince Max and hold him as a hostage, but it was possible to deter them before they reached Salem. Salem boys were prepared to defend Prince Max's house.

The group of Nationalists who had planned and carried out the assassination of Rathenau had also included Kurt Hahn in their list of victims. The plot to murder Hahn came to the ears of a Salem boy, who, in spite of threats, revealed the plan to Hahn, so that he was not caught in the ambush. Quite by accident, it was Hahn himself who later discovered his two would-be assassins and took them into custody. He sympathized at once with them in their grief about the state of Germany while at the same time condemning the methods they had chosen to remedy this state of affairs. He would have liked to help them. Such magnanimity towards mortal enemies set to the school an example of Christian conduct not easily equalled.

Communists and Nationalists waged a kind of war on one another in the district. The Nationalists secretly built up arsenals; and the Communists set fire to isolated farms at night. The Salem Forestry Commission established a guard which patrolled the lonely farms after dark; the older Salem boys belonged to it.

Under Kurt Hahn Salem felt called upon to foster the boys' ability to defend themselves. When the occupation of the Ruhr in 1923 completely violated the rights remaining to Germany after the Treaty of Versailles, the wish to give the boys military discipline became more urgent. Hahn let them drill. This was a kind of prelude to their later participation (at the beginning of the 1930s) in the camps for military sports organized by the *Stahlhelm*.

Before the local fire brigade had acquired a motor vehicle, Salem boys had succeeded in dragging the fire hose on foot to a conflagration two and a half miles away and extinguishing it before the horses could be fetched from the fields and hitched to the fire engine. For this achievement the school earned the official commendation of the local county council for the first time. The formation and equipping of a school fire brigade in the service of the local community did not take place until much later.

In the years 1922 and 1923 the increasing inflation seriously threatened Salem's financial position. The school managed, it is true, to get the funds necessary to keep going from benefactors in the United States, but the original endowment had become worthless, and the school was now dependent almost entirely on fee-paying pupils. Kurt Hahn convinced wealthy parents that it was necessary for their children to be freed from the enervating burden of coming from the wealthy, privileged classes by being educated alongside children who had been familiar with the struggle for existence since their earliest days. He persuaded these parents to pay not only for their own children, but to contribute enough to allow Salem to continue to give reductions in fees or award free places to 40 per cent of the pupils. The parents decided for themselves what they could afford to pay as school fees. This principle has proved its worth in all Salem schools. No one but the directorate at Salem knew which were full-paying pupils and which children were being granted assistance. This, indeed, was a matter of minor importance, for, thanks to the uniform and the fact that the children all received the same pocket money, it was not possible to notice any difference, and the children themselves felt no difference.

Thus the inflation did not impair either the character or the growth of the School. Scarcely was the inflation over than the first Junior School for ten-to-thirteen-year-olds was opened in the former convent of Hermannsberg, far up the Salem Valley. It was followed in 1931 by a second Junior School in Hohenfels, once a castle belonging to the Knights of the Teutonic Order, situated inland from Lake Constance. The juniors were thus given their own realm suited to their own needs and have ever since supplied Salem with a nucleus of pupils, without which it would scarcely have been possible to maintain the Salem tradition in critical times.

After the inflation the world was once more open to German youth. Twenty Salem pupils went on a trip in open boats across the Finnish lakes. They were allowed hunting and fishing permits for the whole area covered by the trip. They steered their boats through almost uninhabited country. It was like a voyage of discovery. For all the participants it was one of the happiest experiences of those years. Because of its success, Kurt Hahn thereafter attached the greatest importance to expeditions carefully planned beforehand and carried out with endurance. They have become an essential part of his educational programme.

The boat trip through Finland meant the realization of a dream for the leader of the expedition, a woman geographer on Salem's staff. Here was an example of how individual enjoyment was linked to principles of education in the development of what has been called 'the Salem method'. The pedagogue wants to pass on to the young his enthusiasm for an activity and the inspiration he derived from it, because for him they have been a lifelong source of strength. Hermann Lietz's affinity with Nature went hand in hand with his doctrine of the evil of urbanization. He loved gardening and farm work and wanted every one of his pupils to share the blessings of such work. Luserke passionately loved sailing: his school on the sea aimed at bestowing on the pupils the strength he derived from the sea. In the early years of Salem, Kurt Hahn placed great importance on hockey because he realized what the game had meant for him in his own development.

Thus the teacher is often in a position to do something beneficial for adolescents when he fulfils his own longings, and he will be successful in this so long as his enthusiasm can sweep his pupils along with him. The crisis in a pioneer school comes when this sweeping force begins to lag. Kurt Hahn tried systematically to free the 'Salem method' from too close a dependence upon his own person, not only in so far as he gained new objective insight from his experience, but also by opening in 1929 a new Senior School, without Greek for thirteen-to-nineteen-year olds, the running of which he delegated to others. This school for another 100 boys and girls was located in Spetzgart, a castle situated on the outskirts of Überlingen on the shores of Lake Constance. Salem always had one stream without Greek, but this was also without Latin. Spetzgart had no Greek, but had Latin. This school raised the total number of pupils at that time to 360. What had been tried out at Salem had to prove its worth in Spetzgart without the prevailing influence of Hahn, although his example as an untiring defender of what he believed to be the right cause had its effect even from a distance.

In three respects Spetzgart developed and evolved the educational line followed at Salem. In the first place, it was possible to go in for water sports on Lake Constance. These were entrusted to retired naval officers and based on proper nautical training. These activities furthered accuracy, enthusiasm, team spirit and the spirit of enterprise—at least as much as Salem's hockey did. Furthermore, sailing encouraged the observation of Nature, developed physique and moreover, gave the girls more chances to excel in sport than were provided for them by hockey.

The greatest achievement in practical work, however, was the building of their own harbour by the pupils of Spetzgart. They tackled the job with zeal, and even asked to stay on in the Easter holidays to complete it in time.

Being less isolated than Salem, Spetzgart provided more and better opportunities for community service; helping on the farms, amongst the old people and in the local hospital, all of which became regular rather than sporadic help in time of need.

In Salem the Upper School had dispensed with lessons on Saturday mornings in 1926 to work on individual academic projects lasting for at least one term. The studies were not assigned by the teachers, but they were on hand to give advice. The projects were unsatisfactory because of the large variety, which made it almost impossible for the teachers to ensure the necessary guidance. At Spetzgart a modified form of the Dalton Plan was used. The last two hours of the morning's time-table were free of lessons for the Upper School. The pupils were given long-term assignments, either individually or in groups, on which they worked independently. During these periods each classroom was set aside for one particular subject. A small reference library was available and a teacher was present to answer questions and give advice and guidance if necessary. Studying in this way had considerable advantages, and its success was proved by the results in the final examinations. Unfortunately, this became impracticable for the staff as the number of pupils grew.

There still remains for Salem to solve the problem of making academic studies the pupils' own responsibility, as the system demands. The project, to which Hahn would like to give importance in the term's syllabus, has practically disappeared in Salem itself.* It survives only in the handicrafts performed by the Salem Juniors.

The endorsement, however, that Salem received from its own pupils, as well as the growing desire among the general public to have their children educated according to Salem methods, led not only to further expansion, but also to plans for making the Salem schools the starting point for a 'Salem movement'.

In 1930 numbers increased again when a new school, Birklehof, was founded. Situated nearly 3,000 feet above sea-level in the Black

---

* It has since been revived.

Forest, it enjoyed a more bracing climate than the schools around Lake Constance. For this reason it was originally intended as a convalescent school for delicate children. Birklehof soon developed into a proper school, financially independent and supplied with pupils and teachers from Salem. Birklehof and Hohenfels now brought the total numbers up to about 500. It was not until Salem became particularly exposed to Nazi attacks that it was decided to make Birklehof entirely independent. It was hoped that thereby the Salem system would survive the Nazi era in at least one school. After the Second World War, Birklehof adopted different educational principles.

An attempt to develop educational influence outside the Salem schools was made in two directions—amongst university students and in suburban schools. At that time Hahn summed up what he thought was important to counter the oncoming danger. He crystallized his precepts for the young in these terms:

Give children the chance to discover themselves.

See to it that children experience both success and defeat.

See to it that children have the chance to forget themselves in the pursuit of a common cause.

See to it that there are periods of silence.

Train the imagination, the ability to anticipate and to plan.

Take sports and games seriously, but only as a part of the whole.

Free the children of rich and influential parents from the paralysing influence of wealth and privilege.

Negotiations were carried out with several cities to expand day schools to meet these precepts; and it looked as though progress was assured when the political events of 1933 put an end to the project for the time being.

Hahn now concentrated his attention on older boys on the verge of manhood. He became increasingly confident that they could develop the necessary public spirit, even if the experiences which develop a sense of responsibility and train the abilities do not occur until the onset of adolescence or even later. He called upon all former pupils of the *Landerziehungsheime* to unite on the basis of three commitments:

1 To carry out a light athletics training programme for four weeks every year and to abstain from toxicants and stimulants during this period.

2 To carry out some form of social work (e.g. in the mines, in distressed areas, amongst the unemployed).
3 To take part in a course with military discipline (e.g. the riding, driving or sailing schools).

He wanted to open a house in Heidelberg for former pupils of *Landerziehungsheime* from which their influence would spread and have its effect upon the other students. But the attempt was premature and failed.

Kurt Hahn felt ever more urgently that it was a race against time as to whether Salem or Nazism would win over Germany's youth, and that unless our little group grew more rapidly it would be swept aside by the oncoming tidal wave of National Socialism. No one was as yet to foresee how soon Salem's voice should be drowned and how many Salem boys were to perish on Hitler's battle-fields or to be driven into exile.

Kurt Hahn of Gordonstoun

Henry Brereton

Before making my contribution to this book I had better declare my qualifications for doing so. I met Kurt Hahn first in June 1934, and went to Scotland to work under him as Director of Studies at Gordonstoun in September 1935. For the next seventeen years we were associated in an intensity of partnership and campaigning that was virtually daily, with the briefest interruptions. (Only those who know Hahn will understand that in using the word 'intensity' I am not guilty of exaggeration.) For sixteen years more I have remained in touch with him, and in my professional work have been largely concerned with helping to give workable forms to his highly original and significant creations, adapting them to play their part in a relevant way against the kaleidoscopic backcloth of the 1950s and 1960s.

When I first met him, Hahn was forty-eight, with a political career in Germany behind him, and was well known as a pioneer schoolmaster, the founder of the Salem schools in Germany which had aroused interest beyond the national frontiers, particularly in both public-school and progressive-school circles in this country. I personally knew very little about him, except that as a man of outspoken liberal principles he had fallen foul of the Nazis and that his innovations in boarding education were in some ways similar to, and yet quite distinct from, the progressive movement in English education which was, professionally, my own chief interest at that time. It was quite easy to detect from talking with friends who had met him that there was something remarkable about this man, and that he did things in a way that was quite his own, that he did things with a certain style. Many years later a friend of his—rather a critical friend—said to me, 'Whatever shortcomings Hahn has, there is an unfailing feeling for quality!' Some such impression was conveyed to me before I met him.

Though Hahn's mind has changed and expanded fundamentally in the years that I have known him, so that to treat him as the same person in the 1930s and in the 1960s is to get him wrong, yet it does help to an understanding of him today to remember how he appeared on the English scene when he arrived here in 1933. To make my account strictly accurate, I must say something about myself at that time.

After two years of teaching in the orthodox conservative atmosphere of the junior department of a Scottish public school I was given the opportunity at the age of twenty-four to conduct an experiment in the teaching of English and History by individual assignments. I was granted a latitude that left me virtually free. This was in a new, company-owned preparatory school in Surrey, the object of the founders being to apply progressive principles within the orthodox framework of the public-school system. All the boys joining Abinger Hill between the ages of eight and eleven were expected to take the public schools Common Entrance examination at age thirteen. Starting with a handful of boys in a beautiful house and estate large enough to accommodate sixty-five boarders, the school quickly reached its complement. There was an exciting atmosphere of freedom in the community life, but always under the remote control that most parents intended their boys to go on to famous traditional schools. Looking back now at the eight years I spent there, I can recognize that we were as much of a period piece as the League of Nations and disarmament, but period in an English way, like Stanley Baldwin and the *Weekend Book*. But our educational achievements were considerable. My own teaching, in its confident reliance on the individual, which led to rather surprising successes in the conservative examinations, won me some small reputation, and when Hahn, in the enforced leisure of his first months of exile, came to see the school, he asked to meet me.

In spite of my success, or possibly because of it, I was beginning to feel restlessly dissatisfied. I looked back to a Victorian grandfather who was a social and educational pioneer after the Dr Arnold pattern,

5   Dr Blendinger, a successor to Hahn as Headmaster of Salem,
takes a class in the open air. In the background are the buildings
of Salem School and Castle, formerly a Cistercian monastery

6 The morning sport and athletic break at Salem. The old monastic granary, now a wing of the school, and the Catholic Abbey itself, which forms one side of a quadrangle of the castle, are in the background

7 The Salem Hockey Team in the 1920s: Kurt Hahn (right); Prince Max von Baden (back middle); Prince Berthold (front middle); boys from Salem village (right) and the Freiburg guest XI (left)

and was impatient for more significant worlds to conquer. From the soft climate of Surrey and the world of the radical intelligentsia whom Abinger Hill attracted, I looked back also to a hard education amongst the middle-class boys and miners' sons of the county of Durham, and felt I was occupying a charming backwater from which in a year or two more I might lose the incentive to detach myself. Of course, like many other Englishmen of my age, I was sensitive to the disturbing tremors from the European mainland which gave warning of the earthquake that was to come.

Hahn and I were immediately drawn to each other. Hahn recognized in me an English traditional ballast, something which has always had an attraction for him, and at the same time a contradictory readiness for not too cautious pioneering. I, on the other hand, was meeting a man who had already been in prison for his principles, who was briefly visiting my backwater from the main stream of European history. Moreover, where my mind was composed of question-marks, he, seventeen years older, seemed to be sure where he stood and where he wanted to go.

But there was another factor in the attraction that Hahn held for me. He had experienced defeat and was at that very time seeking to recharge his batteries, willing to start off again. My grandfather had witnessed the collapse of his ring of pioneer schools fifty years earlier because of a crisis of confidence. Some of his influential supporters who had been urged forward by his drive and enthusiasm had lost such timid sympathy with his liberalism and such hesitant faith in his finances as he had been able to inject into them, at a moment that disastrously corresponded with his involvement in a serious railway accident. This left him in hospital for vital weeks during which the company which controlled the ring of 'County Schools' went into liquidation. The material consequences of this disaster and the family conflict of opinions—matters of principle— which were its legacy, had been the daily background of my boyhood even twenty years after the event. And although three years at Cambridge and ten years of practical schoolmastering had broadened my horizon and purged my adolescent romanticism with a strong dose of realism, they left a gritty, indestructible residue. Short-lived sensation as the shipwreck of the 'County Schools' had seemed to contemporaries in the big national pond, in the mind of a romantic boy it had been monstrous and unnecessary. Had there been a bold

Herminius to support the Reverend Prebendary Joseph Brereton
Horatius upon his left hand—I had early ambitions as a left-arm
bowler—the issue would have been reversed and history altered.
And suddenly in 1934 there was the old story repeating itself. Hahn,
like a Victorian ghost, stood in front of me: the founder of schools,
the liberal visionary, the vulnerable pioneer, willing to start again
with worn-out tools, who might in a future crisis need the tenacity
of support which only someone who shared his dream as a plan
capable of capture into bricks and mortar would be able to sustain.
I decided then and there that if he did carry out what was apparently
still an uncertain project to start a school in Britain, I would try to
persuade him to take me on his staff. As I learnt a few weeks later,
he had decided at the same encounter that he wanted me to become
Director of Studies of his new school.

In my Gordonstoun book I have tried to isolate the influences
which were early at work in Hahn's mind to make him the kind of
headmaster he became. My headings read: 'Plato's Influence',
'Oxford and Moray in Kurt Hahn's Life', 'Prince Max of Baden',
'Influence of Eton', 'Influence of Buildings: The Cistercians'. From
this it is obvious that I think of him as a traditionalist; and indeed he
is proud of the story he tells of Prince Max, Salem's owner and
Hahn's senior partner in the Salem enterprise. After Prince Max
had taken an American visitor round the school the latter asked him:
'Now, what would you say you have here, Prince, that is new?'
'Nothing at all,' was the reply.

It is certain that in the early years of Gordonstoun when I first got
to know him, Hahn shared the Prince's view that in human affairs
what has proved workable in the great classical and European civilizations must be the basis of any successful modern society. It seems
from advertisements of soap powder or orange squash that contemporary man will buy nothing that is not 'new'. And this fashion had
already made a good start in the 1930s. As an instance of Hahn's
innate suspicion of something fashionably new, when I knew him
first he was passionately opposed to the influence on education of the
Freud school of psychologists. I think today that most educated men
would agree that Freud has given an irreversible twist to our attitude
to ourselves, to the young, and to society, which must be accepted
as part of constructive history. But it must be remembered that
schoolmasters between the wars had to cope with an awful lot of

nonsense because of the unintelligent doctrinaire application of Freudian theory by highly educated, unintelligent 'specialists'. Hahn has always been a psychologist himself, a serious student of the workings of the human mind, but his approach to understanding has been more that of the poet than the analyst. The poet in Plato affected him more than the philosopher, and to work on Shakespeare with him was to learn through Hahn's perceptive sympathy a great deal about Shakespeare's own uncanny insight. Hahn himself has surprising insights into the workings of the human mind and emotions, those of the individual in the moments when he is alone, and again when he is under the conflicting pressures of the society of which he is a part. And if his insights are essentially those of the artist rather than the analytical scientist, they run in harness with an honesty of observation and a cold assessment of motive that marks him as just as much of a realist as Shakespeare himself. I stress the point because in writing of Hahn one tends to forget to pass on to those who have never met him the inexhaustible energy of his interest in human beings and more particularly of the young. The great majority of persons who come within his personal orbit get the undistracted attention that most of us can give only to members of our family and a circle of a few friends. I think in his most active years as a schoolmaster both at Salem and Gordonstoun it was this capacity to give personal attention that most astonished both those, such as his colleagues, who knew him best, and others, such as parents paying a visit to the school, who saw him for the first time. Literally scores of the latter have spoken to me about it. Hahn seemed never to forget that this old boy returning to the school after five years had a crippled sister; that this small boy had an elder brother and three younger sisters and, more important, a donkey called Toby; that the gardener's boy once ran away from an orphanage and was missing for three nights. When he listened to what people told him casually about their families or their interests or their illnesses, he really did listen with interest, and it stuck in his mind, not to be expunged by the crisis which was probably already knocking on the restless Headmaster's door.

Those who learn about Hahn by reading what he has written, his theories of education and social philosophy, will get a curiously distorted picture of the real man. It is necessary to remember his extraordinary capacity for personal friendships and the lightness of touch that is so important a part of them, to correct the impression of heavy theorizing and systematization and the formidable moral uplift which much that he has written or formulated as part of his schools gives. It is necessary too as a corrective to the impression of romantic idealizing to remember that he successfully inspired and controlled vigorous school communities for many years, in which, in an astonishing way, boys of a great range of intelligence, temperament, background, physical handicaps and character complications undeniably flourished. In my view, a great part of the man's unique success as a schoolmaster and educationist has been due to the romanticism and realism which are so curiously, so inextricably interwoven in his nature.

I have suggested that Hahn's approach to other human beings smacks much more of the artist than the scientist, of Shakespeare rather than Freud. I should immediately make a reservation. In one sense, he has never used the eyes of an artist in dealing with people. He is much too clinical. He tries to read a boy so that he can give scope to his potential strength and enable him to overcome innate weaknesses—whether physical, mental or moral. In this way he never ceases to be the schoolmaster. Shakespeare penetrates the human identity to explore it with a view to exposing or presenting it. But the clinical schoolmaster explores to improve or ameliorate or cure. As a consequence, Hahn has never been so sure in his touch with adults as with adolescents. The former have become set in their ways, and are almost always resistant to a schoolmaster's patently good intentions. Hahn's ability to penetrate immediately to some basic weakness of the ego, which I have seen pay off again and again with boys whom possibly no one had been able to read correctly before, can err into comic aberrations when applied to adults. I remember once when we interviewed a prospective member of the staff, a man with outstanding achievements to his credit, how Hahn took me aside, saying: 'Henry, we must have this remarkable man. But he has a secret. I am certain of it. Either he drinks or takes drugs.' Now, it required a much less inspired psychological insight than Hahn's to know that this particular man did neither, and I was so convinced of Hahn's error that I was able to reassure him. I could not help being amused when months later the boys saw him snatch at his hair in a gale. Hahn's penetration, as usual, was basically sound. The man did have a carefully nursed secret. He wore a wig.

And this incident led me to wonder years ago whether it is true of all great men that they suffer from lapses just where the ordinary mortal most easily can take things in his stride. But let me give another example of Hahn's psychology at work. In the early days at Gordonstoun a boy of fifteen was sexually assaulted by a tramp as he was going from one of the scattered houses to another. It was, of course, a very disturbing experience for the boy. Hahn felt that for him the memory of such a shock must be associated with a triumph as well, and, resorting to his own characteristic school machinery, he invited him to a coaching session at the long-jump pit that evening, which he took himself. Hahn knew that this item of the Moray Badge, which required a jigsaw puzzle of achievements for qualification, was an obstacle for the boy. Using all his skill as an outstanding jumper himself, and the great encouragement which his personal enthusiasm could generate, he got him over the necessary target even though it was several inches more than he had previously achieved. I am not in a position to say whether the psychology did not have a flaw, like that in the incident previously recorded, but those who know Hahn will recognize that it is typical of the man. There must be hundreds of examples of his personal care for the individual in which he used originality and ingenuity and ignored pressing duties to give direct help on occasions when it might have been wiser administratively to have delegated the task to someone else. Should a headmaster keep important guests waiting for a lunch already served whilst he admits a boy to the room where they are assembled because he had earlier promised him a lesson in pebble exercise to cure flat feet? I was present as the lunch cooled whilst, to the astonishment of the guests, the Headmaster sat on the floor, took off his shoe and threw an india-rubber about the room with his toes!

Hahn founded Gordonstoun in 1934. But in a sense it started life much earlier, before the First World War. It was during a prolonged illness following sunstroke that he conceived the idea of a modern school. During convalescence he was forced to spend long periods in the semi-dark and had much time to think. He was keenly conscious of the shortcomings of his own schooling in Berlin when he compared it with Plato's comprehensive conception of what education of the individual might mean for himself in self-realization and for the common weal through his responsible citizenship. The first three chapters of the *Republic* were what fired his imagination and, after long gestation, inspired the birth first of Salem and then Gordonstoun. I think that increasingly he has turned away from Plato as a social philosopher. After Hitler, the dangers inherent in the conception of an élite selected and educated to govern are too much on top of us, and it is doubtful if that aspect of Plato ever had much appeal for Hahn. But the Socratic conception of the relationship between what one does and why one does it had a profound influence on him later, as he developed his school constitutions like those of small states. When I joined Gordonstoun at the end of its first year, I was told that it was a 'demonstration of the Salem system'. And I think the word 'system' was correctly used, for what Hahn did at Salem had been 'to systematize'. There was a reason—at least in Hahn's mind—for everything that was done. This could easily have led to inflexible rigidity and there was always this tendency, but fortunately the influence of Plato worked also in the opposite direction; the method of dialogue leads to the fluid definition, and in my view this fluidity was reinforced by the transfer of the 'system' to Britain. It was a bit off-putting to someone like myself, to begin with, to find that by using my common sense and experience I might be, unawares, infringing some established principle of Hahn's system. But it was exciting and stimulating too, after being for eight years almost completely my own master in professional matters, to have to justify what I was about. And Hahn too was stimulated by the discussions so long as the dissenter was capable of standing up to the first steam-roller assault of his powerful conviction. The German mind has a tendency to systematize and the English to be suspicious of any such generalization. For that reason, I have the feeling Hahn has always been at his most constructive and most fruitful when working with the British people. He was certainly well aware of their importance to him personally and always surrounded himself with them at Salem. Also they are—or at least the kind he chose for partners—not easily intimidated by steam-rollers.

It may be helpful if I list a number of things which in 1934 Hahn regarded as characteristic of the Salem 'system' which his new Gordonstoun was to 'demonstrate'. The worlds of action and thought must 'no longer be divided into hostile camps'. Special steps were necessary to build up 'the imagination of the boy of decision and the will-power of the dreamer' so that 'wise men will have the nerve to lead, and men of action will have the vision to imagine the consequences of their decisions'. This meant in practice insisting that every boy should use the confidence gained in opportunities the school would provide for each to indulge in what he was good at, to help him to overcome his own defeatism in things distasteful. 'No boys should be compelled into opinions; but it is criminal negligence not to compel them into experience.' The system meant that the keen sailor was liable to be press-ganged into acting in Shakespeare plays and the promising actor into a sailing expedition.

Hahn was driven into exile because he insisted that it was the latent character of the German people to show compassion. He quoted Prince Max as believing that a nation loses itself for long periods, so that its character 'as God wanted it to be' only flares up at rare intervals. Both individual and nation should listen to the Greek poet Pindar's admonition: 'Grow into what you are'. 'The system', with the experience of a Nazi take-over so vividly in Hahn's mind, was vigilantly on the lookout to bring schoolboy incidents of bullying or mob justice into the open and use them as opportunities for education. Hahn, good schoolmaster that he is, has never been fearful of repetition; it is significant that as Headmaster of Gordonstoun he had an almost obsessive preoccupation with the Parable of the Good Samaritan. The desire to have it read to the school seemed to seize him again and again, like the Ancient Mariner's periodic need to tell the adventure of his enlightenment.

To give practical shape to such an ambitious educational ideal, Hahn had conceived the system that all parents should be asked to assess themselves in the highest of a series of fee grades that they could afford, the upper grades being above, and the lower below, what the education cost. We have found a satisfactory formula at Gordonstoun to make this system work successfully for more than thirty years, but it is so contrary to what people have become used to in such matters that no other independent school so far as I know, has ever adopted it. Yet for the school's whole history between a quarter and a fifth of Gordonstoun's parents have voluntarily paid more than they need so that others can pay less. The object was to create a society free enough of the enervating atmosphere of privilege to be a possible medium in which to teach human sympathy and concern. A school society dependent on fee-payers needs to include those 'who have to struggle for existence'. For the same reason, the system demanded that there should be day-boys. It demanded too that there should be girls, but for a public school in Scotland in the 1930s the fluid definition had to save the situation. Gordonstoun to start with had a hard struggle to get enough fee-paying parents willing to send their boys. That number would probably have been quartered had we been co-educational on top of our other innovations. The place could not have lasted a year.

It is interesting to recall that when Hahn gave an explanatory broadcast talk on the B.B.C. entitled 'The Salem System' in January 1934, after a brief introduction, he chose as his first item the attempt which his System had made to humanize the individual and society, and allowed this theme to take up one-third of his allotted time.

It is unnecessary to categorize here all the Gordonstoun characteristics which were part of the System, none of them 'new', as the founder would claim, but all given a new self-consciousness. In the light of more than thirty years' work using the System and adapting it, what shall I say of its virtues and failings? Did Hahn, as suggested in my book on Gordonstoun, often 'show a genius for exploiting the experience of others, thus releasing, by a simple twist, fresh vitality from a tired tradition'? Or was he more liable, as some of his critics think, to impose doctrinaire self-consciousness upon immature minds and unjustified limitations upon their freedom of thought and action? Did he, through the System, seek to forestall the mistakes by which, in fact, young people learn? And, furthermore, did he, by using the Trust System, the colour-bearers and other devices, try to close the safety valves of revolt against discipline which made the traditional British public schools, with their hangover of severe Victorian moral pressures, tolerable? I have spent so much anxious thought on this aspect of the System at Gordonstoun that it would be stupid to deny the inherent danger has been real. The answer is that such a wide variety of people have used this or that idea from the System with success, adapting it to suit their own temperaments and circumstances, that most of the inherently undesirable elements have been eliminated in practice and the System has been fruitful beyond the dreams of all its early protagonists except Hahn himself. Let me add that he has given his blessing to nearly all the adaptations —at least at Gordonstoun. But even in his eighties he is still impatient that what he calls the 'islands of healing' in an inflamed body politic are insufficient to keep pace with an ever more critical decline.

As these doubts, where Hahn is concerned, are in many people's minds, it is as well that they should be clearly faced and answered by his supporters. Man, as he moves into the technological age, is abandoning many of the folk traditions that have been his guide throughout history. Against their relics in the Establishment the young today are in revolt. Even those reluctant to admit that this amounts to a critical situation for contemporary civilized man are no longer in a position to dispute the weight of evidence from all over the world as well as under their noses. There has, of course, always been revolt by the young against their elders. That is a biological necessity and an historical commonplace. But today the breach in sympathy between two generations has no precedent. Family education in morals and religious education in ethics lost their grip between the wars, and after 1945 have ceased as a relevant factor in many countries. Was Kurt Hahn wrong in the 1930s, foreseeing as he did this situation, to try to get the schools to accept responsibility for filling the vacuum this created? It is astonishing that so much thought should have been expended by the teaching profession upon the education of the mind and yet so little upon education for life, for human relations in the new industrial world. Many of the problems facing society today are due to inadequate schooling in a sphere where the family and the Churches have now either abrogated responsibility or lost an effective grip. There is a vacuum which the schools do not think it their job to fill, so that the field is left clear for more willing and more irresponsible educators: the journalists and television personalities.

It is hardly to be expected that, setting out on a fairly lone trail after the First World War, Hahn's steps, when we look back on them from another country and another age, should appear sometimes heavy and blundering. The terrain then still provided the firm going of Christian orthodoxy, supported by the time-hallowed disciplines of loyalty, honour, military order and courage. But today that terrain is notoriously difficult and Hahn's importance for all of us is that he at least stepped in where angels fear to tread and suggested solutions, some that have caught on in a world-wide scale and others that have at least promoted thought and discussion.

The Gordonstoun years were probably the most testing of Hahn's life. To begin with, having been a rich man, he was suddenly bereft of his personal fortune. This frustrated him, but never inhibited him, and in the circumstances he had to call upon reserves of resourcefulness and courage beyond those needed for the founding of Salem. And he was, of course, an exile, a German in a Britain where the legacy of suspicion and even hatred from the First World War was by no means dead. As the danger of a new war increased so the distrust intensified, particularly in Moray, where the vulnerable new school community, after a promising start, found itself struggling to survive financially. When the war began, the situation became critical, particularly after the invasion of Norway. Members of the school were refused service in the Local Defence Volunteers (the early Home Guard). There were a number of good reasons for Gordonstoun's evacuation to central Wales in 1940, but the chief was the antagonism of influential Morayshire people. In Wales, where the school remained till the war was over in 1945, Hahn increasingly, without personal finance, worked himself to the point of nervous prostration. He felt impelled by three separate convictions, any one of which would have sufficiently stretched him:

1   That Gordonstoun must survive against all odds. In 1942, when the school's financial fortunes were at their lowest ebb, he still saw this task in terms of a crusade. He reported to the Governors:

> I am conscious of many who regard our continued existence to be of importance, not only for the reform of the national educational system. They believe in the European tradition which is entrusted to many centres all over Europe. It is also in the keeping of Gordonstoun as it was in that of Salem. . . . I feel, Mr. Chairman, that we shall overcome our difficulties as long as we remain convinced that we have not only the right but the duty to live and grow. I should like to close with Mr. Geoffrey Winthrop-Young's words: 'We are more than a school; we are a movement.'

2   He considered it his duty to transmit to those responsible for the nation's military training what he had learnt from years of thought and experience about basic fitness. Intensive specific training, he claimed, if it were not built on a basis of vital health, would defeat its own ends. It was in Wales and during the war that years of preliminary thought and experiment eventually found practical expression in a series of adventure courses and a centre for them in

Aberdovey, which became the first Outward Bound School. Today there are six in this country, each with a Board of its own and a central Trust to manage and co-ordinate all their complex affairs. The Outward Bound Trust has sponsored more than twenty schools in five continents. But the inception of this great movement, the philosophy behind it, the task of getting practical sailors and moun- taineers to co-operate with educationalists, politicians and captains of industry, the initial experiments for the solution of detailed prob- lems of programme, and the relation between enterprise and safety —all these were for months the daily concern of a busy Headmaster with his own community to manage, who at the same time was campaigning to have his voice heard as one who knew the heart of Germany and believed there were ways to shorten the war and retain the chance of a constructive peace.

3   Hahn was indeed haunted by the prospect that as the struggle became more intense it would become more brutal. His mind was constantly concerned, as a British citizen which he had become before the war, with ways in which the early defeat of the enemy could be accomplished, but more than most men intensely involved in this way, Hahn kept clear the notion that this was a war for a cause rather than a national struggle. It was, for so sensitive a nature, hard to stave off the horror underlying the conflict. He had pupils fighting on both sides, and with many in each category he had, as I have earlier suggested, a bond more like that found in families or between friends. I find it impossible to convey the intense activity of Hahn's mind to keep clear the conflict of loyalties of principle, interwoven as these were with loyalties of friendship at this time. Just as I have often been prompted to think how different history might have been had more Germans in the 1930s shared his long- term loyalty to moral principle and come out, as he did, against Hitler before it was too late, so too I have wished that post-war history could have had a more hopeful basis, that in the later stages of the struggle long-term loyalties of principle had not given way to expediency. Such speculations may be fruitless, but if one has known a man like Hahn they are also irresistible. The young today also speculate; they read of Hiroshima and ask why more of their elders did not take the long view that would have given their own genera- tion a better prospect.

The end of the war saw Gordonstoun more confident, larger than at the start, but still with a tenuous existence financially. Hahn insisted on an immediate return to Scotland, even though the old house had suffered a major fire during Army occupation and was only partially restored. Permits for restoration and for the necessary expansion and adaptation were hard to come by; so was the necessary finance; so was the labour. Boys and masters worked at these practical tasks in school holidays. The school lived partly in Army huts. The place was a mess.

The Headmaster was often away. As soon as it was possible to revisit Germany, he went back in a series of visits. He was campaigning to influence the re-education of German youth. Salem, with a creditable history of resistance, had eventually been taken over by the SA, but was restarted immediately hostilities ceased, with the approval of the French—for Salem was in the French Zone of Occupation. Twice in those years I accompanied him on such visits. Journeys with Hahn never fail to be unusual. Unlike most of us, travelling relaxes and revives him; he is stimulated by the casual encounters.

Intent on the purpose behind the journey, he manages its details casually, as it were nudging the arrangements into place with his foot—but what a knowing, enterprising foot! Time-tables seem to adjust themselves to his whim, engine-drivers are in league with him, and hold up the start of the express whilst he conducts an excited invalid infinitely slowly to her reserved compartment, saying with irritating assurance as guards blow whistles and porters shout and safely seated travellers stare from the windows, 'We have plenty of time, my dear. Don't hurry. There's plenty of time.' And on journeys, at intervals between the opportunities he always finds, whatever the physical restrictions, for deep sleep and the similarly certain spells of deep absorption in thought, or rummaging through a wealth of letters, memoranda, notes, and newspapers, he invariably manages to be gay like a schoolboy on holiday. Travelling in Germany, he has the perspicacity, for instance, to know that his Scottish driver will be miserable following a breakfast of German sausage and ersatz coffee and has remembered to buy a bar of chocolate to appease him. But that happened on the second of my German journeys with him. The first was in a three-seater single-engined hired Proctor aeroplane piloted by a friend, Lord Malcolm Douglas-

Hamilton, who, with his younger son, eventually tragically lost his life piloting an aircraft in Central Africa. It happened to be the first time I had flown, and I wish all subsequent flights could have been as delightful. When we reached Switzerland with about fifty miles still to go, Hahn found it would be necessary to fly the length of Germany, south to north and back, to gain permission to land near Salem. It was April 1947 and, but for Hahn's persistence in getting through the red tape, the whole expedition would have foundered. Lord Malcolm was not in the least put out that we must fly 1,000 miles to cover about fifty. During these frustrating negotiations, similar to those which had already delayed us for ten days in London, Hahn sent Lord Malcolm and me off to enjoy ourselves on interesting visits in Switzerland. Meantime he, typically, stayed in Berne, without pyjamas or toothbrush, to make sure nothing further should go wrong with the awkward permits. He paid visits of kindness before he rejoined us at the Swiss–German border, and we found he had already arranged to break the journey in Hamburg to study the school situation there, and especially the availability of extra food for the children, and then to stay as the guests of the British Regional Commissioner in Schleswig-Holstein, and there take the opportunity to visit a huge camp of refugees from eastern Germany. But, knowing my own interest in Gothic churches, he also saw that I had time to visit the Schleswig *dome* with a guide. On the side he was negotiating about the founding of an Outward Bound School on the Baltic, and an independent boarding school for the region, and when I went next with him by car it was to inspect the house in which it would shortly begin. On the return north we used the freedom of the air to fly low over the Rhine, tracing the bomb damage to miles of end-to-end barges, and then, like liberated tourists, we would circle some turreted mansion, trying to trace on the map what it was. In a day we had gone from summer to winter and now in a day we reversed the process and landed near Salem, where Hahn again busied himself to try to ease the occupation restrictions and increase the supply of food. That was in April 1947. A year later, with our Gordonstoun car and driver, we were in Germany again. On that journey an incident occurred so unusual and yet so typical of aspects of Hahn's personality which are difficult to convey to those who do not know him that I am tempted to recount it.

In 1948 the German main roads were full of foot-travellers, for public transport was still almost non-existent. Clothes were still short too and many of the men wore some sort of uniform. They all thumbed for lifts from anything that passed. All the way from Aachen, where we crossed the border, to Hamburg, we passed them in scores, but could offer no lift because every seat was filled with our luggage. But at Hamburg we were to return for a second night to the same lodgings and left the luggage behind, motoring north via Kiel to Schleswig. In spite of the empty seat beside the driver, we did not at first think of breaking what was now a habit—to ignore appeals for lifts. Hahn was absorbed. He seemed asleep, but his imagination, always practical as well as creative, was, as I knew, deeply involved with the need to offer the German young, affected as many of them had been by the exciting demands of Nazi adventure, some alternative which would demand the same kind of bold initiative and devotion in a more worthy cause. One of the reasons for this journey was to meet the founder of the first German Outward Bound School at Weisenhaus on the Baltic, where it was proposed to train the boys who went for monthly courses to man the Coastguard station. Suddenly from his dreamy apathy Hahn sprang into life and called out to our driver 'Stop! Stop! That man asked for a lift!' Similar uniformed men had been asking for lifts for miles. By the time we stopped we were 100 yards beyond the young man. But he came running up and got in beside the driver. Hahn started to talk to him in German, which I do not understand. The young man turned to him and started talking with excitement. Hahn himself became excited. Staccato, he translated to me without interrupting the dialogue: 'He helped to save two drowning men last night. . . . He's a Coastguard coming off duty and going back to his wife. . . . He works under a British naval officer. . . . The cargo ship struck a mine and they heard the explosion. . . . They searched all night before they found them. . . . A Norwegian and an Italian. . . . They were nearly gone, but saved by artificial respiration. . . . One recovered quickly, but he had to strip for the other and give him "the heat of my body".' Then, with a grin to me: 'When they parted the Italian embraced and kissed him and the Norwegian shook his hand.' The excited exchange went on then for some time and was concluded. The German turned round and was silent. Hahn turned to me: 'He apologized for talking so much. He says when a thing like that happens you just have to tell someone. He's an uneducated man,

but this has had a profound effect on him and he speaks with the insight of Aristotle: "You feel all the time: *it might have been me*." '
Hahn was looking for evidence to convince himself, and so convince others, that to take part in rescue strikes the deep chords of the spirit. By what instinct did he choose to give a lift to that one man in a thousand?

At home post-war Gordonstoun, still quite inadequate materially and with years of insecurity still ahead of it, was proving a healthy pasture for all kinds of boys to grow up in and at the same time a good workshop for testing the practicability of a good many of its founder's ideas. At Salem there had been some sailing on Lake Constance, but it was not till he came to Gordonstoun that Hahn was able to give scope to his ideas of the part that untamed Nature in its more formidable aspects of sea and mountains could play in the education of enterprising individuals. It has seemed to me a curiosity that Britain, with its continuous history of maritime triumphs, should have delayed so long before exploiting the possibilities of seamanship for purposes of general education. Training *for* the sea there has always been, but practically no training *through* the sea. It seems odd that such an innovation should be the work of a foreigner. It is an example of the restricting effect of the separation of education from life that came about when compulsory education was introduced 100 years ago and narrowed its definition to academic teaching in the classroom. The lead that progressive education gave between the wars in correcting the initial error has had its influence on the national policy since 1945. But habits of mind change reluctantly and it seems doubtful whether there is a sufficiently developed technique in the sphere beyond the academic to educate adequately in the present schools those who will be compelled to stay on an extra year against their will.

In the years before the war Hahn's impulse to make a great deal of seamanship in the Gordonstoun curriculum sprang from what he felt to be the need to introduce adventure and danger into the experience of boys who would be starved of some vitamin of the spirit without it. Though he had virtually no science in his own education and modern biology has not directly influenced him, he acted in this as though he had already read Konrad Lorenz's *On Aggression*, for he knew instinctively the need for what Lorenz calls 're-direction' or 're-directed activity'. Lorenz's evidence and arguments are too complex and too massively compiled for me to attempt to compress into a paragraph. But I quote one passage which shows how closely related are the explorations of the classically educated Kurt Hahn and the conscientiously scientific Konrad Lorenz in one area of human experience:

> The noble warrior's typical virtues, such as his readiness to sacrifice himself in the service of a common cause, disciplined submission to the rank order of the group, mutual aid in the face of deadly danger, and, above all, a superlatively strong bond of friendship between men, were obviously indispensable if a small tribe of the type we have to assume for early man was to survive in competition with others. All these virtues are still desirable in modern man and still command our instinctive respect. It is undeniable that there is no situation in which all these virtues shine so brilliantly as in war. . . .
>
> Fortunately, there are other ways in which the above-mentioned, admittedly valuable, virtues can be cultivated. The harder and more dangerous forms of sport, particularly those demanding the working together of larger groups, such as mountain-climbing, diving, off-shore and ocean sailing, but also other dangerous undertakings, like polar expeditions and, above all, the exploration of space, all giving scope for militant enthusiasm, allowing nations to fight each other in hard and dangerous competition without engendering national or political hatred.

Of course, such ideas did not originate with the modern school of behaviourist biologists. Hahn likes to use the phrase which he took from the philosopher William James, 'the moral equivalent of war'. And he finds expression of his own thought in Tennyson's 'The Sailor Boy',

> God help me! Save I take my part
> Of danger on the roaring sea
> A devil rises in my heart. . . .

or in 'Rizpah', where a mother laments her son hanged for robbing a coach. I deliberately set out the over-tuneful Tennyson as a prosaic statement:

> They swore that he dare not rob the mail and he swore that he

8 The School Choir and Orchestra in Salem's Prayer Room,
the Protestant Chapel, formerly the Bishop's breakfast room

9   The complex of Gordonstoun School buildings with Covesea lighthouse and the Moray Firth behind

10 View of Gordonstoun main building from the south

11   Gordonstoun Hockey Team, 1935. From left to right:
Standing: Adam Arnold-Brown; Jocelin Winthrop-Young;
Teddy Sale; Christel Nohl; Commander Lewty; Mr Waylen;
Kurt Hahn
Kneeling: Prince Philip; Jan Weber; Guido Kocherthaler;
Joerg von Bonnet

12   A production of *Macbeth*
in the early days of
Gordonstoun; Kurt Hahn,
the producer, is standing on
the lawn in the centre

would. . . . He was always so wild—and idle—and couldn't be idle. . . . The King should have made him a soldier; he would have been one of the best.

But whilst the war rolled nearer and engulfed the world and passed, leaving in its wake the moral chaos, the disillusion of the young, the situation in which today we all familiarly live, the sea became for Hahn not just an environment of danger and challenge, but one where ever-present potential threat required ever mobilized resources of rescue: coastguards, life-boats, beach rescue, and the skills of resuscitation. At the same time, as more and more people took to the mountains for sport and relaxation, there was a similar need for mobilized rescue, with its own equipment and techniques. As the years have passed, Hahn's belief that a large proportion of young people need adventure as a factor in the 'healthy pasture' which will enable them to reach their full stature in maturity has not grown less; but it has seemed to him to be by itself insufficient. Increasingly, he has become obsessed with the therapeutic value of associating it with rescue and with other kinds of service less dramatic, but more available in an urban civilization.

At Gordonstoun Hahn himself was responsible for starting the school coastguard service before the war. It is part of the pattern of his life that he has been the instigator and others the builders—and better builders than he, because his often romantic dreams had to be fitted to the limitations of all kinds of commonplace boys and men. The Gordonstoun services that have sprung up in the wake of the Coastguard Watchers have this in common: they are recognized, and sometimes supported, by regional or national organizations. The Watchers man a station of Her Majesty's Coastguard Service, the firemen belong to the North-eastern Fire Brigade, the Mountain Rescue work in collaboration with the R.A.F., and the school's Beach Rescue service is now part of a growing national organization. Whilst they lasted, the school's bloodhounds, trained to follow cold trails, were at the disposal of the police. On the other hand, the youngest and one of the most successful of these school services is the Gordonstoun Community Service, which has put itself at the disposal of the old and sick and poor in the immediate vicinity of the school. As yet this service is not linked to any central organization.

Although Gordonstoun, catching the bug from Kurt Hahn, has

experienced rescue service earlier and more intensely, as an epidemic, than has been the case elsewhere, the infection is today widespread, and Hahn is by no means the only 'carrier'. The Royal Life-saving Society had been spreading it for years before Hahn came on the scene. The Beach Rescue Service in Australia had been highly organized for many years before it overspread its national boundaries. Such services as V.S.O. have only indirect connections with Hahn's work. And today organizations like the Outward Bound Trust and the Atlantic Colleges, and many schools like Sevenoaks in Kent, have become dynamos of ideas and experiment and effective achievement, developing our simple Gordonstoun formula in directions and on a scale which is quite outside the range of a single school.

Two years after the war as Headmaster of a school still woefully short of capital, which, quite apart from its task of educating 400 boys, he required to be a volcano of educational ideas that should run like lava throughout the British Isles and the continents of Europe and North America, Hahn had not allowed the strain which he thus imposed on himself to ease. In an appeal for funds, I wrote in January 1947:

> In many ways Gordonstoun's problems would be simplified if the Greater Gordonstoun projects could be postponed to allow for a two-year period of consolidation and administrative overhaul which the boarding school needs after twelve years 'living in tents'. But this is scarcely practicable because Hahn feels justified in remaining Headmaster only if we can proceed with these plans forthwith: and because Greater Gordonstoun is one of our main grounds of appeal for material support of one kind or another. At the present time education is in the melting-pot and there is a search for new moulds. There are many indications that the trend of enlightened thought today is in a direction which Gordonstoun has taken for a decade.

The actual campaign to try to get funds, not only for Gordonstoun, but for all the other institutions and schemes he had at heart, which took him to London constantly, to Germany and the USA, was the last straw that cracked him. In 1952 his health broke down, and he retired as Headmaster of Gordonstoun a year later at the age of sixty-seven. But by this time Gordonstoun was sufficiently on its feet to work out its own salvation and Hahn, recovering quickly, was set free to think, to travel, lecture, campaign and inspire. In his eighties he is almost as active as he was ten years earlier, and during the last decade has been able to forward the work in which he so passionately believes and watch it prosper to an extent that would satisfy any but himself. But he, like many great schoolmasters, has himself never quite grown up. He is as impatient as the students who will not wait for their middle-aged elders to introduce the reforms they regard as urgent, and as improvident of his own security and safety.

Widely scattered now are a host of friends, collaborators and admirers whom he has inspired or encouraged or helped in more practical ways. A loose circle of schools, some well-established, such as the Salem and Gordonstoun schools and Anavryta in Greece, which acknowledge him directly as their founder, others which have in their foundation direct personal connections, such as Luisenlund in Schleswig-Holstein, Box Hill in Surrey, Rannoch in Perthshire, Dunrobin in Sutherland, Battisborough in Devon and the International School at Ibadan in Nigeria, look to him with respect and affection. A much wider circle of schools acknowledge his influence. There are Outward Bound schools now all over the world, to most of which his name is still more than a legend. The movement which has founded the first of a series of Atlantic Colleges acknowledges his inspiration. Dons and schoolmasters, directors of education, famous seamen, mountaineers and explorers, captains of industry, bankers, politicians, peers of the realm and princes have delighted in his company. And these come from many lands and races, for Kurt Hahn, who often appears so Victorian in manners and language, belongs in a deep sense to the new age of hope. Like the great artists and scientists, like the astronauts, he is a citizen of global mankind.

The establishment of the First Outward Bound School at Aberdovey, Merionethshire

James M. Hogan

From the middle of the 1930s Kurt Hahn became increasingly dedicated to the idea of extending the influence of Gordonstoun in two important respects. The regular training in simple athletic skills which had been practised with notable success at Salem had been linked with an expedition test which required a demonstration of stamina, determination and some knowledge of map-reading and route-finding. Gradually a fairly complex syllabus had evolved whereby boys were able to work for an award which came to be known as the Moray Badge. Patently, it was Hahn's hope that eventually this might provide a pattern to be adopted progressively by other counties throughout England and Scotland—and even ultimately by the Commonwealth countries.

The first obstacle to be overcome was the objection of those who argued that Hahn's achievements with selected pupils in a specially favoured boarding school were quite irrelevant to the tasks to be accomplished elsewhere. So Hahn issued an open invitation to the young people living in the neighbourhood of Gordonstoun to use the human and physical resources of the school and train alongside the full-time pupils. On the basis of this proposal, the King George V Foundation were persuaded to promise a sum of £2,000 to assist in providing a cinder running-track for an all-the-year-round training programme.

Hahn's efforts to generalize the Moray Badge idea resulted in an increasing flow of articles and speeches; from time to time intensive bursts of correspondence in the more influential newspapers and periodicals indicated that he was making important converts.

While the campaign for the badge was pursued with energy, Hahn was equally concerned with a second cause, both being complementary and essential the one to the other.

In November 1938, in a letter to the Chairman of his Governors, Hahn asked, 'Can a community of adolescent males be kept spiritually healthy?' and he himself provided the answer:

> It can, on condition that such a community gives up its isolation and renders public service to the district in which it is located. I consider one of the chief dangers in an isolated school the turning of the eye inward. Boys observe each other too closely, domestic events are exaggerated, gossip fills every empty moment.

Consequently, Hahn began the attempt to interest a variety of trusts in the idea of founding an adolescent college near to the school. He visualized that some 100 boys aged from fourteen to eighteen would be sent by voluntary organizations for courses lasting four weeks. They would specialize in agriculture or seamanship or horsemanship, but in addition would enjoy the physical training and the community life of the boarding school. Hahn believed that the school would benefit from a widening of its horizons and its responsibilities, while the boys from day-schools or industry would be given an encouraging start in a programme of training which in less promising circumstances might have been unduly daunting.

As long as Gordonstoun remained in Morayshire, none of the appeals for assistance met with success. In part this must be attributed to the form in which Hahn presented his applications for financial support. These were characterized by his imaginative ideas, his ambitious proposals and his colourful style of writing—but they contained no estimates of cost or positive indications that any detailed planning had been undertaken. Only isolated projects, such as the Summer Schools, existed as a demonstration of what Hahn had in mind. When war came and the school settled temporarily in Wales, it was not long before Hahn had renewed the attack, but received no support for anything more than a short course for Fire Service messengers and pre-service cadets.

I first met Hahn when such a course was in progress at Plas Dinam in the summer of 1940. Because of my own previous experience as a schoolmaster and Scoutmaster, I was able to comment constructively on what I saw. At this time also a number of conferences were being arranged to commend the County Badge idea to youth organizations and education authorities. At the end of 1940 this resulted in the establishment of a County Badge Experimental Committee composed of a group of distinguished educationists. Henceforward appeals were being made for funds for two separate enterprises: first, the extension of the badge idea to day-schools and youth organizations generally, and second, the establishment of a boarding school for demonstration of the County Badge form of training, preferably in close association with Gordonstoun itself.

In the summer of 1941 Hahn suggested that I should become the Secretary of the County Badge Experimental Committee. An anonymous donor had made it possible for a simple secretariat to be established, though it could operate fully for only three months unless further funds were immediately raised. I arranged to be seconded for three months from my normal job, and soon reached a number of conclusions. At this period of the war most active young teachers had entered military service, and those who remained were finding it difficult to maintain even the well-established practices. It was idle to expect the rapid adoption and development of a pioneer venture which would only be likely to succeed if young people could be guided and assisted by enthusiastic teachers and leaders. Furthermore, there was no good reason to expect sufficient financial support to provide adequate stimulus and advice to such teachers and youth leaders as were prepared to attempt to apply Hahn's ideas. Bitterly disappointed, therefore, I felt obliged to warn Hahn that at the end of the three months I should have no alternative but to return to my normal work. He then formed the idea that my services could be retained if I were to become the Warden of a training centre; to demonstrate the method rather than be Secretary of a committee merely commending it. It seemed to me that if we were unable to raise the funds needed to maintain a modest secretariat we could scarcely hope to attract the vastly greater sum of money necessary to launch a permanent school, with its buildings, furniture, special equipment and the expense of staffing it, until a regular income was assured. Hahn was entirely undaunted by difficulties of this kind. It was obvious that he had long been nursing an idea, which now for the first time he judged to be ripe for development.

Plas Dinam, the war-time home of Gordonstoun, was nearly thirty miles inland from the sea. Seamanship was nevertheless such a well-established activity of the school that boys had been sent for short periods to live in a rented house at Aberdovey, a village on the north shore of an attractive estuary which provided the nearest access to the sea. Some of the school's small craft had been transported from Scotland, and during the summer of 1941 the schooner *Prince Louis* had been sailed down. There was, therefore, at Aberdovey a modest nucleus around which training in seamanship could be developed. The boats, however, were all in very poor condition and much expenditure would be necessary to bring them into a sound state. And if a sea-going craft such as the *Prince Louis* were to be employed as well as the smaller cutters and dinghies, a generous staff of experienced seamen would be absolutely essential. Furthermore, Hahn had discovered a house which he thought suitable as a future training headquarters; a cursory examination revealed that considerable capital expenditure would be necessary to fit it for any such purpose.

One could perhaps be forgiven for viewing Hahn's idea of establishing a training demonstration at Aberdovey as totally unrealistic. Replies to appeals he had previously made to Government departments and to private trusts alike had been such as to discourage all but the most determined. There was no doubt, however, about Hahn's determination. He revealed now the hopes he had pinned on Mr Lawrence Holt, senior member of the family firm of Alfred Holt & Company. Lawrence Holt had long been an admirer of Hahn's educational practice. He had sent one of his own sons to Gordonstoun and had financed scholarships there for the sons of local people who might ultimately look to the sea for their careers. He was Chairman of the Governors of the training ship, HMS *Conway*, at that time moored off Bangor in the Menai Straits, and he had met Hahn there when the *Prince Louis* had anchored nearby on her war-time passage from the north of Scotland to Aberdovey. Possibly there had been some discussion then about a combination of the tradition of *Conway*, the inspiration of Gordonstoun and the Holt resources. There was, however, no record nor any evidence whatsoever of any undertaking by Mr Holt that he would be prepared to provide support on the scale that would be needed if even the most limited experiment were to be set on foot. For this reason, I found Hahn's optimism difficult to understand, and was full of misgiving when he insisted that I should prepare a scheme showing how an effective training scheme could be established and financed.

Hahn had two great advantages in this project. First of all there was Holt's tremendous admiration for his educational vision. Secondly, Hahn knew of Holt's faith in the virtues of sail-training. His own company was quite exceptional in that it ran its very large merchant shipping fleet with its vessels uninsured. The view was that it was cheaper to try to deserve freedom from accidents than to insure against them. Thus everything possible was done through staff selection and training to ensure that Holt's ships were manned by the finest officers they could attract. But in the Battle of the Atlantic it was becoming clear that the men whose training had been obtained only in steam and motor-ships were unprepared technically and physically for the hazards they were being called upon to face. When their ships were sunk many who took safely to the boats were unable to survive the ordeal of ocean voyaging in small craft.

When once one knew of Lawrence Holt's deep concern about these matters it was comparatively easy to present a proposal which would give young seamen the preparation for emergency which Holt regarded as imperative, and at the same time demonstrate Hahn's County Badge training scheme idea under favourable conditions.

By the autumn of 1941 the County Badge scheme had been firmly formalized, and a publication had been issued under the title *The Fourfold Achievement*. Candidates were required to pass physical tests (involving swimming, sprinting, distance-running, jumping and throwing), to undertake a project demanding prolonged study or reputable performance in some art or craft or skill, an expedition requiring care in preparation and some stamina in execution and, finally, training for defined service to their fellows.

It was easy to relate this to the Aberdovey project. Small-boat sailing and elementary seamanship could offer a common basis for project work. Physical training would assist the development of stamina, which, together with technical skill, would be tested in expeditions both afloat and in the exposed mountainous country which lay readily to hand. As for service, there would be constant preparation for rescue operations in the form of lifeboat drills, rocket apparatus and later the techniques of evacuating casualties in mountainous terrain.

Lawrence Holt was immediately captivated by the possibilities. He undertook to purchase the house for the school base, to supply such experienced seamen as were required for the nautical side of the training and to provide a capital sum of £1,000.

Generous as this was, it was patently insufficient to ensure the safety of the venture. To Hahn, however, after years of frustrated hope, this was enough. Nothing could puncture his confidence that support would now begin to flow. In October 1941 the school was launched. Immediately, accommodation existed for no more than twenty-four boys. Eight of these came from Gordonstoun, eight from *Conway* and eight from Alfred Holt & Company. Progressively fresh accommodation came into use until within a year or so over 100 boys were being accepted on eleven courses a year, each lasting for twenty-eight days.

The enterprise was not brought into being without strain. Though Hahn's faith was fully justified and further sources of financial support were tapped, the early years were by no means free from anxiety. Recruitment of trainees had to be expanded from the small but secure initial flow to such a figure as was necessary to maintain a reasonable balance between income and unavoidably heavy outgoings.

The training itself presented difficulties enough. Dr Zimmermann, who directed the physical-training programme with unparalleled humour and skill bordering on genius, had to establish the essential facilities on a rocky hillside; his running tracks perforce were main roads, fortunately denuded of fast traffic by the exigencies of war-time. The small boats were obliged to operate in a tidal estuary without confidence that they could be supported, as they are today, by a fast, powerful and reliable motor vessel. The schooner operated in the unlit waters of a bay round which were situated no less than seven military establishments training men in anti-aircraft and anti-tank gunnery, bombing, rocket-firing and other highly lethal prac-tices. Thus each cruise presented problems and anxieties vastly in excess of those thrown up by the normal struggle with the natural elements. Later the mountain country used for expedition training also became an area selected for battle-training by marine com-mandos and others, all of whom scattered a quantity of unexploded ammunition to add to our concern.

Only those who have worked closely with Hahn have any conception of the strain under which he labours when young people are put in hazard because of the interpretation of his educational ideas in exciting practical forms. Certainly the early operations at Aberdovey gave ample material for concern, and there were periods when Hahn telephoned hourly for news of our adventures. There is no doubt that the Outward Bound schools could not conceivably have established themselves with their remarkable record of freedom from accidents had it not been for Hahn's almost obsessive concern that there should be no trace of carelessness or recklessness in our affairs.

There were other important respects, however, in which his personal influence was plainly felt. He was enormously conscious of the subtle effect of environment, and chose the houses in which his enterprises were to be accommodated as much, I am sure, for their atmosphere and outlook as for their physical suitability. I recall his rage when, depressed by damage to wall surfaces in overcrowded and congested premises, I had ordered redecoration in a drab and utilitarian manner. At the time I thought it inexcusable that Hahn should have countermanded my instructions and insisted on the obliteration of what he felt to be my grave error of judgment. Today I know that he was right.

The evolution of Outward Bound practice illustrated a balance between the ideas of the co-founders. Holt felt that there was a duty to create emergencies in order to train people to react to the unexpected. Hahn, who was not essentially a practical man, plainly believed that emergencies represented the consequences of lack of prudence and foresight. In the tension between these two different approaches in the Outward Bound schools, there undoubtedly evolved an attitude and a body of practice which made it possible for them to grow and spread to four continents. Others will write of the process of growth. I must content myself with this simple statement of how the first of the schools came to be established and how, through Hahn's unswerving determination and attention to fundamentals, the bases were laid on which a whole series of interesting variations could ultimately be planned.

The Outward Bound Movement

Sir Spencer Summers

By the time the war was over, four years had passed since the Outward Bound Sea School at Aberdovey was first established. It had already attracted considerable attention, and had been highly recommended to the Admiralty by Commander Bedwell, who was to do so much for its subsequent development. A number of firms were sending boys for twenty-six days' challenging experience, in addition to those whose boys were destined for the Merchant Navy. The fee was £15 a course, and between 500 and 600 boys a year were taking the training.

The future of the school depended on the goodwill of Alfred Holt & Company, through whose foresight and generosity it had been started in the first place. Apart from the hidden subsidy in the form of staff and galley-boys seconded for months at a time, the school was running at a loss. Clearly it must go forward or go back.

It was in these circumstances that, in 1946, at Kurt Hahn's suggestion, a group of those of us who were keen to harvest the experience to date and establish a more sure foundation for future development met at Trinity College, Cambridge, under the auspices of the Master, George Trevelyan. The outcome was a decision to found the Outward Bound Trust, to which the school was in due course given by Alfred Holt & Company.

By degrees more boys were recruited, and gradually the school became an economic proposition. The support that was enlisted in the form of boys and money came mainly from industry. There were so many sides to the case that could be put, and so many ways in which firms could gain, albeit differently with different boys, that we met with few disappointments.

To some, the idea of receiving a confidential report on a boy's behaviour and performance when under pressure was regarded as a valuable independent assessment of his prospects of promotion. Others recognized that, as labour became more scarce and industrial methods of manufacture and administration more sophisticated, it became more important than ever to pay attention to the quality of the labour force. If an Outward Bound course enabled a young man to discover latent qualities he scarcely knew he possessed, then his time away from the factory would be time well spent. As the pay of men in production came nearer to the pay of supervisors, it became more difficult to induce young men to accept responsibility. If, through successful accomplishment and encouragement given by hand-picked staff, ambition was fired, even the idea of paying wages whilst the young men were on the course was seen to be worthwhile.

The war, with its opportunities for turning boys into men almost overnight through the enforced acceptance of responsibility and the need for self-help, was still fresh in many minds. Perhaps something of what the war had made possible could be provided in peace-time. For these and other reasons, industry came to regard Outward Bound as an investment rather than a charity.

In 1951 HRH the Duke of Edinburgh graciously consented to attend a public dinner to raise funds for expansion. The proceeds, augmented by a substantial interest-free loan from an anonymous well-wisher, enabled us to establish the second school, at Eskdale in Cumberland. Since then, development has been consistently maintained until in 1968, we had five boys' schools and one girls' school in the United Kingdom, and sixteen others abroad directly associated with us, as well as nine more giving comparable training.

OUTWARD BOUND BOYS' TRAINING

At home the fee is uniform, and certain characteristics are common to all, but the forms in which challenge is presented naturally differ according to the facilities available locally. During the first week of each course, the time is spent in basic training associated with the sea or the mountains, map and compass work, first aid, and athletics or 'circuit' training to help the boys to get fit. In the second week more ambitious expeditions are embarked upon. At the mountain schools in the Lake District—Eskdale and Ullswater—the training is designed to enable the boys nearing the end of the course to undertake safely a three-day expedition unaccompanied by instructors, but passing through various check-points by means of which their progress can be observed. At Aberdovey forestry activities and riding play a notable part in the varied training programme, whilst at the Devon School full use is made of the rivers Dart and Tamar for canoeing.

Each course is divided into watches (at the sea schools) or patrols (at the mountain schools) of ten to twelve boys, under the care of a particular member of the staff, with a Captain and Vice-Captain selected initially by the staff, and subsequently changed or confirmed by a direct ballot of the boys concerned. Team rivalry is encouraged in a variety of ways, ranging from marks for tidiness in the dormitories to the results of the cross-country run in which everyone takes part. The teams are so selected that boys from the same firm, or the same locality or occupation, are, as far as possible, separated.

Athletics, or 'circuit training', is part of the training at all Outward Bound schools as a means whereby a boy may not only become fit, but also as a means to measure improvement. Standards are set in each of the five events such as will suit the average boy, and a higher one suitable for the gifted boy. To pass at either level, however, it is necessary to attain the requisite target in all five events. Thus, a most valuable incentive is provided for a boy to master those sections in which he is weakest, be it short- or long-distance running, or high- or long-jumping. In athletics, as in all other aspects of the training, one boy never competes with another. He is competing against his own previous best. Thus improvement is the hallmark of success.

Proficiency in rescue training of all kinds plays an important part in the training, not least because of the purpose which such training is seen to have—namely, to stimulate that compassion and consideration for others which is essential to a proper set of values. The mountain schools are recognized rescue posts, whose help is frequently enlisted to cope with accidents to climbers and hill-walkers, and those in difficulties on the lakes. Many a sheep has also been rescued. Artificial respiration is taught universally, and in the summer the busy beach at Aberdovey is guarded by relays of boys from the Sea School, who are ready to go to the help of any swimmer in difficulties. Cliff rescue is practised at Devon, and in the summer surf life-saving instruction is given on the Cornish coast. In addition, community service of varying kinds is regularly carried out, such as carrying up fencing materials needed by local farmers in otherwise inaccessible places, mending damaged stone walls or preserving the banks of a river by means of judiciously placed boulders.

At the end of each course, not only do the boys write an account of their experiences, which are frequently illuminating, but a confidential report on each boy is compiled and sent to each sponsor.

Halfway through the course a staff conference is held under the Warden, when the attitude and performance of every boy is discussed. Where necessary, advice or criticism is subsequently given, so that whilst there is still time boys may be given a chance to overcome weaknesses. The effort put in during the second half of the course may well determine the tone of his final report.

All boys must undertake as an exercise in self-discipline to do their best to give up smoking and drinking for the duration of the course. It should be noted that this subject is not treated as a rule to be observed (which automatically would set up a conflict between the school and the staff on the one hand and the boys on the other), but it is presented in the Warden's initial talk, on the first night of the course, as an obligation voluntarily accepted for the sake of the other boys. It is assumed that they wish to accept this challenge, and in the process greatly help their fitness, which will be tested to the full.

Undenominational prayers are held every morning, whether it be in the school precincts or in the hills or at sea, and opportunities are normally available for the boys to attend a service of their own choice on Sundays. It is of interest to note how the 'things of the spirit' are frequently, and for the first time, acceptable when presented to the boys by men of action whom they respect.

With boys from so many different backgrounds, occupations, localities and aptitudes, different aspects of the training will provide differing challenges. To some, the idea of lecturing to his contemporaries on even a chosen subject for five minutes is much more frightening than climbing a steep rock-face; to others the morning daily dip or cold shower is more nerve-racking than spending twenty-four hours alone in a self-made bivouac on a hillside. Those who can endure a long-distance run across country comparatively easily may, nevertheless, find the initiative test very revealing. The training is thus varied, and yet intense, exciting at times and very demanding, with little time left for writing or home-sickness. If the courses were longer, the rate of acceleration would have to be modified, but if they were shorter it could not be stepped up without running severe risks of strain. Indeed, even in twenty-six days great care has to be taken to see that boys are not subjected to unreasonable physical demands, quite apart from the compulsory medical examination on arrival at the school. It is, however, important to emphasize that any healthy boy can safely embark on an Outward Bound course, any special physical prowess or aptitude being quite unnecessary.

OUTWARD BOUND GIRLS' TRAINING

It was not long after the pioneering days that pressure grew to introduce Outward Bound training for girls. For some years two courses were held each year, sometimes instead of a boys' course, and more often at an outside centre loaned or rented for the purpose. The staff were recruited specially, and some of the instructors were seconded from one or other of the boys' schools. They were highly successful.

In 1959 it was decided to allot half the courses at the new school in Devon to girls, and to have a dual-purpose staff until such time as it was thought possible to recruit enough girls to warrant a school for girls only. That time came in 1963, and was greatly helped by a Government grant of half the cost of the new school near Towyn (not far from Aberdovey), which, including equipment, vehicles and canoes, in addition to building and domestic needs, exceeded £100,000.

It had become clear some time before that it was not satisfactory to water-down the main features of the boys' course and call it a girls' course. With this in mind, the school was built and furnished to a standard of taste and comfort which it was thought would instil into the girls a sense of pride in and care for their surroundings. This hope has been entirely fulfilled, and the appearance of the furnishings and decorations after five years of hard wear is much admired by visitors. The training had to be re-thought and built up from first principles in ways suitable for girls. This meant that team competitions played little part, endurance was modified and greater emphasis placed on indoor challenges, such as drama and individual dancing. Emphasis is also placed on individual service to others in such fields as home nursing, in addition to community-service projects such as are common to all Outward Bound schools. Nevertheless, expeditions, rock-climbing and canoeing continued to play a notable part in each course.

THE STAFF

In all this the staff play an absolutely crucial part. It is they who show how everything should be done. It is they who must teach each boy how to do the unfamiliar. It is they who, by a judicious mixture of praise and prodding, enticement and enforcement, induce boys to give all they have got, which invariably is a great deal more than they ever knew they possessed. As a result, the most frequent comment in what a boy writes at the end of the course is some reference to the fact that he has accomplished more than he ever thought possible.

The standard establishment of staff is a warden, a chief instructor, and one for each watch or patrol, plus a spare. For them life is very exacting, even though the ten courses held at each School every year only take up 260 out of 365 days. There is much to be done between courses. They must constantly give of their personality, and just when they are really getting to know their group and to understand them, they are off, and another group comes to replace them. Salary scales are related to those paid to teachers, and there is a recognized ladder of promotion. Even so, it is exceptional for staff to remain more than a few years unless they are already in line for rapid promotion.

In addition to the regular staff, each school takes a number of temporary staff. They may come from the services, the police, the universities or elsewhere, or be schoolmasters coming during their own holidays. Usually they have had some experience of one or other of the outdoor activities practised in Outward Bound. They are paid a modest fee and, of course, their keep. Their help is invaluable, and it is not uncommon for a man who has been a 'temp.' on a number of courses to join the staff permanently.

Reference will be made in another chapter to the development of Outward Bound overseas. Here it is only necessary to refer to the effect in the United Kingdom of the very considerable development

13 Boys working on a mural at Gordonstoun during their art
lesson, 1954

14 The ketch, *Henrietta*, in a Norwegian fjord, where she was
sailed from the Moray Firth by a crew of Gordonstoun boys,
summer 1937

15 Prince Charles as a pupil at Gordonstoun

16 Fire Service practice at Gordonstoun. Robert Chew, the Headmaster, is on the right

17   1942: the schooner, *Prince Louis*, at Aberdovey, Wales.
Kurt Hahn is standing on deck wearing a hat, on the right of the
picture. This fine ex-pilot boat was first owned by Gordonstoun
and then passed on to the Outward Bound

18   Climbing above Barmouth, during an Outward Bound Course at Aberdovey

that has taken place overseas. It has been agreed that the Trust will pay the travelling costs of instructors or other authorized people going abroad to help with Outward Bound overseas, and of those recruited abroad coming to this country for training. The demand for instructors has been so great that considerable difficulty has been found in meeting it without denuding the British schools of their more experienced staff.

Recently, steps have been taken to increase the collaboration between all Outward Bound schools so that the knowledge and experience gained at each may be available to all. An International Secretariat has been established in London, and a magazine under the title *Strive* is published twice a year to provide a means of regular communication between those practising Outward Bound in different parts of the world.

THE TYPES OF FULL-LENGTH COURSES AND THEIR
COMPOSITION

Most of those who come on standard Outward Bound courses are at work. They come in their firms' time without affecting their holidays, and usually continue to receive their wages. Others may be police cadets, junior firemen, older schoolboys sponsored either by local education authorities or privately, and they are normally between sixteen and twenty years old. In the summer there is a big waiting-list, but vacancies still exist in the winter, when so many who would like to come are prevented by attendance at night schools, continuation classes and other forms of further education.

To help with the problem of winter recruiting, and at the request of many local education authorities, six junior courses are run annually for those at secondary modern schools in term time. They must be over fourteen and a half and under sixteen. These courses, though popular with the sponsors, nevertheless present a great problem to the staff. The young people are much less mature, and so need a great deal more supervision. The training has to be modified and pitched to suit the more juvenile type. It is doubtful if the result is as profound or as lasting as it is with the over seventeen-year-old.

Then, in response to demand, two courses for seniors are held each year—seniors being those over twenty and up to twenty-five. They are usually less fit, but are no less keen to observe training conditions. Such courses tax the staff in a different way, because it is not unusual for them to have to defend, before a critic or a sceptic, the demands that are made on the young men. All agree it is a very stimulating affair.

BADGES

In the early days the badges awarded at the end of each course were graded. The best, which was earned by no more than about 5 per cent of the people on each course, were known as honours badges; the next, given originally to about half those on the course, were known as merit badges, and the balance, unless specifically withheld, received membership.

This arrangement prevailed for some years until it was challenged. In the process of stressing the value and importance of an honours badge (as a means to encourage boys to give of their best), it was found that there was a real danger of too much importance being attached to something which recorded a young person's performance over only four weeks of his life. Moreover, boys tended to claim a good badge as a justification for promotion. To whatever extent firms might take that into account, it was not healthy for boys to be tempted to see what they could get out of an Outward Bound course. There were many instances, too, when the difference between a boy's performance who had just reached, say, an honours badge and a boy who had just failed to reach it was so small that the final divisions were thought to be somewhat unrealistic.

It was therefore eventually decided to make only one exception to the Outward Bound badge which all boys obtain unless it is specifically withheld. This exception is known as the warden's badge, and is given only for a quite exceptional performance, either in absolute terms or in relation to his or her own handicaps.

SAFETY

Great attention is paid to safety, and all young people are taught that risks unnecessary to the attainment of the object should not be taken, and that preparation for the risks that must be taken is no less essential, be it by becoming proficient in the art of rock-climbing, cliff-rescue or canoeing, or by seeing that the equipment used is suitable and in good order. All schools provide protective clothing, and in addition to the first aid normally taught everyone is acquainted with the latest information on the prevention and, if necessary, the treatment of exposure.

A special Safety Committee has been established to advise all schools of the best practice, and to study the independent reports produced if there should be a serious accident or near miss. They have recently revised the Trust safety regulations, which, in addition to those needed to suit local conditions, must be incorporated in each school's safety regulations.

SPECIAL COURSES

Since 1963, when the sixth Outward Bound school in the United Kingdom was completed, the Trust has become more and more convinced that further expansion in this country is not desirable. A broad enough base has already been established from which to draw proper conclusions from the experience gained; the impact of geography or personality has been eliminated and the 'art of multiplication' adequately acquired. Such a situation has enabled special attention to be paid to quality and to experiment.

It is felt that, having a variety of sites, specially selected and dedicated staff and first-class equipment, opportunities should deliberately be made to see in what ways other than courses lasting twenty-six days—be they junior, standard or senior—such facilities can with advantage be utilized.

To this end, the following types of 'diversification' are being developed:

Rover Courses These are of the customary length and are based on a particular school in respect of staff, supplies and administration, but comprise only from twenty-four to thirty-six boys, have a base camp in the neighbourhood, and after the first week are mostly on the move, covering a considerable area in the process. They are held in August or September, when the demand for Outward Bound training is at its highest. The discipline engendered by the atmosphere of an expedition becomes possible, and an especially close relationship between staff and boys is a welcome advantage.

Extension Courses These are usually of ten days' or two weeks' duration, and take place away from any of the existing schools.

They give a high priority in the programme to scope for local service, and are offered mainly, but not exclusively, to those who have previously taken an orthodox course. Those who come have testified to their wish to recapture some of the stimulus they formerly experienced, and to be reminded of those standards to which Outward Bound aspires and which are not always to be found or acknowledged in the workaday world outside.

Apprentice Courses   These are designed as part of the training encouraged by industrial training boards with a view to influencing attitudes, determination and fitness in a way that is complementary to the technical training provided by others. Even in the ten days allotted for this purpose much has been gained of mutual advantage.

Athletic Courses   These short courses, which require special knowledge and experience of physical training, have been attended by promising young tennis-players sponsored by the Lawn Tennis Association on one course and by the British Olympic hockey squad on another. Such courses seem to emphasize the mental impact on those participating, and have been found to lead to quite dramatic changes in the general approach to that concentration and dedication needed by those who succeed in such fields of endeavour.

Mountain Leadership Courses   These are attended by those who seek to pass the newly created mountain leadership proficiency tests. They are necessarily specialist courses, and can only be offered at certain schools.

Executive Courses   These are designed to enable up to twenty-four executives of any age to participate for up to ten days in a full-length course of standard-age boys. The object is to provide an opportunity for sponsors or potential sponsors to understand what Outward Bound is trying to do by experiencing for themselves something of the impact on boys, whilst at the same time seeing from within just how the standard course operates. As a by-product, and a most valuable one, the executives and the boys are given a chance—which it is almost impossible to find elsewhere—to exchange ideas, and in the process acquire a wider knowledge of the other's point of view.

All these courses are additional to the normal programme at each school—namely, the twenty-six-day courses for juniors (from fourteen and a half to sixteen), standard age (from sixteen to twenty) and seniors (over twenty). There are, however, two other types of course which do not fall into either of these main categories. They are:

Mixed Courses Such a course was tried out at Rhowniar (the girls' school) in January 1969. The regular staff there already has several male instructors, including the Chief Instructor, but for this course the numbers were increased to suit the relative numbers of young men and girls attending the course. It was highly successful.

City Challenge These courses are run in partnership with the host Local Authority. Instead of the traditional forms, such as the sea and the mountains, challenge—the essential ingredient in an Outward Bound course—takes the form of a variety of dramatic types of social service. The course lasts three weeks and accepts twenty-four young men and twenty-four young women aged seventeen to twenty-one. They are accommodated in a training college or day school during the Easter or summer holidays. Activities which are carried out for two or three consecutive days include participation in the work at mental hospitals, work with spastics or geriatric patients, helping in the Salvation Army hostels, redecorating and cleaning out substandard accommodation, looking after immigrant children and so on. Each group of six has its own tutor with whom frank discussion takes place each evening about the day's experience. Whenever possible, arrangements are made for follow up by local schools or organizations so that the good work initiated is continued. There is little doubt that such courses which have been outstandingly successful in Leeds, Batley and Cardiff will be followed by others. Already provisional arrangements have been made with the authorities in Pontefract, Manchester and Edinburgh and others such as Bristol and Birmingham are expected to follow later. This whole concept of challenge in an urban context is regarded as a major breakthrough into fresh territory from which very important developments may well occur.

RESEARCH

In 1965 a two-day Conference was held at Harrogate attended by the wardens, members of the Management Committee and school boards, and a number of sponsors. The object was twofold:

1   To seek, by a better understanding of what was meant by Outward Bound, to eliminate public criticisms based on misunderstanding.

2 To consider what changes, if any, in our practice were called for in the light of the changes in modern Britain, and thus the changing needs of those attending our courses.

Important addresses were given by Sir Alec Clegg, Dr Kurt Hahn and Mr Jim Parsons.

Whilst no specific changes were recommended as a result of the Conference, it was widely felt that the time had come for a study in depth to be made of what we were doing, and its effect on those participating in the experience. Accordingly, arrangements were completed in 1968 for such a piece of research to be undertaken. It is divided into two parts. How we operate is being studied by Mr Martin Hardcastle, formerly Deputy Headmaster of Clifton College. To do this, he is spending most of the time during one year staying at the several schools, talking to the boys and girls during courses, discussing the methods used with the staff and noting the differing practices at each school resulting from variations in the facilities and personality peculiar to each.

The effect of what we do is being studied by Professor Fletcher and his colleagues at Bristol University. They will collaborate extensively with Mr Hardcastle, and will make contact with sponsors and with boys and girls who have already taken courses.

It is intended to make this information available to others besides the Outward Bound Trust to whom it would be of interest. The Trust is greatly indebted to the Joseph Rowntree Memorial Trust, who have provided the finance to make this research possible.

ADMINISTRATION

The pattern of administration in force in the Trust has changed little since the second school was founded. It is designed to reconcile the need for a degree of local autonomy with uniformity in essentials. Each school has its own board of directors responsible for the training, the staff, the amenities and the accounts of a non-profit-making company, whose shares are held by the Trust itself. The Council of the Trust, consisting of some thirty people under the Chairmanship of Lord Cobham, meets only once a year unless there is some very important decision to be taken. Their authority, in practice, is delegated to a Management Committee, of which I have been Chairman since 1947. This Committee is responsible for general policy, public relations, recruiting and finance, and employs a headquarters staff to discharge these functions.

Normally, the Trust owns the land and buildings at each school, and rents them to each school company. Equipment, boats, vehicles, etc., are provided to each school by grant from the Trust in the first instance, and are subsequently maintained and replaced when necessary out of the fees charged and paid to each school. Capital requirements are submitted to the Trust at least annually, and dealt with in the light of agreed priorities and the resources available.

The Management Committee consists of the Chairman and two other members nominated by each school board, plus others specifically invited. No written limits are laid down defining where the authority of a school board ends and that of the Management Committee begins, save in the realm of staff, but at no time has any problem arisen on that account. In the realm of staff, the warden is a Trust appointment, but only someone approved by the school board concerned is considered. The bursars are appointed by the school board in consultation with the warden, and the rest of the staff are engaged by the warden.

As a contribution towards the cost of the work done by Headquarters on behalf of the schools, the latter are required to pay any surplus income up to £4 a student, and 75 per cent of any further surplus to the Trust. The full £4 per student, which has not so far been available, plus the rents received, would cover nearly two-thirds of the total expenditure at Headquarters. Thus the Trust relies heavily on covenants, donations and grants from trusts both to cover running costs and to provide the capital with which to finance improvements and expansion.

GENERAL

Up to the end of 1969 in the United Kingdom over 900 courses have been held, through which some 70,000 boys and 7,500 girls have passed. Each year just over 5,000 young people are having the benefit of an Outward Bound course in the United Kingdom, and a further 9,000 overseas—a total of about 14,000 a year. The demonstration of how such an impact can be made in a young person's character and outlook in even one month has prompted others abroad to adapt the training to local conditions—a process which is by no means complete yet.

In addition, the success of using the sea and the mountains as instruments of challenge has induced other organizations to be more adventurous, and has led to no less than twenty-five residential centres being established by local authorities and others, where young people may have a disciplined and exciting experience through which to discover themselves. Education authorities have testified to the contribution which Outward Bound has made to the art of developing young people.

Hitherto, the emphasis has tended to be on the needs of those in industry. The fact that schooldays have been left behind has tended to encourage the view that the schoolmaster's knowledge and experience is no longer so relevant.

The recent Conference at Harrogate prompted some fresh thinking on this subject, and it is fully expected that, in a desire to improve our methods of communication and inspiration, we will look more earnestly and with more confidence to the world of education for help.

This, in effect, brings the wheel full circle. Dr Hahn evolved Outward Bound out of the County Badge Scheme as a means of bringing to the under-privileged boy and girl those ideas designed to create the 'whole man', which he had applied to the privileged few at his residential schools. Outward Bound was established to fulfil an educational need, and by its example to influence others. After twenty years of evolution and adaptation, during which, for a time, its educational origin and purpose was sometimes forgotten, it is returning to its spiritual home.

Dr Hahn has described the art of the educator as being 'to preserve into manhood the attributes of childhood'. If we have contributed to that art, we shall have done something to repay the immense debt that we, and indeed all in Britain who are concerned with young people, owe to him.

Some aspects of character-building

The Edmund Rich Memorial Lecture to the Royal Society of Arts

Tom Price

Character-training, as it is called, now fills a very considerable part of the educational scene. The various bodies engaged in this kind of work include the Scouts, the British Schools Exploring Society, the Duke of Edinburgh's Award Scheme, the innumerable schools and colleges which devote time to outdoor pursuits, the adventure schools set up by education authorities, the training bases for boy soldiers and police cadets, the schools most directly inspired by Dr Kurt Hahn—Gordonstoun, the Outward Bound schools and Atlantic College—the Central Council for Physical Recreation, the physical education colleges, which now include in their curricula such sports as rock-climbing, canoeing, and camping, and the large firms whose apprentice-training schemes include camp-craft and hill-walking. One must also mention the spread of the Outward Bound schools in other countries such as Holland, Germany, Norway, Malaya, Kenya, Uganda, Nigeria and the United States.

But I propose to confine myself to what I have first-hand knowledge of, and that is the present work of the Outward Bound schools, and the aims and ideas which underlie all such training.

The first Outward Bound school, in 1941, at Aberdovey, had a specific aim, to train Merchant Navy cadets how to survive in the event of being torpedoed. The intention was to teach the techniques of survival, boat-handling, physical fitness and the like, but also to rm the cadets against the enemies within—fear, defeatism, apathy,

selfishness. It was thus as much a moral as a practical training, and
it was from the start realized that such training had a general application. In the words of the late Lawrence Holt of the Blue Funnel
Line, 'the training at Aberdovey must be less a training for the sea,
than a training *through* the sea, and can benefit all walks of life'.
A present-day Outward Bound school may still take Merchant Navy
cadets, but in addition it takes industrial apprentices, clerks,
labourers, police cadets, fire service cadets, Borstal boys, Etonians,
grammar and modern school boys—any boy, in fact, between the
ages of sixteen and a half and twenty who can produce a medical
certificate stating that he is in normal health. (Courses are also held
for the age-group fourteen to sixteen and the age-group over twenty,
and there is one school for girls.) The original aim of survival
training and improvement of morale is still present, but there is now
much more diversity than in the original concept. Each of the six
schools in this country is run according to the vision of its warden,
the capacities of its staff, and the opportunities offered by its hinter-
land. Each one is therefore different, except in essence, which seems
to me an excellent thing, for there is always strength in diversity.
Each school runs ten one-month courses a year. Some of the merits
of such courses are, I imagine, quite obvious. Since they are residential, they provide that sudden, stimulating break from normal
environment and habits which puts a boy in an alert and receptive
frame of mind. Many lads have never been away from home before,
and clearly gain from being broken out of their ruts. As the course
lasts only one month they have no time to settle into another rut.
And this I believe is the great merit of the short course: it retains its
novelty and excitement throughout, and can keep up a pitch of
intensity impossible over a longer period. As Wordsworth said, it is
in moments of feeling and excitement that one's deepest lessons are
learned, and every teacher knows that it is only by capturing the
interest, and engaging the emotions, of children, that they can be
effectively taught. An Outward Bound course provides a month of
intense awareness, and I have never met a former student who has
not remembered vividly his experiences at the school. I meet large
numbers of ex-students, the oldest being a man who had attended
Course 2 in 1950. Thirteen years later he came eighty miles out of
his way while motoring from Scotland to the south, in order to see
the school, and he bored us with a description of every minute of his

course, which had evidently been burned into his memory. It is my belief that if the course is not memorable, it has failed.

The social value of the course is equally clear. Boys from different towns, with different occupations, different educations, different creeds, are mixed up together and find themselves embarking on a common enterprise. These are the home towns of a patrol chosen at random: Leeds, Torquay, Birmingham, London, Chelmsford, Kenton, Merthyr Tydfil, Bristol, Manchester, Bromley. And the jobs: plasterer, police cadet, engineer, trainee engineer, junior fireman, plater, draughtsman, Approved schoolboy, stocks clerk, student. A striking variety, and it does not include any of the foreign boys, or any of the more remarkable occupations that we frequently encounter. But if there is variety in their home towns and occupations, how much more variety is there in outlook and personality, and who can tell what clashes, conflicts and adjustments take place when such a group live together for a month, under some stress, and under the necessity of working together to a common end.

For, of course, since we have lured these lads out of the security of their own homes and social circles, we enjoy an advantage that no youth club can attain—that of being able to orient the course towards effort and achievement rather than mere entertainment. The training is presented as a hard one. It is full of enjoyment, but the enjoyment is incidental, as indeed most true enjoyment is, and the main object is work and discovery, not a holiday. A boy makes a first step by consenting to come. This consent is sometimes eagerly given, sometimes grudgingly, but once he has bought a pair of boots, and kissed his girl goodbye for a month, and travelled two or three hundred miles, and made a few new acquaintances, he is not likely to back down from the first difficulty he encounters. Nothing in the course is compulsory, but there are no easy ways out. This I think is a very satisfactory state of affairs, for as Kurt Hahn has said, 'It is wrong to coerce people into opinions, but it is right to impel them into experience.' Impel is just the right word. Compel would be too strong.

For this reason, when talking to the boys on their arrival I insist on the voluntary nature of the activities. On a recent senior course I laid particular stress on this point, and it gave rise to a good deal of ironic pleasantry later in the course as they sweated round the steeplechase or struggled over the ropes course. Yet they were greatly heartened by reminding themselves that it did depend upon themselves. On every course there are a few, who if they lived round the corner and could easily do so, would go home. But they stay, and usually do very well.

Another evident merit is improvement in physical fitness. To most boys this is a revelation; they attain a state of fitness which is an entirely new experience. They regretfully realize they can never maintain it once they return to work, but they at any rate never forget that it is possible.

With this fitness, often gained only after many days of struggle, there comes more keenly the impact of natural beauty and the pleasures of fresh air. Only a few lads are articulate enough to be able to express their appreciation of this, but hardly anyone, I believe, is altogether insensible of it. I once took a group of schoolboys on a week's camping journey across a remote part of Scotland. And a hard journey we had of it, meeting no one, seeing nothing but deer, doing nothing but camp and travel. One boy complained incessantly, particularly about the absence of shops and other pleasures. Yet the following year he wanted to come again. The big, empty spaces had made an impression upon him which outlasted the discomforts and petty deprivations he had suffered. Boys do not always know what they want.

There comes also the impact of new sports and pursuits. Everything is done to encourage boys to keep their eyes open and take an interest in the landforms and natural history of the region, and good safe technical instruction is given in the dangerous but greatly rewarding sports of mountaineering, sailing, potholing and the like. Boys who perhaps have never shone at football and cricket find a new world of physical activity and achievement.

In sum, the course provides a memorable month of new experience, a mental and physical shake-up and tonic.

These claims for Outward Bound no one would quarrel with. But there are a number of reservations I think you may well have and which I shall try to anticipate and answer. In this I am guided by recalling my own reactions when I first heard of Outward Bound, but had no knowledge of it or connection with it. Furthermore, I have, since I have been engaged in this work, come across a number of misconceptions. The most common is that it is primarily a training in physical hardihood and toughness, suitable for a commando. Of course it is tough, and it does call for hardihood, but that is because the students are boys of from sixteen to twenty, and boys from sixteen to twenty are tough, especially when you challenge them to give of their very best. No boy is excluded, however unfit, except on grounds of actual disease. And no boy fails through lack of physical strength or aptitude. In fact, it is emphatically not a question of success or failure. The experience is what counts. Direct competition, such as exists in most team games, plays a small part in an Outward Bound course, where for the most part a boy is competing against his own previous best. The course then is only as tough as the boys can be persuaded to make it. Much of the value, I do believe, lies in the fact that the boys know they are going to have a testing time of it. It puts them on their mettle, gives them something to rise to and something to be proud of when it is finished. It appeals to boys' natural idealism, to their need to put themselves to the test. Youths are for ever putting themselves to the test, trying to do the ton, testing their capacity for beer, trying anything that is forbidden or hazardous and which demands strength and nerve. There is with us, however, no cult of toughness. It is never suggested that toughness is an end in itself. If instructors are fit, it is the accidental result of their interests and way of life, and the things they value are the things of civilization and ordinary cultivated life.

Outward Bound may easily be construed as a romantic escape from the ills of civilization into a sort of Arcadia, or, rather, a pantisocracy, where plain living and high thinking prevail. I am reminded of Thomas Love Peacock's comment on those early devotees of the Lake District: 'The cities are bad, therefore we live out of the cities. The mountains are good, therefore we live in the mountains. And there we shall pass each day in the amiable occupation of going up and down hill, exclaiming at the views, and communicating our thoughts in immortal verse to admiring generations.'

Perhaps it is an escape, but it is not escapism. And there is the best of all precedents for retiring for a limited period into the wilderness. The romantic poets, even Wordsworth, and especially Byron, only looked at mountains. Boys camping in them, in all weathers, may well get a 'sense sublime of something far more deeply interfused', and so on—indeed, I am certain that many do—but they also see the realities of cold, danger, fatigue, companionship, and the like. Life in the hills tends to show a boy the unromanticized truth about himself and his world. One of the biggest and most difficult tasks confronting a young person today is to distinguish between the romantic, the specious, the flattering—and the plain truth.

Another impression it is easy to get, especially if one has reflected too much upon the implications of that phrase 'character-training', and heard that the training conditions in the school preclude drinking and smoking, is that there is something narrowly puritanical and restrictive about the course, that it is in fact a month's discipline. The quickest way to disabuse oneself of this idea is to spend a day or two at one of the schools. Formal discipline is kept to a minimum. Rules are few. Boys are called by their Christian names, and in my school the staff too, including myself. The only discipline we know is the discipline imposed by dangerous undertakings, and the self-discipline of responsible and considerate people living together. Consequently, the prevailing atmosphere is one of freedom, friendliness and good spirits. Early brochures bore the legend, 'Character-training through adventure and testing experience'. The adventure and the testing experience are certainly present, but in my view 'character-training' is an inadequate description of present-day aims, and, furthermore, open to grave misinterpretation.

The word 'training' in this context can suggest an attempt to mould opinions, to impose behaviour-patterns. One pictures a group of boys arriving full of personal oddities and idiosyncrasies, and leaving at the end of the month uniformly clean-limbed, keen-eyed and self-confident, 'the finished product', as one booklet on Outward Bound actually put it. How terrifying! One is inclined to draw analogies with obedience-training suitable only for dogs, and management-training, which can, of course, be justified by being vocational. Since large numbers of our boys are sponsored by firms, there is always a danger of assuming that character-training is vocational too. Which it isn't. Its aim is simply to help the individual boy. That he thereby becomes a better employee is true but purely incidental. I do not like the term 'character-training'. It makes me think immediately of the Stiff Upper Lip and the Right Type. Phrases from the war stir uneasily in the memory, O.L.Q. and L.M.F. (Officer-Like Qualities and Lack of Moral Fibre). It was thought-associations like this that caused one writer to suggest that 'character-training' 'provided willing N.C.O.s for the Gordonstoun officer-class', a quip which has caused more delight and hilarity at

Eskdale than anything I can remember, even including 'the finished product'. Had this man visited a school, instead of brooding about character-training, he could never by any stretch of the imagination have picked up that idea. Naturally, we try to suggest sound values and teach Christian precepts, but for the most part boys simply discover their own powers and personalities. Far from attempting to tell a boy what he should be like, we hope, as all teachers should, that our pupils will turn out far better and wiser than we can even guess how to be. I also firmly believe that too much uniformity and conformity can be the death of any society. If we were intended to be all alike we should be propagated by spores instead of by the present system.

But in any case 'character-training' as a term has now been discarded. Character-building is preferred, and character-development. But in my view the word 'character' itself is objectionable: it is at once too imprecise and too narrow for our purposes.

By character we evidently mean good character, but of all the qualities that are good qualities who am I to presume to say which are the best? Do we put honesty, probity, courage first, or tolerance, warmth, affection? As Christians we should perhaps say 'love and humility', but are 'character-trainers' really thinking of love and humility when they use the term?

Usually when we say a person is of good character we mean that he is not a drunkard and has not been in prison. If, on the other hand, we say he is a character, we mean he probably has been in prison, but only for poaching. When, however, we say he has 'character', we surely mean that he will stand firm and stick to his code. Now, it seems to me that if we go to the trouble and expense to have a hundred boys brought away from homes and work for a whole month and all we attempt to teach them is to stand firm and stick to a code, I think we should be ashamed of ourselves. It means we have made no progress in our educational philosophy since Dr Arnold. We should at least try to examine the code we stick to. Our aim surely should be—and is, in spite of character-training—that of discovery, of enlargement of mind and spirit, it is that young people might have life and have it more abundantly. And they can do this only by discovering for themselves, with our help and encouragement, what are life's truest values. The endurance, the hard work, the facing of dangers, the abstinence, the plodding on in rigorous conditions, these are merely the means. They are not ends. The term 'character-training' suggests they are ends.

The true end is freedom and light. And, in the words of Clemenceau, 'Liberty is the right to discipline ourselves in order not to be disciplined by others'.

Character-training is closely allied to leadership-training. Yet, like character-training, leadership-training is an expression which has curiously little real meaning but a large number of connotations, some of them rather unpleasant. As Sir Alec Clegg has pointed out, it readily suggests the assumption of superiority. It suggests the kind of man whose sole stock-in-trade is that he has the training and temerity to order people about effectively. Such men may be valuable, but only in a limited way. And if they happen to be fools or rogues, they can be dangerous. Clearly it is good if a boy shows a willingness to accept responsibility and take the lead. But to suggest by one's teaching that this is the prime quality seems to me quite wrong.

The only concession to leadership training in this narrow sense that I am willing to make is in trying to help boys to overcome the diffidence that most of them suffer from, and I have never seen anything more competent to do this than the Outward Bound course. If boys can gain confidence in themselves, they will emerge as leaders when leadership is needed. And not before.

But, of course, there is a wider sense in which leadership is used, and that is as a synonym for energy, enterprise, and originality of mind, and here our training can be of the greatest possible use to industry, which, I am told, is so much in need of what it will call leaders, but what I would call responsible and public-spirited men with minds of their own. In the past, before educational opportunities existed for everyone, each stratum of society had its first-class men who were the natural leaders and advisers of their groups. Now they are all creamed off into the better schools and better jobs, so that there is no one left to leaven the lump. Outward Bound, I believe, can help here by giving encouragement and confidence to lads who have made no mark in academic work, or whose talents have never been realized.

It seems to me that the task of education and of the Outward Bound schools is not so much to make leaders as to ensure that leaders lead in the right direction. In fact whether one is thinking of character or leadership one always comes round to this funda-

19   City Challenge, an adaptation of Outward Bound. A
member of the course takes part in Community Service

20   Dipping-lug sailing cutter sailed by a watch from the
Outward Bound School at Aberdovey, Wales

mental question of values, and if I were asked to say in one sentence what is the most important thing that my school can do for a boy I would say that it can help him, through the vivid experience of twenty-six demanding days, to establish his values. For there is intense confusion in the minds of young people: they need to find an answer to Auden's question,

> Here am I, there are you
> What is it all for? What are we going to do?

And they get precious little clue from the adult world; in whom consequently, they have lost faith. It is interesting to consider how a young man of eighteen or so sees the adult world. I believe he sees adults as more strong, confident, and firmly established, more secure than he can imagine himself to be. He may feel for them anything from admiration for their achievements to baffled rage at their insensibility, smugness and unassailability, but he seldom sees us as the failures, or part failures, that we all are. I mean failures in the sense that we have nowhere near used all our potentialities, or made the most of our brief sojourn on earth. It is this, I think, that is at the root of his diffidence. He is insecure and vulnerable because his attitudes have not hardened, his idealism is still active. If only he could gain the confidence of maturity without sacrificing his youthfulness.

I come finally to the concept of adventure as a training aid, and I should like to preface my remarks with a quotation from Seneca: 'The good things which belong to prosperity are to be wished: but the good things which belong to adversity are to be admired.' Simply stated, adventure training as practised means persisting towards a given objective in spite of the dangers and hardships. It means discarding prosperity, and accepting adversity. And it usually involves burning one's boats too. More than once, on a rock-climb, I have bitterly regretted ever starting, but the assuagement and calm which has followed the facing of a disagreeable series of moves has always made it worth it. Frequently boys bitterly regret having volunteered for some mountain expedition, but necessity is the mother of invention; they cope somehow, and come out of it bigger and better versions of themselves. I am convinced that everyone has a wealth of potentialities which are never tapped because the extreme exigency or the kindling spark of interest that would do it never arises. A man might imagine all his life that he cannot jump a five-bar gate, until chased by a bull. Or, to change to a different beast and to quote from the comment of an Irish boy on a course last year, 'It reminds me,' he wrote, 'of the saying of Confucius: "A lion chased me up a tree, and I greatly enjoyed the view from the top." '

Outward Bound has become notorious for this aspect of its training, and there are dangers in it. There is a need for moderation and discretion. But undoubtedly it is one of the most important elements of the course and one of the most fruitful of startling results. It is as Francis Bacon said, 'Prosperity doth best discover Vice: but Adversity doth best discover Vertue'. Wardens and instructors in Outward Bound schools may vary greatly in outlook and opinion, but one thing they have in common is the conviction, through experience, that in adventure there is to be found the greatest significance and fulfilment. By adventure I mean the stepping out into the unknown, having completely committed oneself to an enterprise. The man who, without recklessness and with the most sober and careful provision against mishap and accident, sets out on an adventure is a practising optimist. He is a man of faith, and he is man who can put something before self and before personal safety. It is indeed this escape from selfish interest and morbid anxiety which is the liberating and enlarging force of adventure. In the words of Lucien Devies on the desperate climbing of the first 8,000 metre peak, Annapurna, 'A flame so kindled can never be extinguished. When we have lost everything, it is then that we find ourselves most rich.' An adventure strips a man of the trappings of his self-importance, and of his illusory material security. Like King Lear, he realizes he is just a 'poor naked, forked creature', unless he has some spiritual resources.

A clear sign of the lack of spiritual resource is the fact that anxiety is one of the greatest of modern ills. And it flourishes most in the fat soil of security. It is a middle-class disease, endemic in those countries which enjoy the highest standards of living and greatest stability. We have banished fear, which is a healthy emotion, only to admit anxiety, which is a morbid one. We no longer wake up in the morning mildly astonished and delighted to have been safely brought to the beginning of this day. We no longer spring to our feet to satisfy ourselves that there is no immediate threat. Instead, we come gradually to consciousness, and lie in bed in complete safety, gnawed by anxiety. The man, however, who has retained a spirit of adventure has that true optimism which regards disaster and failure as the norm from which he, through the Grace of God and his own vigilance and devotion, has temporarily and joyously escaped. G. K. Chesterton wrote feelingly of the miracle of the eight o'clock train, how wonderful it was that it managed to run every single day. He had the true spirit of adventure. The man who on the other hand pins his faith on security is bound to suffer from anxiety, for he knows in his heart that however many insurance policies he takes out, he can never really be safe. This very night his soul may be required of him. It is only when he turns outward, to some end outside himself, in other words embarks on life's adventures, that he saves himself, and exchanges anxiety for mere fear.

It seems to me wholly good that young people should be encouraged to be adventurous, to plan boldly and optimistically, to dare to commit themselves instead of hoarding themselves. By doing so they attain maturity without losing their youth.

But of course the great thing is to stay alive if possible. One must distinguish clearly between adventurousness and recklessness. When boys are deliberately encouraged to take part in activities in which there is a danger to life and limb, there is a heavy responsibility to ensure that safety precautions are taken. The principle here should be not to restrict activities within safe limits. Anyone can make adventure training safe by taking all the adventure out of it. It should be to prepare boys by technical training and physical fitness to deal with danger competently. If one disregards safety, one in effect holds life cheap, and that is contrary to the whole spirit of a training which devotes so much time to first aid, mountain rescue, life-boat work, and other forms of service.

The Duke of Edinburgh's Award Scheme

Peter Carpenter

DESCRIPTION

To anyone familiar with Hahn's ideas it is clear why so soon after the foundation of Gordonstoun in 1934 he decided that his programme of character-developing activities should culminate in an award. The award was to be in four fields, to combat what Hahn believed to be the four main dangers confronting young people: the decline of physical fitness, of the spirit of initiative and enterprise, of care and skill, and, most serious of all, the decline of compassion.

To qualify for the award, boys had to qualify in all four fields. There was, however, a choice from a range of activities within one field. In each activity there were objectives in the form of standards of achievement; and so that these objectives should be within reach and at the same time stretch the boys as they grew older, the standards were set at successively higher levels.

The story of this award—from the Gordonstoun Badge to the Moray Badge and from the Moray Badge to the County Badge, the programme of which formed the basis for the first Outward Bound courses at Aberdovey—has been sketched in by J. M. Hogan on pp. 60–6. Hopes of such a programme taking roots elsewhere were dashed, but the idea lived on.

I should like to pick up the story in 1954. In that year, at Hahn's instigation, a committee of interested parties was called together, and the outcome of their deliberations was the Duke of Edinburgh's Award Scheme, launched two years later. In appointing Sir John (now Lord) Hunt to be the first Director no more inspiring choice could have been made.

That Prince Philip should have taken a lead is not surprising if one remembers that he was a pupil at Gordonstoun and if one knows of his special interest in the welfare of the youth of this country. With his own experience behind him, he wanted to realize Hahn's dream of making available to the many what had hitherto been available only to the few, and in particular extend it to the post-school years.

The time was opportune. In the mid-1950s the Youth Service—or what there was of it—had reached a low ebb. Young people, the majority of whom left school as soon as they attained the age of fifteen, faced many problems; and these problems were aggravated by the period of unsettledness between leaving school and entering National Service at the age of eighteen.

More will be said about the aims of the Award Scheme anon. Basically it was designed (so Prince Philip wrote in the Preface to the *Leaders' Handbook*) as 'an introduction to leisure time activities, a challenge to the individual to personal achievement'. From the outset it was made quite clear that the Scheme was not set up in competition with existing agencies, but (to quote Prince Philip again) as 'a guide to those people and organisations who are concerned about the development of our future citizens'.

The Award was to be operated on an experimental basis for the first few years for boys only. During those years the number of organizations which tested it out was to be limited. If successful, the intention was to make it available to any organization which wished to adopt it, and institute a similar venture for girls. Both intentions were fulfilled, the girls' Scheme being launched before the trial period came to an end in 1959.

Not only during the experimental years, but throughout its existence, the Award Scheme has been subjected to changes. This was to ensure that as far as possible all boys and girls should stand an equal chance of success, whatever their special interests or abilities or the circumstances under which they entered.

So the standards of achievement and endeavour which were demanded of them were constantly adjusted in the light of experience gained. New activities were incorporated into the Scheme and techniques evolved by which it could be made to work more smoothly. The most radical revision came into force in 1969, the object of which was to simplify the requirements and, in particular, to unify the boys' and girls' Schemes. Until then the two had run in close association, drawing ever closer together until they were finally merged.

To describe why and how the Award Scheme has been modified over the years would take up too much space. Although important in themselves, the changes have not affected its essential features. The real importance lies in the fact that changes *have* taken place. For the world of the 1970s is not the same world as that of the 1950s, and if the Scheme had not been prepared to take into account the demands of a rapidly changing society it would soon have outlived its usefulness.

Not long after its inception the Award found its way into countries overseas. It started in one or two individual schools and was taken up by voluntary youth organizations in different parts of the Commonwealth, where, being the flexible instrument it is, it was soon adapted to local conditions.

Today we find the Scheme established in a growing number of countries (28 in 1970) as far apart as Ghana and Malta, Grenada and Hong Kong. In some it is represented only in one or two groups, but most have national committees responsible for the operation of the Award throughout the country under the general direction of the Trustees. Australia, Canada and New Zealand have their own Schemes operating under their own national councils. There are even countries in which it is known by a different name, such as the 'President's Award' in Kenya.

Having briefly outlined the origin and development of the Duke of Edinburgh's Award Scheme, it is proposed to explain what it consists of and how it is operated. The Scheme offers a programme of purposeful leisure activities which have been grouped into the following four sections:

> Service
> Expeditions
> Interests
> ⎧Physical Activity ⎫
> ⎨Design for Living ⎬

Entry is open to all young people between the ages of fourteen and twenty-one. If they fulfil the appropriate requirements in the above four sections, they qualify for the Award. They can do so at three levels: Bronze, Silver, Gold. Without going into all the details, the requirements are as follows:

Bronze Award The minimum age for starting is the fourteenth birthday, and the qualifying age any time between fourteen and a half and twenty-one.

The Service section takes the form of either practical service to the community or following a course of training in, say, first aid, life-saving or child care and taking the appropriate qualification.

Expeditions consist of preliminary training in the use of map and compass, camp-craft, safety precautions, etc., one practice expedition and, finally, a cross-country journey, the duration of which depends on whether it is undertaken by boys or girls, on foot or by bicycle.

In the Interests section candidates can pick either one or two activities from an approved list of over 200—which could be archaeology or pop music, judo or bee-keeping—and pursue them for a period of six months.

When we come to the fourth component of the Award we find that there are different sections for boys and girls. Boys go in for Physical Activity, in which they must reach the score of eighteen points; of these a minimum of six points must be for standards passed in either athletics, physical efficiency or swimming, and six points for participation in organized physical activity.

Design for Living is for girls, who follow a course of instruction in one of the following subjects: making the most of yourself; you and your surroundings; you and your money; you and your friends; fun with flowers.

Silver Award Here the minimum age for direct entry is fifteen, and the qualifying age between sixteen and twenty-one.

In the Service section there is a wider choice of activity and the level of attainment required is higher.

In the Expeditions section more is required in the way of preliminary training and practice expeditions, and the cross-country journey is longer, both in time and distance. The journeys may also be on horse-back or water.

In the Interest section the period of participation has been extended to twelve months.

In Physical Activity (boys) the score is twenty-four points and individual sports are included in the choice of groups.

In Design for Living (girls) there are new subjects, mainly connected with the setting up, furnishing and running a home.

Gold Award   A start for this may be made from the age of sixteen upwards, and the assessment is made between the ages of seventeen and a half and twenty-one.

In the Service section training is to an advanced level and, with practical service now mandatory, must take at least twelve months.

In the Expeditions, the journey has been extended to four days. As an alternative, girls may undertake a 'worthwhile project'.

In the Interests section the stipulated period is now eighteen months.

For their fourth section boys and girls this time have a choice between Physical Activity and Design for Living. If they go in for the former, they must reach a score of thirty points, and games is another group from which to choose. The latter consists of the practical study of a topic, such as family relationships or the social services.

Gold Award holders will also be expected to have had residential experience of at least five days.

Boys and girls are encouraged to progress from one level to the next, the conditions being graded accordingly. For those who have completed the Bronze Award and enter for the Silver, certain exemptions apply, in time and for ground already covered. The same applies for Gold. However, provided they fall within the appropriate age-range, they are free to enter direct for the higher levels.

Whatever mode is adopted, at all three levels the all-round nature of the Award is ensured by the stipulation that the appropriate conditions are met in each of the four sections. To avoid the danger of such a stipulation forcing everyone into the same strait-jacket, a vast choice of activities is offered within each section. Thus the boy who is not good at sprinting may go in for the mile, and the girl who loathes cooking has the option of doing make-up instead.

Allowance is therefore made for individual differences, both in ability and interest. Nor is anyone penalized if an essential facility (say, for swimming) is lacking in the locality. There are always alternative activities to choose from, making it possible for anyone to enter wherever he may live, in a village or city, in the Scottish Highlands or on the South Coast.

How *does* one enter for the Award Scheme? That takes us straight to the administration of the Scheme, and here it is important to remember that it is not an organization in itself, but a programme put at the service of existing organizations. Policy decisions are reached by a body of Trustees (of which Prince Philip is Chairman), aided by an Advisory Committee and a General Council. The responsibility for announcing these policies and seeing that they are carried out rests with the Award Office in London. This has a small senior staff, consisting of the Director, Alfred Blake (Lord Hunt's successor); two Assistant Directors, Mrs P. Gordon-Spencer and Commander D. L. Cobb; and the General Secretary, F. A. Evans.

The Award Office is helped in its work by subsidiary offices in Cardiff, Edinburgh and Belfast, and there are seven Regional Officers, who between them cover the whole of England. However, neither the staff of the Award Office, nor the Regional Officers, nor the Honorary Liaison Officers (of whom there are some forty up and down the country) are involved in the actual running of the Scheme.

The responsibility for the organization of running the Scheme has been delegated to what are termed Operating Authorities. The main Operating Authorities are: local education authorities, voluntary youth organizations, independent schools, armed services, industrial firms, and police forces. By accepting this responsibility, they make it possible for any young person under their aegis to go in for the Award.

The Operating Authorities in turn have placed the effective day-to-day running of the Scheme firmly in the hands of local groups: youth clubs, secondary schools, factories, cadet units, and so on. It is up to such people as the school-teacher, club leader and personnel officer to conduct or supervise the various courses of instruction and arrange for the assessments to be made. Subject to certain safeguards to maintain standards they can do all these things as fit in best with their particular local circumstances.

It may well be asked how, when there are no 'officials', it is decided whether a participant is deserving of an Award or not? There are handbooks giving detailed information about the programmes and conditions which have to be fulfilled.

The conditions are of two kinds. Some demand a definite standard of achievement; others look for endeavour and progress. The former are mainly objective; the latter relative. To give an illustration of the former: if first aid is chosen as a Service, an examination must be passed in the theory and practice of first aid as laid down by the British Red Cross or similar national organization. No such unequivocal demands can be made of the candidate who, say, decides to do pottery as an Interest. Here the standard must be relative to the level of proficiency at which he started; and when, after a period of time, he is assessed, it will be according to the effort he has shown and progress made.

The outward form of the Award are a badge and certificate, signed by the Duke of Edinburgh in facsimile and bearing his personal cypher. These are presented locally, except for the Gold Award certificate, for which ceremonies are arranged at one of the royal palaces, with Prince Philip himself being present. This is but one example of his personal involvement and the keen interest he takes in the fortunes of his Scheme.

It is one of the features of the Scheme that the activities can be followed concurrently or consecutively, and tests taken whenever a candidate is ready. In all these matters the adults in charge, working at first in isolation, soon discovered for themselves the advantages of co-operation. In this way local Award Committees have sprung up on which representatives of the various participating organizations in the area meet in order to, for example, find instructors and assessors, arrange joint classes, or simply compare notes.

The secretaries of these committees are mainly officers in the employ of the local education authorities. It is appropriate at this point to pay tribute to those LEAs who have given generous support, financially and in many other ways. Without this support, the Award Scheme would be in a sorry state.

Indeed, by its voluntary nature the Scheme is entirely dependent on the goodwill of numerous organizations and individuals. Something of how they have responded and what it has been able to offer them in return, follows in the next section.

ASSESSMENT

Has the Award Scheme exerted a positive influence on young people, and if so what is it? The question can never be answered satisfactorily. People react to the same situation in different ways, and the Scheme has not been in existence long enough for us to know how lasting the reactions are. Even in later life there is no means of ascertaining whether those who have been through the Scheme would have been any different if they had not.

However, these are difficulties which occur anywhere in the field of education in which measurable results are hard to obtain. All one can hope for is to draw some tentative conclusions based on what impressions one may legitimately gather. There is one way of putting these impressions into some sort of order: that is, to review the Scheme in the light of its avowed aims, section by section.

Beginning with Physical Activity, the intention is to encourage young people to go in for physical activities and improve their physical fitness. This was done at first by laying down certain standards of achievement.

However, the plight of those—a minority—who were genuinely incapable of measuring up to the accepted norm was underestimated. To put this right there has been a substantial shift of emphasis in the requirements, rewarding attendance as well as the achievement of a minimum standard. What the results will be is too early to say, but it is probably right to regard the feeling of satisfaction which participation in purposeful physical activity engenders as more important (because more lasting) than the purely organic benefits.

As far as the girls are concerned, the decision to offer them a different section was a wise one. The object of Design for Living (interchangeable with Physical Activity at Gold level) is to encourage young people to care about their health and personal appearance and contribute to the life at home and the community.

These are matters which, in secondary education, where the emphasis tends to be on academic learning, and further education, where it tends to be on vocational training, are often overlooked. Yet they are matters which, to girls in particular, are of the utmost relevance in their 'teens. Hence it is not difficult to see why they have applied themselves to this section with great enthusiasm, as well as see the benefits they have derived from doing so.

The Expeditions section aims to encourage the spirit of adventure in young people by presenting them with a challenge both in terms of physical effort and completion of a purpose (e.g. visiting a place of interest or collecting a piece of information).

Making their own plans and preparations and matching these against unknown territory and uncertain weather do present a challenge. It is not unreasonable to suppose, even if one cannot prove it, that those who have experienced that sort of challenge have gained something from it. Certainly, going on an expedition has proved extremely popular with the younger generation.

The purpose of the Interests section is to act as an incentive for the discovery and development of leisure activities which are purposeful and creative.

Some youngsters have utilized an existing interest and, one hopes, enriched it by devoting themselves to it for a stated length of time under guidance. Others succumb only too easily to the mass entertainments and have no interests of their own, and it is thanks to the Award Scheme that they have picked one up. On account of the time clause and insistence on 'stickability', the casualty rate is higher here than elsewhere. This is right: a test which makes no demands is not worth having.

Our final question is: Has the Scheme helped young people to realize that as members of a community they have responsibilities towards others? Here, at its most triumphant, is the justification for those who have always held that the young are as willing, and as able, to render help to their fellows as are their elders, as long as they can see for themselves that their help is needed.

The Award Scheme has provided them with the opportunity to undergo *training* in a variety of forms of service and then *giving* service in a practical way. It is possible, of course, that experience in this field over an extended period of time may leave the participants totally unaffected. But it is not likely, and there are many close observers who would put it more strongly than that.

So much for an assessment of what the Award Scheme may, or may not, have accomplished, made to correspond to its four constituent parts. But, of course, the Scheme must be considered as a whole.

Here one can only say, by way of summing up, that in an age in which the problem of leisure looms larger and larger the Scheme has compelled attention to opportunities of spending this leisure productively; that but for the Scheme many boys and girls would not have grasped these opportunities; and that those who have done so not only enjoyed it but appear to be the better for it. There is a sufficiently large number of persons concerned with the education of young people who will claim that this is so.

By 1970 some 600,000 boys and girls had been involved in the Scheme in the United Kingdom and 240,000 Awards granted. Growth there has been, but it has been slow and participation over the country patchy. There are a number of reasons to account for this.

Participation has always been purely voluntary. From the start the Award Office applied no pressure, but took the line that, if it is to last, the Scheme must be allowed to make its own way in its own time.

The standards may be exacting, but not unduly so. They have been carefully designed to be within the capacity of the average boy or girl. With some determination, they can be reached by practically everyone, particularly at Bronze level. That determination, it is true, has often been lacking, with which are linked two factors: the comprehensive nature of the Scheme and the problem of continuity.

As regards the former, the more ambitious the Scheme becomes the more educationally desirable it may be; but also the greater the degree of commitment it imposes on young people in the face of the many demands which are already made upon them. Continuity is not easy to achieve because of the inevitable break (both in physical and psychological terms) which occurs at the time of leaving school, and the increasing mobility of the population, causing many a well-laid plan to be discarded or connection severed.

There are always those who refuse to join in any pursuit which is organized; on them the Award Scheme has made no impression. But by and large, because of the natural appeal of most of the activities offered, young people have responded readily when given the opportunity. In many cases that opportunity simply has not existed. Here we come to the crux of the matter.

For any one youngster gaining an Award, a number of adults are involved who in some way or other have helped him to gain it. The fact that thousands and thousands of them give, and continue to give, this help, in their own time and without pay, is in itself a measure of the success of the Scheme. They would hardly do so if they were not convinced that what they are doing is worthwhile.

On the other hand, this essential adult help needs organizing, and those who are in a position to organize do not necessarily have the time (and often not the enthusiasm) to apply themselves to the Scheme.

In view of what has just been said, it is hardly surprising that where the Scheme has made most headway is in the secondary schools. More than half of those who take part do so while still at school—as an extra-curricular activity, of course.

The schools enjoy all kinds of advantages. This is not so with the average youth club which functions twice a week and where the club leader is an unpaid part-timer and resources are often lacking. However, with inspired leadership, some remarkable results have been achieved within the Youth Service too.

Progress in the sphere of industry and commerce has so far been slow. This is partly due to the fact that most firms are small and have few recreational facilities, and partly a matter of attitude. Where training is offered it is mainly of a vocational nature.

The observations made so far apply in the main to those boys and girls who have had direct experience of the Scheme. In view of the difficulties it has to face—difficulties which apply to any voluntary venture—I consider it unlikely that, in its present form, the Scheme will ever make a significant impact, speaking in purely statistical terms.

There remain what may be described as the 'indirect' effects. These are perhaps more important and affect the adults as much as the young people. It has often been remarked that the Award is no less a challenge to the former as to the latter, if not more so. There are many directions in which the influence of the Award Scheme has extended. To discuss them in detail is outside the compass of this essay, but there are a number of points that can be made.

Mention has already been made of adults concerned with the running of the Scheme within a locality joining forces. Though they may have been engaged in similar jobs or had similar outside interests, for many of them this has provided the first point of contact. This contact has not been confined to persons professionally involved with young people, such as teachers and youth leaders, but, because of the extensive range of the Scheme, all kinds of persons have been drawn together. Once established, such contact has frequently led to co-operation in other spheres.

The Scheme has drawn attention to the curious situation whereby there are many organizations with almost identical aims which are either ignorant of each others' existence, indifferent, or even hostile to one another. Within the Youth Service, certainly, it was not so long ago that a partnership between statutory and voluntary bodies was virtually non-existent. This is no longer true, and some credit for it must go to the Award Scheme.

The Scheme has also provided a platform for people of different ages to meet and get to know one another. The grown-ups young people come across usually represent to them authority—parents, teachers, employers—and authority tends to be resented. However, to the adults who have been called in, in connection with matters affecting their leisure, they are under no such obligation and appreciate that they, too, give up some of their free time. These adults would not normally have occasion to work with young people, and they have been glad to help because the call for their services has been in specific terms. Once common ground has been found and a happy relationship built upon it, it is not so easy to destroy that relationship. In this way the Award Scheme is doing something towards bridging the gap which separates the generations.

The repercussions of its influence can also be felt within agencies specifically concerned with the welfare of the young. To take the voluntary youth organizations as an example: many of them had run out of ideas and failed to attract new members. It is not that they have all necessarily taken up the Award Scheme, but in many cases inspiration has been derived from the example of a programme of purposeful activities.

In secondary education, too, a silent revolution has been taking place. There is a greater awareness nowadays of the importance of the informal side of education and the social function of the school, as is shown by a gradual broadening of the traditional curriculum and the introduction into many schools of 'extra'-curricular activities such as community projects.

Over the country as a whole there is much better provision for young people to take part in enterprising activities and be of service. To suggest that but for the Award Scheme these things would not have come about would be absurd. But whether the role of the Scheme has been to initiate or to reinforce, of the importance of its role there can be no question.

It can certainly be said that the ideas which underlie it appear to be fulfilling certain needs which are basic. If it were not so, the Scheme would not have lasted. Nor are these needs peculiar to this country, otherwise it would not have met with so much success in societies different from our own.

Nothing has been said in this section about Hahn. Although he was involved in the discussions which preceded the setting up of the Award in 1956, he has played no part in it since then. This is characteristic.

Hahn does not like being in the limelight (and, conversely, there have been some who, for various reasons, preferred to keep him out of it). He is essentially a visionary whose prime concern is not with the implementation of his ideas. But he has an uncanny gift for finding people who will take up—and develop—his ideas, and of inspiring them to do what might well seem an impossibility.

Finally, once having launched a project, his restless and fertile mind soon turns to other matters. Whatever they are—and the present book is an eloquent tribute to the wealth of his achievements—there can be little doubt that there is no more far-reaching medium through which Hahn has made his influence felt than the Duke of Edinburgh's Award.

United World College of the Atlantic

Anne Corbett

The most recent school to be associated with Kurt Hahn is Atlantic College. As its co-founder, he has shaped its aims. But here he has never been responsible for the school's day-to-day running. Its different relationship to him is reflected in its differences from Salem and Gordonstoun. Atlantic College, however, shares one distinction with them. It is in British—and even international—terms unusual. Intended as the first of a series, it has pioneered the idea of an international pre-university college, taking boarding students for two years between the ages of sixteen and eighteen. It is now (in 1970) at a watershed. Hahn's co-founder, Sir Lawrence Darvall, died at the end of 1968. The college's first Headmaster, Desmond Hoare, retired at the end of the academic year, 1969. He saw the college grow from 56 students when it opened in 1962 to 269 in September 1968. Now he has handed over to David Sutcliffe, a young member of the Atlantic College staff. But Sutcliffe's links with Hahn schools go deep: he has taught at both Salem and Gordonstoun.

The Atlantic College project is also poised for change. Lord Mountbatten took over as Chairman of the newly-created International Council of the Atlantic Colleges in 1968. It has already been announced that to emphasize its world-wide interests the project is being renamed 'The United World Colleges Project'. It is also likely now that further colleges will be set up in West Germany and

Canada. The Canadian one will probably be sponsored jointly by Canada and the USA.

Atlantic College was never intended to be like State schools, a characteristic it shares with other schools with Hahn links. But it tries to use its independent line and scholarship structure to make itself different from the traditional public school. The particular points its founders tried to avoid are a narrowly middle-class intake, a hierarchical prefect organization for the school, an over-specialized academic curriculum and an obsession with team games. These are precisely the points that many of the public schools are also modifying. And immediate impressions that it is much like a public school are strengthened by the fact that Atlantic College shares two attributes with many of the more successful public schools: it has a memorable environment and a wealth of facilities.

If you go down to St Donat's on the south coast of Wales to see the college, you visit a medieval castle complete with everything but a drawbridge. The staff common-room is the old castle hall, with a minstrel's gallery and a wide stone fireplace. Students eat in a dining-room with a moulded plaster ceiling and a Gothic screen. The class-rooms are wood-panelled. The decorations are all period, bought from churches and country homes. It was restored in the 1920s and 1930s. Its owner, William Randolph Hearst, the newspaper baron, had made restoring castles a hobby, each done more magnificently than the last. The attention to the detail in the castle extends to the grounds, with their terraced gardens leading down to the Bristol Channel. The site—again in common with many public boarding schools—is isolated. The nearest big town is Cardiff, nearly twenty miles away. It is sixty miles from Bristol, the cultural centre of the area. London is 170 miles away, but, with a good train service, is almost as accessible.

The specialized facilities for students include a modern language laboratory. With students from various nations, language teaching has an obviously important role. There is a science block, just completed. Maths and languages centres are being built in the castle grounds. Where specialized space and equipment is needed, it is aimed to provide it outside the castle. Students live outside the castle. There are six Scandinavian-style boarding-houses, landscaped in with trees, at the top of the estate. They are supposed to be social as well as residential centres. Some of the staff live in the college grounds with their families. The outdoor facilities include a heated swimming pool and a range of boats. There are in addition the usual opportunities for football, athletics, tennis, and so on. In return for this the annual fees are £800. These are about £100 to £150 above most public schools.

But if in style Atlantic College seems like a public school, the aims are patently different. These are two-pronged. First, as its Governing Council puts it, the aim is 'to promote international understanding through education. To break down national educational barriers, especially in the field of university admission, and to make education a force which unites, and not divides nations'. Secondly, Atlantic College aims to 'provide a pioneer experiment in a pattern of education adapted to meet the special needs of our time'. Underlying these aims is the belief in the importance of the age-group. 'Students at this age are old enough to be influenced by national or racial prejudices and to understand the causes of international conflict. They are still young enough to live together in residential communities, and have not yet come under the intense pressure of specialized studies combined with concern for their careers, which normally affect them at university level. Idealism is still strong: attitudes of mind can be cast at this time as at no other age.'

The analysis of Atlantic College's objectives remains much the same as first expressed by Kurt Hahn. Indeed, the analysis seems almost unique to the schools with which he has been involved:

The essential aim is to counteract some of the evils which have accompanied advancing material prosperity. Among these are the decline in physical fitness, insufficient satisfaction of the youthful instinct for adventure, boredom and a loss of the quality of compassion. Students [the council's statement goes on] must be encouraged to achieve physical fitness and learn the necessary skills which will fit them to work for others and to do this in conditions which tap their hidden resources. When students from many nations do this together, it is likely to be especially effective in removing national prejudices and awakening a recognition of the common humanity of all men. Through this recognition by the rising generation may emerge a real contribution to the future peace of the world.

Atlantic College looks to three means to achieve these objectives:

through a broadly based and academically demanding curriculum, through preventing the proportion of British students rising above a third, and ensuring that the different nationalities are housed together and mix in classes and the outdoor activities, especially the rescue services. Atlantic College is famous for its rescue services along the cliffs and shore of this rocky stretch of coast.

The idea for Atlantic College dates back to the mid-1950s. It seems to have been very much the joint brain-child of Sir Lawrence Darvall and Kurt Hahn. Darvall, an Air Marshal in the Royal Air Force and at that time the first British commandant of the North Atlantic Treaty Organization Staff Training College, had been friendly with Hahn for years. Says Desmond Hoare, the first Head-master, describing the germ of the idea: 'Darvall suggested that the successful NATO Staff College experience in training together in the business of defence mature men of several nations might well be applied to intelligent boys in their pre-university years, with an aim very different in nature—the creation of understanding which would in time supplant the use of force in international affairs.'

By 1960, Hahn and Darvall had inspired enthusiasm for the idea in Britain, in other parts of Europe, and in North America. A Pro-motion Committee was formed. Besides Hahn and Darvall, it included well-known industrialists and City of London figures— Lord Fleck (a former Chairman of Imperial Chemical Industries), Sir Michael Denney, Ronald Grierson and Eric Warburg; Conserva-tive M.P.s Richard Hornby and Sir Spencer Summers; the Bishop of Norwich, and the Director of the Institute of Education of Oxford University, A. D. C. Peterson. The committee had three jobs—to find a site and raise money, to appoint a Headmaster and start to build up the staff, and to work out the administrative structure of the project.

In 1960 the committee appointed a Headmaster. Hoare, a Rear-Admiral, found his naval experience gave him many Hahn-type ideas. He is an engineer, and training apprentices (as well as volun-tary work with boys' clubs) convinced him of the value of getting adolescents together to learn skills. The value, he feels, lies largely in the co-operative spirit that this can lead to.

The first Deputy Head, Robert Blackburn, was appointed at the beginning of 1962. Blackburn, now chief executive officer of the

International Council of the United World Colleges, had been teaching at Merchant Taylors, an independent school near London. He was attracted to Atlantic College by the idea of an international education. A history teacher himself, he had already tried to give his history an international approach.

By September 1968 the staff had grown to thirty-two full-timers. Many of them are young. The majority are English. It is a continuing aim to make the staff more international. There have in fact been teachers at various times from the Scandinavian countries and from Germany, France and Spain. But it was on Hoare and Blackburn alone that much of the initial planning of the college devolved. Robert Blackburn looks back on the nine months between his appointment and the opening of the college in September 1962 as exhilarating but nerve-racking. 'Our inheritance from Hahn', he says, 'was the nature of the college's entry—intellectual, international —and the activities programme with its emphasis on service. But *we* worked out how these ideas should be applied. Hahn was a midwife. But we had to keep the baby going.'

St Donat's had been bought in 1960. This was largely thanks to a gift of £65,000 from Antonin Besse (son of the founder of St Antony's College, Oxford). After Besse's gift, an appeal was made to British and foreign sources for funds. After a slow start and a tight period soon after the college opened, the appeal has now reached over £1·5 million. This excludes amounts made available for scholarships. Four-fifths of the money comes from British sources, including the Government (£100,000), the Dulverton Trust (£270,000), the Bernard Sunley Foundation (£100,000) and Sir George Schuster (£63,000). The Federal German Government has contributed £72,000. Other large benefactors include the Ford Foundation, the Steel Company of Wales, Guest, Keen & Nettlefolds, Marks and Spencer, ICI, Unilevers, Cadburys, and the clearing banks.

The success of this appeal is not the Promotion Committee's achievement. By common consent, that seems to rest with one man who joined the college Governors at the critical period in 1964—Sir George Schuster. Schuster, now in his eighties, came on the Board of Governors on his retirement as director of the Westminster Bank and after a distinguished career of financial advisory work, much of it to countries overseas. Schuster is now Chairman of the Board of Governors of Atlantic College. He also takes an active part in the

International Council as one of the Deputy Chairmen. This is the body of which Lord Mountbatten became Chairman in 1968. Its members include the chairmen of the foreign promotion committees for similar colleges in Canada, the USA, Austria, Denmark, Norway, Sweden, Spain and West Germany.

Why did all these people become involved with the Atlantic College project? What was the appeal?

Hahn's name is prominent. Says Sir George Schuster: 'I have such an admiration for Kurt Hahn. And Atlantic College, with its internationalism, its emphasis on social service seems to me to be such a hopeful cause.' Of his own part in keeping the idea alive he says modestly that on his retirement he wanted 'to get involved' in some worthy causes.

Lord Hankey, a former diplomat and both a college Governor and a member of the International Council, talks enthusiastically about Atlantic College as a 'yeast'. He sees the colleges spreading worldwide. 'How can such an idea fail?' he asks. He sees the appeal of the type of education to an era of big international businesses. But he sees as most significant the co-operative ideals. 'If you have one of those little boats out in the Bristol Channel,' he says, 'and a storm blows up, what happens? You don't think about whether you like the fellow in charge or that he's a German and that your father may have fought his father in the war. You co-operate—or that boat sinks. That sort of experience doesn't leave you.'

Alec Peterson, the director of the Oxford University Institute of Education, talks about another aspect. He too was attracted to Atlantic College by what he describes as Kurt Hahn's charisma. But he also felt the intellectual challenge of educating together an international range of students. Earlier, as Headmaster of Dover College, he himself had taken foreign students into the sixth form. He sees Atlantic College as a more ambitious experiment along these lines. Educationally too, he thinks, it offers an exciting opportunity to find a new pre-university course less general than some of the Continental courses and less specialized than the G.C.E. Advanced level requirements of the British sixth form. It is also a testing-ground for a new concept in examinations—an internationally acceptable qualification for university entry. In fact, through Peterson, Atlantic College has been playing a key role in the development of the International Baccalauréat. This is designed to fit the varied demands of systems as different as the American on the one hand and the British and German on the other.

The formal aims of the school and the expectations of these men sum up much of what the college stands for. How does it work in practice?

First, who are the students? The original 56—all boys—came from Europe and North America. They were all from countries bordering the Atlantic, hence in part the name of the college. By September 1968 there were 269 students, of whom 37 were girls. They came from 35 countries, the original students from only 12.

About a third are British (81), the expected proportion. About half the students have English as their mother-tongue (there are 28 students from Canada and 26 from the USA, though only one from Australia). The Scandinavians form a substantial group (24 from Norway, 10 each from Denmark and Sweden, 5 from Finland). The countries of Western Europe, other than France and Belgium, where there are university entrance complications, are also well-represented (25 from West Germany, 15 from the Netherlands, 8 from Spain, 2 each from Austria, Greece, Italy and Turkey). There are now students from Eastern Europe (3 from Yugoslavia, 2 from Czechoslovakia), from the Middle East, the Far East (India, Pakistan, Tibet and Malaysia), from Latin America and the West Indies. South Africa is the only part of Africa represented at present, though there is no bar on any country. There is one proviso only: that students have the academic qualifications. They do not even have to be able to meet the £800 annually for fees. It is fundamental to the college's aim of a wide social mix that most students should have scholarships. Except for the Canadians and Americans, most students do indeed have scholarships. Funds are generally provided by industry, banks and charitable trusts in the country concerned. Outside help has been given to students from Czechoslovakia, Yugoslavia, Tibet, Turkey and South Africa. Most of the British students get grants from their local education authority.

Not surprisingly, given the almost exclusively middle-class appeal of boarding education, the social mix aim does not seem to have been achieved. There's much talk at the college of parents' occupations ranging from King in Libya to taxi-driver in Greece. But the students I talked to produced a solidly professional catalogue—businessman, doctor, lawyer, and so on.

But if not socially, at least academically, the college can claim to be breaking out of the traditional mould. It faces a great challenge. It has to make sure that students from the countries with the most competitive systems of university entrance do not lose out by breaking with their conventional schooling. It has to bridge the gap with students from countries with an almost automatic right to higher education and thus no tradition of pre-university specialization.

The college has already persuaded a number of foreign ministries of education to accept the British G.C.E. qualifications. There are two hazards in particular: that it will over-examine students in order to give them ample safeguards, and that it will provide merely a watered-down version of G.C.E. 'A' level courses.

There's progress on the examination front. A number of overseas countries now accept the British G.C.E. results for entry to higher education. There's hope for a simpler future with the International Baccalauréat. Peterson, as acting Director of the I.B. organization, has involved Atlantic College in the trials for this examination, and the college will take part in the six-year full-scale experiment which starts in 1970. Meanwhile, the students do have to put up with a battery of exams. They take the American Scholastic and Aptitude and Achievement tests as well as the G.C.E. and the I.B. trial exams., so that all the results can be compared. But this is clearly only a phase.

In practice, it's a greater problem for the college not to provide an unattractive and irrelevantly insular education for its non-British students. The college tries to overcome this narrowness of the traditional English pattern of three or four G.C.E. 'A' levels by making students take three subsidiary courses in their first year and two in their second. There is some choice. Nevertheless, so that all students will have a broadly-based education, they have to complete one course from each of certain categories—their mother tongue, one of a wealth of foreign languages, a further course related to the language and literature of another country, social studies, maths and science, and art and music. There are project weeks, which may be centred on academic work, during both the school terms. (Atlantic College has two terms annually, not the normal three.)

Educational experts have been impressed by the academic range. A report by the H.M. Inspectors of Schools, the Department of Education inspectors, which was completed in 1966, concluded that the teaching was almost all good; it was often outstanding. They were impressed by the breadth of approach of so many of the staff. Nevertheless, said the H.M.I.s, in practice few students are in a position to benefit fully from the courses, the students' different educational backgrounds, varied competence in English and diverse national university requirements lead to compromises. In some cases students take fewer than the intended nine subjects. Where they do take them all, the H.M.I.s found that their studies were often restricted, so they could not effectively counter the specialized 'A' level studies. Certainly I was told by students—Scandinavian and Canadians especially—that they had to put all their energies and many of their evenings into the unfamiliar 'A' level courses. They had no time to worry about their non-examination subsidiary courses. In fact, as far as 'A' level results are concerned, they do well. Both British and overseas students do better than the British average. In 1968, 36 per cent of the Atlantic College students got passes in the top two grades of 'A' level: the British average was 25 per cent.

An integral part of Atlantic College life—and this is one of its most distinctive features—are the 'activities'. They owe much to Hahn and his Outward Bound schools. But the form they have taken also springs from Hoare's Navy experience, and more recently from changing ideas of social service, making it more community-based. Each student has to spend four afternoons a week on activities. Two of these afternoons must be spent on some form of service. They may choose between the beach, inshore and cliff rescue services, or they may take on some form of community service, such as visiting old people in the nearby villages. The other two afternoons must be spent on games or crafts or something cultural—photography or printing, for instance. 'Not less' than two afternoons weekly have to be spent out of doors, 'for health reasons', say the rules. The project weeks can be spent on activities.

American educationists, including the Dean of Harvard, visited the college in 1967. They were assessing it on behalf of the Commission for Atlantic Colleges Inc., an American promotional body. They had this to say of the activities programme: 'I went a sceptic . . . but returned a convert.' 'The thing that is great about these activities is that there is a reality about them not found in the usual sports programme.'

The beach rescue service is actually responsible for patrolling local beaches during the summer months. The cliff rescue unit is a recognized part of the Coastguards. The inshore rescue boats unit is affiliated to the Royal National Life-Boat Institution. The H.M. Inspectors were impressed by the thorough professional approach to practice and training. It seems to be a professionalism that is needed. The rescue services may be called out dozens of times in a year. Even in midwinter they have to help people trapped by the tide against the cliffs. A school with such an outdoor emphasis may attract a special type of student. But I was impressed that so many of the students seemed quite so keen on the rescue services. This even applied to the girls.

What, finally, of Atlantic College's most ambitious aspect—its internationalism? The long-term effects are obviously immeasurable. But it is also difficult to measure how enriching it is at the time. As a visitor, one is struck by the fact that there you are at lunch talking to two Americans, an Indian boy, a Swedish girl and a Czechoslovakian. Or that you find a Finn and a Swede and a Canadian working on the boats, helped by the English and German wives of two members of the staff. Staff and students talk of how genuinely the nationalities mix in the boarding-houses or in the rescue services.

But some students and ex-students argue that Atlantic College makes you more conscious of nationality, since so many of the social and cultural experiences of the college start with reference to one's country. A visitor can see that there must be occasions when this national awareness gives rise to unbearable strains, when youngsters are driven to defending their country, right or wrong. You are told, for instance, of the 1968 Middle Eastern war and how there were two Jordanian students and an Israeli at the college. One of the Jordanians had to live through almost a week of college tension not knowing what had happened to his parents after one of the raids.

However, on the whole students do not seem to be so aware of international tensions as of social tensions. At this stage the college still seems to be finding its way towards a social system appropriate for these near-adults. It is complicated by the fact that they come to the college with many different expectations. But they do, for instance, still have to wear a uniform. There are strict rules about when they may go out and what time they should be in bed. Though there is a student council, it is not allowed to discuss any matter impinging on the teaching—and this includes the content of courses, which must often be puzzling for foreign students. Moreover, the council is not directly elected, but brings together the officials of college clubs and societies. These are issues, of course, which many English schools are grappling with, so Atlantic College is not unusual.

In general, it is clear that in its eight years' existence Atlantic College has made progress in its aims. Now it has almost its full complement of students, and has moved away from its NATO connotations. It will inevitably change under the personality of a new Headmaster. No doubt the next few years will be a period of consolidation while the pressure for development turns to the West German college and possibly one in North America.

While outsiders watch with interest to see whether Atlantic College becomes more consciously an international 'junior college' and less of a school-oriented sixth-form college, Kurt Hahn must look at Atlantic College with a special feeling of involvement. In Blackburn's metaphor, it will be the feeling of a midwife or guardian —whereas at Salem and Gordonstoun he's the parent. But there is no reason why he should not be pleased.

Anavryta

πεῖρά τοι μαδησιος ἀρχά
Trial is the beginning of wisdom—ALCMAN

Jocelin Winthrop-Young

Anavryta was founded by the King and Queen of Greece in 1949. It was to be a boys' boarding school on the lines of Gordonstoun and, in the event, the system was nearly identical to that current in Gordonstoun under Mr Hahn before the war. Four of the first Greek masters were sent to Scotland for a term to see for themselves how it all worked.

The choice of a site for the school was limited, as the country was still in a state of civil war, and we were restricted to an island or the immediate neighbourhood of the capital. By good fortune, we found a large wood at Kifissia, ten miles north of Athens, with a large house, gutted by fire, which we rebuilt for the first boys. The wood lay on the southern slopes of Mt Pentelicon, and the estate of some twenty-five acres allowed us to space out the buildings much as we liked.

It was the first time that a Hahn school was built from the ground up. The classrooms were concentrated in one block and the houses, for fifty boys each, were spaced out in the woods; on the principle that they could not be seen from one another in day-time, but that their lights should be visible through the trees at night. This allowed sufficient isolation and independence for each community and its housemaster.

We started with twenty-five boys, and the total grew to 180 by the end of the first eight years. They were divided into three houses: a junior house taking the age-group ten to twelve and the two senior houses taking them up to the final exams at eighteen.

A healthy spirit of competition grew up between the senior houses Anatolikon and Hymettus, and each developed its own character, largely dependent on that of its housemaster. Each house also had an assistant housemaster, normally a young Greek and, in the later years, often a former pupil who wished to take up teaching as a career.

The boys came from all parts of Greece and from the large Greek communities overseas: from Alexandria, Cyprus and Constantinople, from Europe, Africa and India. Only a very few were foreigners, as we taught in Greek, and this also ruled out the possibility of exchanges with schools abroad. Extreme poverty was widespread in the country, and we had many boys who came from the poorest homes. We therefore kept a simple way of life in the school and restricted the items that the richer boys might bring with them. This seldom led to difficulties, as there is no feeling of class difference in the country, and we found that the boys mixed well from whatever background they came.

One third of the boys were non-paying scholars; these we selected on journeys through the poorest provinces: the Epirus, Thrace, Thessaly and Macedonia. The local village schoolmasters collected their most promising boys together, and we would spend three or four hours examining them before moving on to the next small town. Once they had been selected, the boys had everything, including clothing, provided for them, but they were expected to find their own way to and from Anavryta; this was severely criticized at first, as it was argued that it often led to hardship for the family. I nevertheless considered it important that the parents should feel that they had made some contribution towards their sons' education. We kept the scholars for the full nine years. We also considered ourselves partly responsible for seeing that they completed their studies at university in Greece or abroad. In this we were soon helped by a very active Old Boys' Association: they have spacious club rooms in Athens and help some of the scholars through university by paying them for organizing and servicing the Club.

Academically we were able to compete successfully with other schools from the start. We had small classes in a country where classes were normally far too large and often included two or even three school years together, due to lack of teachers. We had most able Directors of Studies and were close enough to Athens to have easy access to extra teachers and lecturers when required. Above all, we had enough applications to allow a careful choice among the paying pupils and a free hand to pick the non-paying scholars. There was also a keenness to learn, partly due to the necessity for the scholars to succeed in their exams and partly due to a more lively attitude to studying than is often found in Western Europe.

We celebrated the services and festivals of the Greek Orthodox Church. There was a small chapel in the grounds and we attended the local church from time to time. Religious instruction was given by members of the staff and by a priest who was a theological scholar of national repute.

Most of the staff were Greek State teachers, but there were also American, English, Swiss and German masters teaching languages. There was considerable enthusiasm for modern languages among the boys and reasonably high standards were reached.

We built an open-air theatre, and drama, as was only right in Greece, played a large part in the school life in summer. The works of Sophocles, Shakespeare and Molière were performed in their original tongue with great enthusiasm and resulted in a perceptible rise in the knowledge of each language. A memorable occasion was the first performance ever of *A Midsummer Night's Dream* in 'a wood near Athens'.

The country itself we exploited by taking the boys to visit as many historical sites as possible and by inviting distinguished historians and archaeologists to come with us and lecture on the spot. In this way the boys learned thoroughly about Delphi, Chaeronea, Olympia, Sparta, Mistra and the Argolid. We even chartered a ship to take us round the Aegean, visiting Crete, Delos, Tinos, Rhodes and other islands.

The heat in summer forced us to alter the daily programme so as to keep the boys indoors between the morning break and five in the afternoon; Prep was therefore carried out before the afternoon activities. For the same reason, the summer holidays were three months, which is too long a break in the working routine, but unavoidable in that climate.

The winters were cold and we were able to set up a skiing school in the Pindus Mountains in collaboration with the Greek Commandos. Groups of boys were sent up there with members of the staff, and the courses proved very popular. The conditions were fairly primitive, so that not only technique, but also endurance were acquired by this experience.

Expeditions were carried out each weekend with groups taken alternately from the different houses, and most of the mountains in Attica were well known to the boys by the time they left. Some rock-climbing was done and training in mountain rescue was practised regularly and proved very successful: a pair of boys would be 'lost' in a given area of hills and the entire organization of the search and recovery left to the boys. During these exercises they developed a system of visual signals that was most effective. With this one exception, the services were not developed as far as in Salem or Gordonstoun. A fire brigade was not possible so close to the capital and seamanship was not a regular part of the school programme during my time there, although it has now become so under my successor, who was previously a distinguished Greek naval officer. Perhaps we relied too much on the occurrence of emergencies in the country, when the boys could always be counted on to help to their utmost ability. An example was the International Boys' Camp on Cephalonia after the great earthquake in the Ionian Islands; here Prince George of Hanover led a team, including boys from Gordonstoun, Salem and Anavryta, and the three Guardians were able to work together for the first time.

In the early days of the school there was much practical work to be done and the boys were employed building the obstacle run, garages and other necessary projects. We also did a lot of tree-planting and levelling of ground for the playing fields. This slackened off as the necessary jobs were completed and we were, for financial reasons, unable to compensate by providing carpentry and metal workshops. Mr Hahn criticized this development during his later visits and we managed, as a result, to start up pottery on a small scale.

The morning break was carried out daily and athletics, swimming, and cross-country running, hockey, basket-ball and volley-ball were compulsory for all boys. There was a lengthy argument as to whether hockey was an ancient Greek game or not; but in any case we kept a high standard and used to play the teams from visiting British naval ships. The running track and games fields were cleared out from old olive groves in the woods, and we later built a large closed gymnasium at the highest point of the estate; alongside we put a squash court and this game became most popular with both masters and boys. In half a dozen years we achieved a dominant position in school sport in Greece and were able to influence the development of sport among the young throughout the country. The first Olympic Gold Medallist from our schools came from Anavryta; this was indeed appropriate. It was also some reward for the effort put into sport in the school. The success of all these activities was largely due to their Director, the Deputy Headmaster, Ioannis Neris, who was ably supported by three sports masters and a very active group of young housemasters.

The school was run on the same lines as Gordonstoun. The training plan, Colour Bearers, Helpers and Guardians were introduced gradually as the boys grew into their responsibilities. We made one change. I had always felt unhappy over the practice of awarding the school uniform only after a trial period. It seemed hard to me that a young boy leaving home for the first time should thus appear different from the rest of the school; it also seemed to me questionable, in a school basing itself on trust, that we were not ready to entrust our uniform to a newcomer on arrival. Hence we gave the school uniform to all at once, but took it away as a punishment if the boy was dishonest.

The training plan worked well, but its effectiveness seemed to me to fall off after the boy had reached sixteen or seventeen; either self-discipline had been achieved by then or the training plan did not seem the right means of helping a boy to achieve it. It tended to be an unnecessary chore for the senior boy who carried out his responsibilities conscientiously, whether he noted them down afterwards or not. Nevertheless, it was compulsory for all boys to whom it had been awarded until they left; but I am not certain that we were right in this.

On the whole, the Colour Bearers and Helpers worked well, and their sense of responsibility for the younger boys was outstanding. It meant a lot to them that they were carrying out the same responsibilities as their counterparts in Scotland and in Germany, and all Colour Bearer meetings were held in a special Assembly Room, where the flags of the three schools hung.

That there should be Guardians in Attica was romantic enough in itself; the boys felt this, and the staff and other supporters of the school were eager to point out that the system was partly based on the thinking of a Greek, Plato. Indeed, there was a strong feeling of patriotism that often helped the educator, providing an extra spur to the boys' interest that is often absent in Western European countries. At times it also increased our difficulties. The Cyprus question provided the school with its first real crisis; loyalties were divided and the boys were incited by the press and radio to disown their Headmaster—because he was an Englishman. Once again, as earlier in Salem, the Guardian and Helpers held the school together, while many of the staff were unable or unwilling to help. Once again the Colour Bearers were ready to accept unpopularity and abuse rather than abandon those principles for which they had been elected. Afterwards, when quiet had come to the country again, there was a feeling of confidence that if the school could live through such a crisis so early in its life, it must have grown strong roots.

In fact, the survival of the school at this time was entirely due to the direct support of the King and Queen. They always kept in close contact with the school, whether in time of trouble or success. They demanded that we maintain those principles for which they themselves stood as living symbols in the country.

Perhaps we were too much in the public eye, due to the Crown Prince's being in the school from its foundation until he left as Guardian in 1958. This meant a constant stream of journalists and newspaper articles—many of them most critical and ill-informed. But it also meant that a large number of distinguished visitors came, who often provided most valuable advice and well-deserved criticism. Of particular value were the visits of the Headmasters of Salem and Gordonstoun.

Mr Hahn visited us three times, in 1952, 1956 and 1958. He never stayed for more than a week, but these were visits that were always great events in the life of the school. Groups of boys were summoned to him and he took part in many lessons and activities. His encouragement was exhilarating and his criticism penetrating; and criticism was, no doubt, much needed during the first years, for we were learning as we went along and the age of the Headmaster and the Deputy Head added together barely topped fifty years. We should certainly go about it differently were we to start again; I suspect that we should not achieve so much. For the effort needed to start up a school of this type and form its traditions demands the enthusiasm and energy of youth. The more amazing does it seem that Mr Hahn should have been able to accomplish this twice in a lifetime, in addition to all his other enterprises.

We took the opportunity of these, his only visits to Greece to show him something of the country, and drove to see some of the historical sites. Two pictures remain clear in the memory: the one of him standing on top of the Grave Mound at Marathon, listening to a description of the campaign, the broad-rimmed hat drawn low over his eyes as he looked across the straits to Euboea. The other of a visit to Mycenae on a cold, clear winter's day with the snow showing on the Arcadian Mountains in the distance. We walked up to the Lion Gate. There Mr Hahn stopped and asked us to go on without him. With his companion, I completed the round of the Citadel and we returned outside the walls on the west side half an hour later. As the Lion Gate came into view we saw a solitary figure seated on a stone in the shadow. He rose and came down to us at a half-run, chanting Homer and full of the possibility of skiing courses in the mountains.

Despite the inspiration provided by these visits, I believe that the significance of Anavryta as a Hahn school lies in the success of the system in the absence of its originator. We applied the same principles and methods as in Gordonstoun and Salem and, despite the great differences of race, temperament and climate, they worked. This should, surely, be an encouragement to those intending to start similar schools elsewhere.

It is still too early to assess the contribution made by Anavryta to Greek education. The influence of the school may, however, be seen in certain spheres, as in the case of sport mentioned above. The Old Boys keep in close contact and support the school and its objectives. In their own lives they try to remain loyal to the principles they have been taught, and this must have some effect, however slight, in a small country like Greece. Few have, as yet, assumed responsible positions. Yet one should not forget that the young King Constantine, in his first speech to his people, spoke of himself as a 'vigilant guardian'. I believe that he chose these words intentionally and that he was thinking then of his earlier responsibility as Guardian of a much smaller community.

The Educational Thought of Kurt Hahn

Hermann Röhrs

Time and again the most powerful stimuli to educational thought and strategy have originated from great educational outsiders—men who were not bound to any academic school, and so were in a position to challenge ideas which had become an accepted part of the establishment of their time. They did not confine themselves to the orthodox academic side of education and to problems of classroom technique; for them education had to do with the whole man, with his fulfilment and development—his renaissance. If we list some names of recent pioneers in education, Kurt Hahn can justly claim a place alongside Thomas Arnold and Cecil Reddie, Hermann Lietz and Paul Geheeb. In this context Kurt Hahn stands out as one of those important personalities who warn and inspire, as a man who, convinced of the moral and spiritual decline of certain sections of society, is fired by a deep sense of responsibility to change society by means of educational reforms.

Like other headmasters associated with the Liberal School movement and the New Education Fellowship[1] before and since the turn of the century, Hahn starts out with a criticism of contemporary culture. Against the background of the bitter experience of the First World War, his criticisms are striking in their realism and urgency, in disquieting contrast to the already familiar line of the 'professional educationists' and the German State schools, from which Hahn has always sought to dissociate himself. Our State system is often stigmatized as a teaching machine, accused of setting tasks for the

children which bear little relation to their age and stage of development, their tastes and interests. And in spite of innumerable attempts
to make the curriculum attractive and more commensurate with the
sensibility and experience of children, the reforms themselves have
retained an air of artificiality, of being imposed from outside. They
are not spontaneous. This is one of the limitations of the German
State system of education which can perhaps be modified and its
rigidity relaxed, but which in principle can never be altered.

With this always in mind, Hahn has repeatedly emphasized the
fact that young people will take pleasure in learning if the environment is attractive, and the lessons both interesting and worthwhile.
From the start his educational thought had a broad intellectual basis
and contained in embryo all the elements and ideas that were
gradually to be developed and institutionalized in his schools. For
instance, both the concept of 'rescue' and 'internationalism' were
present from the first, embodied in the sayings 'Help your neighbour' and 'Give service for peace'. The fact that he was compelled
for political reasons to emigrate only accelerated a process he had
already intended; but at the same time it deprived Salem School,
the parent cell, of nurture, while the new off-shoot was founded in
Britain at Gordonstoun.

The development of the two schools on these lines was a next to
impossible task when they were separated from each other by war.
It was due in no small measure to the co-operation of a body of alert
and positive teachers that the continuity of educational purpose was
preserved across political frontiers and eventually across the frontline
of war. What Marina Ewald, Karl Reinhardt, Wilhelm Schmidle and
Kurt Blendinger signified for Salem, Erich Meissner (starting with
valuable experience of Salem), Henry Brereton and Bobby Chew
came to signify for Gordonstoun. They were all pioneers of progressive schooling backed by sound educational theory—and prepared to experiment with extremely unconventional methods.
Progressive schools depend for their success upon the enterprising
spirit of those who run them. Hahn has a rare gift for finding such
men and enlisting them, and the genius to make each find in this
service the full realization of his own personal gifts.

So we have experienced educationists, with excellent academic and
organizational qualifications, high-ranking officers (whose position
would have excluded any thought of a teaching career), leading

businessmen, members of the aristocracy, scientists and scholars of distinction in their own fields, all finding fulfilment in this environment. One could claim that only in the context of these independent schools did they find their vocation. Hahn has always had a remarkable gift of being able to guide men and women to prove themselves as individuals while very often renouncing economic advantage. His circle of colleagues, individualists of the most varied types, had a sense of purpose and corporateness which took them far beyond the limits of which is normally possible.

In retrospect, Hahn has made some revealing comments on the way the two main concepts of his education have been handled:

> Before Gordonstoun was opened, I had the leisure to reflect on the course of Salem's evolution; it became clear to me where we had been on the right track and where we had gone astray. Of one thing I was certain: we had not made enough effort to emulate the Cistercian model;[2] true, we had indeed seized some dramatic opportunities to show ourselves helpful to the neighbourhood, but there was lacking the epic constancy of daily service such as the Cistercians had practised and preached.

Again, many years later in 1950, he makes a critical comparison of the work in the meantime accomplished in Gordonstoun: 'Has Gordonstoun succeeded in the way Salem succeeded, or has it even perhaps succeeded where Salem failed? My answer will surprise you. We have succeeded at those points where the parent school failed, and we have failed just where Salem succeeded.'[3] This paradox is essentially the result of the separate development of the two institutions and of their different educational preconditions.

The whole range of ideas characterizing Hahn's educational theory, which from 1941, along with Salem and Gordonstoun, also embraced the first Outward Bound School at Aberdovey in Wales, would probably never have materialized in the normal run of events. The necessity of making a fresh start gave a powerful impetus to their evolution. Hahn's ideas proved in the course of time to be extraordinarily fertile, so that beside Anavryta, the public school near Athens founded in 1949, Outward Bound schools (offering a few weeks' training) were opened in many countries in rapid succession. From now on the various elements in Hahn's theory began to emerge more clearly. Two years after the foundation of the first Outward

Bound school in Aberdovey, when Sir George Trevelyan named the school's schooner *Garibaldi*, he said: 'If ever youth loses the thirst for adventure, any civilization, however enlightened, and any state, however well-ordered, must wither and dry up.'

Where modern industrial society fails, Hahn saw it an ever more urgent imperative to provide youth with an urge for adventure. Looking back over his experience at Salem and Gordonstoun, he has always opposed the conventional view that the crises and lethargy of adolescence are an inevitable stage in development. In accordance with Rousseau's belief that tasks motivated by social and moral concern help to alleviate the problems of puberty, Hahn devised the various facets of his 'experience therapy', the cultivation of innate fights and absorbing personal interests, and training in self-discipline.[4]

'Experience therapy' is one of the basic tenets of Hahn's conception of education. In modern society, in view of the complicated requirements of life, young people are kept in the dependent position of learners well into the age of adulthood; yet they need to test and prove themselves if they are to discover and realize themselves. Youth is socially sick because in the framework of modern society it is not led by natural challenge to its powers to develop the basic human capacities. In this situation a corrective is required, and it is provided in Hahn's scheme by an elastic system of training devices: the break for athletics, the expedition, the project and the rescue service; these can be used either singly or in combination. For this a strong mutual respect between teacher and pupil is necessary and an acceptance of sensible limits to freedom—such as Pestalozzi called for in opposition to Rousseau's supposedly unlimited concept of freedom. Spiritually akin to him, Kurt Hahn asserts even more emphatically that a personal renewal in the young can take place only if 'voluntariness is supported by compulsion'.[5]

Athletics are the basis of the therapy, since the acquisition of physical dexterity, strength and endurance reinforces the sense of honour and of chivalrous readiness to help. Team games are of capital importance, for they inculcate a 'feeling of the good ally' and thus train boys to co-operate. These qualities are elementary prerequisites for the expedition and rescue service. The expeditions offer a wide field for boys to prove themselves, whether it takes the form of a mountain-climb, a sea-voyage, or help in a foreign country. An example of the last was the building of an old people's home in Cephalonia in Greece by a group of schoolboys from seven different nations, including members of Salem, Gordonstoun and Anavryta. This took place in 1954 under the leadership of Prince George William of Hanover.

The rescue service is the most remarkable of these activities, because here the youth, by risking his own safety for his neighbour, gains an entirely new attitude towards life. The essential services are sea and mountain rescue, which present young people with a sense of isolation and insignificance in the face of Nature, which inevitably summons up the idea of mutual help and interdependence. In Salem and Gordonstoun the school's own fire brigade, manned entirely by the boys, is one of the main services. Its long tradition makes it a distinction to belong to the brigade, a distinction which must be confirmed and proven when the brigade is called out for an emergency in the neighbourhood.

In the last analysis, all these forms of helping and rescue training are a preparation for the real emergency, and it is looking forward to the opportunity to prove himself in action that gives a boy the impetus to carry out the necessary practice. If no such opportunities arise for a considerable period of time, then enthusiasm may flag, and what was conceived as an experience totally different from anything in the world of formal schooling becomes once again a matter of mere routine. When we were staying in Gordonstoun a year or two back, the fire service had been called out to fight a fire after a long period of inaction. When the boys returned they were full of the service they had performed, which had been both dangerous and successful. The morale of the whole school was given a noticeable stimulus as a result. The infrequency of such serious emergencies leads one to ask whether the more obvious types of 'rescue' from social distress, such as help for old people, families and farmers, ought not to be included too. Certainly these forms of social assistance and rescue would require very much more preparatory training before they could be successful in the same way.

The complement of the services as a principle of education is the 'project' which is specifically intellectual. Besides the scientific projects are those of craftsmanship, artistic projects and projects involving social enquiry, but all alike involve intellectual planning. The project exercises the ability to form judgments methodically, and gives wide scope to a boy's initiative and inventiveness. It makes him work on his own to a great extent, developing his independence and sense of responsibility.

The sharp impact of an event or a deeply felt personal experience can rouse a man from complacency, and the taking of a risk can have a similar result. So the acceptance of risk becomes a means of education: the ultimate form is in the rescue services when a man is involved in giving help to other people. The Outward Bound schools play a major part in providing a practical opportunity to youth all over the world to experience the impact of this kind of education, and they are in a very effective position to do so, since they bring together a very wide cross-section of the community and of class and intellect. After Aberdovey had stood the test, further schools were opened in rapid succession in many parts of the world: in Britain in 1949 the Moray Sea School in Burghead in north-east Scotland, in 1950 the Mountain School in Eskdale in the Lake District, in 1954 in Ullswater, Cumberland, and, finally, the Outward Bound School in Rhowniar, Merionethshire; in 1953 at Man o'War Bay, Nigeria, and subsequently similar schools in Kenya, Malaysia and Australia. In Germany the Weissenhaus Sea School was founded in 1952 on the Baltic coast, in 1956 the Mountain School at Baad in the Kleines Walsertal. In 1961 Holland's first Outward Bound School was opened in Moermond Castle, near Renesse, on Schouwen Island; and, finally, in the United States Outward Bound schools were founded in Colorado in 1963, in Minnesota in 1964, and on Hurricane Island in 1964.

Despite the spiritual affinity of the various Outward Bound schools, one can discern natural differences of emphasis, representing sometimes special national or regional conditions, sometimes different stages in the evolution of the school. The short-course schools in the various countries differ not as much in their aims as in the fact that each concentrates on a few particular tasks in the framework of what is generally binding on them all. Under the influence of Trevelyan's ideas, adventure and risk occupy a central position in the first schools founded in Britain—though these always revert to the idea of rescue. The motto of this type of education runs: character development through adventure.

In the German short-course schools daring and adventure are unambiguously placed in the service of one's neighbour—a logical development from the principles of the original schools. Only in the framework of selfless enterprise do adventure and daring acquire their educative significance and go to the forming of an ethical personality. The American Outward Bound schools, on the other hand, require hard tests directly reminiscent of the life of the early settlers of their country. In no other country are these tests of endurance so inexorably severe—whether it be in the Colorado mountains, in the forests and rapids of the Canadian border or on Hurricane Island off the Atlantic coast, north-west of Boston.

In 1962 the first Atlantic College was established in the magnificent St Donat's Castle on the south coast of Wales. As an international sixth-form school, it prepares boys (and now girls as well) from various countries for university entry. The international setting certainly does encourage the boys to come to terms with the problems of other peoples in a practical way on the simple level of everyday school life, and to learn their languages. Here, too, rescue service, which is carried out in the very difficult sea conditions of the Bristol Channel, from Aberthaw as far as the mouth of the River Ogmore, forms an integrating link in the two-year course.

A rather different training scheme which is not linked specifically to any institution, and which Kurt Hahn helped to found, is the Duke of Edinburgh Award Scheme. It is open to a much wider public, and for this reason has had a national impact. Its object is to promote a continuous course of athletic training and other activities as a valuable contribution to young people growing up. On its introduction in 1957, 7,000 boys took part; in 1963 the number of participants had already risen to 43,000 boys and 19,600 girls. This notable movement grew out of the so-called 'Moray Badge', which Hahn had already initiated at Gordonstoun in 1936, and which in a few years, as a 'County Badge', had found a remarkable measure of acceptance far beyond the precincts of Gordonstoun. The Duke of Edinburgh Award has initiated a real movement for popular education. Despite its great stress on physical efficiency, it nevertheless provides an intellectual counterbalance in the form of the varied projects. The tests of the Award are viewed as an educational whole, and the project in particular is designed to strengthen a boy's personality. By arousing some form of intellectual interest, it offsets the danger of 'spiritual deafness', against which Hahn has given constant warning in connection with the present cult of sport.

In considering the impact of this educational concept, one inevitably seeks for its origins. Lines of thought on the one hand, running from Plato and the British public schools to the late nineteenth-century critics of contemporary culture, appear to intersect on the other hand with the influence of the American pragmatism of William James and the development of the *Landerziehungsheime* (German public schools)—the Lietz foundations in particular. The aim, so to speak, is derived from Plato, while the psychological motivation as an aid to self-knowledge is taken from James.

One can only do justice to Hahn's various foundations if one views them against the background of traditional notions and institutions. In this connection, what is most important is to consider the significant line of development of the public schools, from Cecil Reddie's Abbotsholme down to the German schools of Hermann Lietz and Paul Geheeb, which were inspired by Reddie. Hahn has repeatedly stated that the as yet undefined ideas for a new school which he had long had in mind gained clearer outline through his reading of Lietz's highly individual study, *Emlohstobba*.

Nevertheless, Hahn is certainly not a disciple of Lietz, and Salem is far more independent from an educational standpoint than one might be led to suppose from the remark of Prince Max of Baden, which Hahn is fond of quoting with approval, that in education, as in medicine, traditional and proven methods should be preferred to originality. A certain kinship—with Lietz in particular—shows itself in Hahn's belief in the power of education, whose task is to bring about the regeneration of large sections of the people through certain insulated institutions which should be kept as far as possible isolated. In both cases, the style of education is definitely of an exacting nature; in spite of the physical isolation, it is outgoing and world-affirming and it employs risks and enterprise as a means.

Lietz, who travelled with his schoolboys in the holidays on voyages to Scandinavia on the iron-ore ships or cycled to Paris with a group of boys to visit the World Exhibition, showed Hahn these new paths and deepened his understanding for simple forms of youth leadership; but also made him critical of the 'flattering' promises of 'youth culture'. The simple and natural way of life in Ilsenburg, Haubinda and Biederstein, having its educational pivots in sport, practical work and the hour of recollection in the 'chapel', must certainly be borne in mind when judging Salem, Gordonstoun and Anavryta.

But behind what seems at first a Spartan style of education which values what is bold and daring is concealed a carefulness to do justice to the needs of each individual. Hahn's aim is to suggest and to lead from the sidelines, by contrast with Lietz's patriarchal style of direction modelled upon the management of a farm. Thus the elements of 'experience therapy' are directed less towards intellectual and emotional toughening than towards producing, in Platonic fashion, integrity of soul. In this respect, Hahn comes nearer to Paul Geheeb than Hermann Lietz. What Lietz possessed might be called educational passion, capable indeed of arousing enthusiasm and discipleship, but making favourites of the particularly able. Hahn, by contrast, would be said to have an educational attitude to life, always on the look-out to find forms of activity for the physically less-capable pupils. Lietz was unmistakably nationalistic in outlook: he had the flag run up on his own initiative after hearing of the murder of Rosa Luxemburg, and also developed a form of pre-military training. In Salem the drill that was introduced for a time primarily served the cause of self-discipline and so of peace.

The cultivation of 'Germanism', however—whether in Fichte's or in the philosophic-cosmopolitan sense of the word—was never Hahn's goal, but rather the simple and unpretentious self-commitment of individuals to the welfare of their neighbour, and a 'sense of responsibility towards humanity'. This quotation from Prince Max (December 1917), chosen by Hahn as a *leitmotiv* of his work, may strike one at first as pretentious, but it is convincing when one takes into account the fateful time at which it was spoken.

The originality and power of these imperatives in Hahn's teaching lies in their awareness of the problems of our time, spiritual insensitivity and rigidity, due to living in a civilization which makes us helplessly dependent in all sorts of ways without our realizing it. Materialist civilization on the one hand gives us physical freedom and leisure, but brings with it a sense of alienation. In trying to give the direct answer to this dilemma, Kurt Hahn neither exaggerates nor ignores it. The manner in which he deals with the problem reveals the essence of his thought; he does not lecture or analyse or lament, but sets out appropriate concrete remedies. This positive and constructive quality is already evident in the literary novel, *Frau Elses Verheissung* ('Else's Promise', published 1910),[6] in which severe criticism of contemporary schools and education is countered by the sound educational principles embodied in the mother's personality.

In its fully developed form, Hahn's answer to the problem is, as we have seen, 'experience therapy'—a form of fresh youthful experience which makes it possible for young people once again to feel wonder and astonishment, and so, contemplating, to look outwards and upwards to new horizons. The experience itself has no more than an ancillary function—namely, to uncover the deeper layers of the human personality, which in our everyday life have all too often been overlaid by conventions of civilization. The educative softening of hardened souls and their remoulding in beauty in accordance with the Idea of Man is the Platonic picture of this process. And so, by way of example, success in holding out to the end of a contest, rescue service, the completion of a task, a shared adventure can bring the growing youth into a fresh relationship with the basic forces of life, and so lead him back to Nature, his neighbour and himself.

This principle of dialogue, which ultimately links the urge to self-realization with active service of his neighbour, is the educationally constructive element. It also gives Hahn's concept of education a dynamic aspect: an appearance of perpetual outgoing, of a deep restlessness in the service of outward or inward suffering. This background explains the relative lack of hard contours in this thought and its high degree of receptiveness for any ideas that might be serviceable. Its goal remains essentially the renewal of life by imposing conscious and binding form upon the pupil's experience and relations with his fellow-men. Thanks to this quite new kind of confidence in the world and himself, hitherto unrealized forces can be released and fresh tasks envisaged. The Platonic image of a conversion of souls away from the realm of the shadow into clear light seems to be thoroughly appropriate here. This form of 'experience therapy' is the central link connecting Salem, Gordonstoun, Atlantic College and Anavryta and the short-course schools.

In so far as the concept of an élite is at all appropriate, it can only signify this new kind of 'nobility of soul' which has no connection with rank. It was an integral part of the founder's aim in establishing Salem to provide a school for *all* children of the Salem Valley, since for full human development the children of all classes in society must be educated together. It is a misinterpretation to conclude from this that the working-class children are just a leavening added to enrich the intellectual climate which is exclusively designed for the professional and upper classes. This is to misunderstand the basic approach of Hahn and of the Prince, too, for on educational matters both of them thought in democratic—indeed, comprehensive—not patriarchal terms.

It follows that Hahn's schools were orientated towards the integrity and strength of the growing personality, without any regard to the parents' social position. Accordingly, there has always been a system of free places, based upon a confidential estimate by the parents themselves of the fees they should pay. As a necessary correlative to this, all have to share the same style of living at the schools, including the same uniform and the same amount of pocket-money. Given this equality, differentiation develops only where some take an alert and active part in the various fields of school life, instruction in class being only one among others of equal importance.

No great value is placed on the accumulation of knowledge as an end in itself. The fundamental reason given for this is that the development of powers of judgment is deemed more important than the acquisition of knowledge; and, secondly, that the services, expeditions, the projects and daily training and participation in the running of the school are regarded as equally constituent parts of education. Essential to the practical working out of such a programme is a new technique in the classroom whereby a limited amount of subject-matter is analysed intensively; this would relieve the pressure on the time-table. While expecting a higher educative result from these measures, Hahn says, 'I am by no means advocating a lowering of intellectual requirements—on the contrary, less would achieve more, while demanding more training of thought, less factual knowledge. Depth is what matters. Curricula overloaded with subject-matter were the source of intellectual shallowness.'[7]

Fundamentally the intention is to rescue the gaining of knowledge from the distorted perspective of the teaching of school 'subjects', and to link it up again with its natural and original motivation in practical needs, personal inclination, the desire to dwell on and think through some topic or other. The knowledge acquired through this living connection with practical need is able to affect the pupil's life and his responsible shaping of it. To have learnt to restrict one's knowledge in face of the demands of what is ultimately valuable and worthwhile in life is the objective criterion, and can be ethically justified. A young person who grows up into a clear pattern of life of this kind cannot give up this integral framework again without a struggle, because it has become for him a habit or, in Hegelian terms, second nature.

Thus the morally responsible man, not the scholar or artist, is the educational ideal of this school—that is, the man who is committed to the idea of the good and to justice and who regards professional skill as a part of his task as a citizen in society. The training aims to inculcate an intelligent adaptation and, where necessary, subordination of his personal interests and desires to the larger context of the whole. And so, even outstanding sporting achievements—despite the recognition that fitness must complement academic study—have only a limited justification. Like scholarship or artistic skill, they are only by-products in a course of education that strives to achieve much wider aims in the service of the whole man.

The goal remains 'energetic action', which in a democracy forms a vitally necessary correlative to sound moral sentiments. To this end the Salem 'Rule', which has influenced the basic educational outlook of the rest of the educational world, demands that the following requirements be fulfilled: 'Ability to effect what (he) has recognized to be right, despite hardships, despite dangers, despite inner scepticism, despite boredom, despite mockery from the world, despite emotion of the moment'.[8] Courage becomes general human capacity 'to overcome fear'.[9] This courage meets its supreme test in risking all for one's fellow-men.

In this respect, the idea of education through the rescue services is capable of great development. In Germany possible spheres of activity could include care for the aged, many forms of probation work, service in hospitals and educative and welfare work in rural areas. The fact that on a superficial view these forms of assistance recall the pre-war German Labour Service must not prevent us from recognizing the possibilities for social education through bringing young people into this work.

Here we have a starting-point for an educational and development-aid programme in my own country that could become a real testing-ground for many of our young people. In these forms of social assistance they would be confronted daily with many a tough task; but that could be extremely effective educationally if the circumstances had been thoroughly thought out and the ground prepared beforehand. Short-course schools could become centres of social education and bases for a civil assistance corps of young people, which, by appealing to their sense of moral responsibility, could be an effective means of combating neglect and delinquency in the young.

So here too, as in the Platonic *paideia*, the ideal of 'development of energetic participation', remains the objective which finds its fulfilment in the idea of rescue. But the real keystone of this educational system is the conquest of war by harnessing all energies to an honourable service of peace. The quest for an 'equivalent for war', as James called it, is evident in all Hahn's later writings. It has always been linked with a striving after international understanding—especially in the period of intensified nationalistic feeling that prevailed during the war.

His writings and speeches of the war years bear eloquent testimony to this. The address 'On Pity', a long sermon that was given in 1943 in the Anglican Cathedral in Liverpool, is an example. This deeply moving sermon, which Hahn as a recently naturalized British subject was preaching to his fellow-countrymen, might well be entitled 'On loving one's neighbour in wartime'. In an atmosphere of hysteria, while bitter fighting was in progress and mutual distrust was verging on the fanatical, Hahn preached to the congregation on the theme of 'Reverence for life', and made the war appear utterly senseless. Here as in his later writings service towards the physical and spiritual well-being of his fellow-man is shown, in a manner exemplary by its modest simplicity, to be the only truly satisfactory way of life.

War on war is therefore a central preoccupation of this educational reformer. That Hahn finds the remedy in devoted service for peace is due not only to his personal conviction, but also to the influence of the psychology of James, who sought to motivate and guide the attitudes, interests and strivings of men. The passion for service to his neighbour is meant, as it were, so to possess the soul of a young person that every aggressive or warlike instinct is smothered or redirected into new and peaceful channels.

NOTES

1   The New Education movement had its origin in the quarter-century before the First World War, and was based on cultural criticism and dissatisfaction with acknowledged education system. The main representatives of this global movement were Dewey, Kilpatrick, Ferrière, Decroly, Kerschensteiner, and Blonsky. The idea of founding new schools, in which children could grow up in free conditions, spread all over Europe and North America (county boarding schools, Landerziehungsheime, country day schools, laboratory schools). It even reached India, where Tagore set up his Sanctuary School. In 1921 the New Education Fellowship, with sections in several countries, was founded as an organizing centre of the movement.

2   Salem School is accommodated in a castle monastery, built by the Cistercians. Here Hahn refers to the industry and charity of the Order, which he wished to be a *leitmotiv* in the life of the school.

3   Hahn, Kurt, *Education to Responsibility*, p. 67.

4   Hahn, Kurt, *At the Crossroads*, p. 18, a confidential letter of 9 January 1965 (twenty copies published).

5   Hahn, Kurt, 'Juvenile Irresponsibility', in *Gordonstoun Record*, 6.12.1961; also *At the Crossroads*, p. 21.

6   Hahn, Kurt, *Frau Elses Verheissung*, München: A. Langen, 1910.

7   *Education to Responsibility*, p. 87.

8   Hahn, Kurt, *Education and the Crisis of Democracy*, p. 30. Speech delivered on the occasion of being awarded the Freiherr vom Stein Prize, 1962.

9   *Education to Responsibility*, p. 60.

Kurt Hahn amongst Children and Adults

Hellmut Becker

I first met Kurt Hahn when, at the age of seven, I was sent for a term to Salem. Hahn had founded Salem a year previously, after changing from politics to education. The school at that time had only twenty pupils, the first class being the Upper Fourth (fourteen-year-olds). Much to the amusement of the other pupils, I received my instruction sitting at the very back of that class. From this moment and throughout forty-five years I have met Kurt Hahn many times at the various stages in his and my development: first as a schoolboy in the Middle School at Salem, then as student helping out as a teacher in his schools during my vacations, later as a lawyer after the war in intense argument about public financial assistance for the independent schools, which he was against at first, and then during the last ten years on the boards and consulting committees of his schools and in constant discussion about the central problems in our educational system. We often disagreed about questions of content and theoretical problems, but again and again we were always prepared to participate in mutual undertakings. Once it was the founding of a school or a finance plan; another time a reform project concerning the State school system; often simply a question from one of his schools concerning personnel; and most of all help for a particular child or a grown-up. Hahn belongs to that group of people capable of co-operation and friendship in a high degree, a quality which has only been enhanced by time. During a lifetime, when others have become stolid and indurate, he has become more dynamic and discriminating.

Why do the customary attempts to classify Kurt Hahn according to some specific philosophy or educational development fail? He is close to many of them, but when taken at their true value they are all inappropriate and do not stand up to any thorough examination. Hahn has called himself a pupil of Plato. This is certainly true subjectively, but when one enters his school one does not get the impression of being in a Platonic environment. Some of Kurt Hahn's words sound like quotations from William James, and yet Hahn's educational philosophy and his attitude to justice could not be expressed in James's words, 'truth is what works', and the Outward Bound schools could not be described in terms of William James's famous lecture as the 'moral equivalent of war'. Since its foundation, Salem has been regarded as the most impressive attempt to establish the English type of public school in Germany. However, everyone who knows the public schools is immediately aware of the fundamental differences between Salem and even Hahn's English foundations and the public schools. Hahn often refers to the influence of Hermann Lietz on him, and the literature of education is in the habit of pointing to this influence; and yet how distant Hahn's schools are from the theories of Lietz, not to mention his practice!

The attempt, then, to place Hahn in the usual categories is not possible, because his impact is determined by an attitude to justice and present needs and not by a relationship with theory. Reflection serves the moment and theory is subordinate to it. For this very reason, the constitution plays an important part in his schools; fixed rules, the long-term durability of a constitution, are all the more important, due to the lack of educational or social theory. Therefore Hahn is not done justice by descriptions which attempt dogmatically to create from his widely scattered theoretical observations some system, which may be used whenever necessary to contradict this dynamic educator who has no system. The lack of theory makes it possible for Hahn to admit to educational mistakes in such an impressive way, even in the face of those children who have suffered from his errors. In this connection, it is therefore worth noting how much his attitude to the educational role of the teacher and the lesson could change, firstly in England and even more as he became older. There is no special formula for each individual child. Instead, a new approach is ever at the ready; he can wait long and humbly to see how the child develops. It seems to me that one of the strongest motives of the Hahn approach lies in a pre-Christian humility in the face of the suffering of his fellow-man. Intellectuals, whether children or adults, provide difficulties for Hahn: they seem to lack—especially when young—that basic virtue, humility. But all people, whether intellectuals or not, can never be indifferent in their relationship to Hahn. They are either his friends or his opponents. Hahn has a great respect for all achievement, even when at first he is not familiar with its every detail.

The ability to apply his own potential in dealing with children and grown-ups Hahn acquired but slowly. There are many people who were at one time his pupils or who worked with him who now speak his language or who have adopted his way of thinking, but as clichés, because his effect upon them as children or colleagues was too immediate, too direct. No one is more disconcerted by this than Hahn himself, just as he is extremely annoyed when his own educational methods, which he is constantly able to modify in the presence of the actual case, become dogmas in the hands of unoriginal imitators.

It has often been inferred that the staff in Hahn's schools did not have an easy time. He was not one of those who looked for easygoing and respectful colleagues. It was people with powerful and complex personalities like Karl Reinhardt, Erich Meissner and Desmond Hoare whom he chose to work with him. The basis for friendship and co-operation lay in their often conflicting views. The same applies to the close educational co-operation with the socialist Minna Specht, of whom Kurt Hahn spoke so highly in the book dedicated to her on her eightieth birthday.

Hahn's untiring ability to be constantly at the ready to offer help does not derive alone—as with many educators—from the problems the child experiences. Again and again with like intensity he has applied himself to those unmastered situations in life in which grown-ups find themselves. Of course, this zeal, when directed towards the individual case, whether child or adult, caused his attention to stray from those children or colleagues who were also dependent upon him. There were always teachers on his staff to whom he rarely spoke and pupils to whom he paid little attention. And it is perhaps amongst these very people that some of his most faithful followers are to be found.

Kurt Hahn's educational approach has been called non-intellectual.

Its inclination towards a Good Samaritan service, its preoccupation with health and its sense of adventure, have been described as irrational. Some critics have even labelled his attitude pre-Fascistic. It must be admitted that Hahn, for whom intelligence is a matter of course, was always especially interested in developing those abilities which can supplement intelligence. His choice of educational methods and their verification has been quite eclectic. The forces which drive him on are to be found in the desire to help the one who is weak now and an untiring concern that justice be done. In this way he might be unjust towards some individual, but there is no justice without injustice. And one of the most decisive things about Hahn is the constant determination to right the wrongs which have been done.

Hahn will not leave us a particular educational code. Indeed, there is a danger that the constitutions of the schools he has established will lead his pupils astray into Pharisaism when his dynamism has faded away from them. One often asks oneself what causes princes and Nobel Prize-winners, millionaires and politicians, scholars and industrialists, trade unionists and artists to constantly stand up for Hahn's creations. Hahn's social criticism was concerned with actual phenomena and with the effects of those phenomena on groups or individuals. I don't think that his solutions aroused great fascination, however right they may have been in each case. There was nothing sensationally new in the sea or mountain rescue services, nor in the 'poisonous passions', nor in self-education derived from responsibility for others: these would not have sufficed in engaging between 1920 and 1970 men of all kinds for Hahn's enterprises. The desire to be original Hahn regards as 'one of the greatest sources of error in education'. Again, his effectiveness cannot be explained by reference to his unusual gift for rhetoric, his ability to tell stories and his dramatic powers. Perhaps one has to go back to his Jewish roots in order to comprehend how he was able, through knowledge of his own weakness and the weaknesses of others, to develop a policy of strength through action for the benefit of others, and how from his own timidity and gentleness came the persevering tenacity of his actions, and how, in spite of his own impatience, there unfolded an ability to wait with great patience—perhaps the greatest virtue of an educator—which showed itself again and again in the presence of children and adults.

Kurt Hahn has no family of his own, but he has a definite feel for family life. The greatest praise he has for a woman is that she reminds him of his mother, and he feels completely at ease with a large family. A difficult childhood, much influenced by a remarkable mother, became a life dedicated to youth, which finds the world of today and yesterday difficult to comprehend, and whom he himself sometimes misunderstands, but to whom he is always capable even in old age of offering direct help. The responsibility for this youth gives him no rest. He feels obliged to awake in each individual, wherever he may be, a feeling of responsibility for his fellow-men. It seems to me that the phantasy, the diversity of his efforts to help, the intensity of his engagement, the seriousness and the wit which Hahn invests in each single case or institution he has fostered these last forty-five years is unique in the history of education. We realize that his intensity is not without its dangers, but all our traditional educational institutions can learn from it.

Hahn's educational actions seem always to stem from two poles—justice and love. Should these two ever be in conflict, then love conquers. That may sound somewhat banal, but the directness of his actions allows for only this interpretation.

In contrast to the great majority of German educators, Hahn has always been an educator within the context of 'one world'. It still seems amazing even today that when we read Hahn's German speeches we regard him as a true German, yet his English ones stamp him a true Englishman. The fate of emigration unfolded something latent within him, which found its full fruition in his last and perhaps greatest foundation, Atlantic College, a school of international character, the predominant aim of which is the realization of an international curriculum. Just as the dangers and problems experienced in his own youth caused him to be ever ready to come to the aid of others in danger, so has his twofold involvement broadened the horizon of international education. Kurt Hahn has demonstrated to us that education today is doomed to failure if it neglects to acknowledge an international context. It was not by chance that he was born in Berlin—the only metropolis Germany has ever known.

Kurt Hahn's Political Activities

Professor Golo Mann

Old people find that they have lived through times which are now beyond the ken of the younger generation, but which are still in a way part of their own present. Anyone who describes the political life of an eighty-year-old must refer to people and events known only to his contemporaries, or else to the specialist. They are not quite history yet; they are no longer topical; they are in the twilight between the present and history.

Kurt Hahn never entered politics as a profession. Politics was for him only a link with his primary aim as an educator. However, following his classical models, education and politics were inseparable, and at times he was directly and consciously involved politically; at others, only indirectly. He was a man of action who got things done, which is evident from the way in which, amidst the poverty of the 1920s, he developed the Salem School system when it was no small task to find staff and raise funds. More recently we can see this practical nature at work in the founding of Atlantic College. Here a tough and cunning will, capable of turning dreams into reality, was at work.

In practical politics he usually failed, close though he came to success once or twice. He was, moreover, a man the degree of whose influence cannot always be clearly ascertained. It was the destiny of Hahn, as a politician, to work not directly but through others. He did not choose the medium of publicity, which would have been open to him, perhaps because he knew what little effect even the most gifted publicists have ever had, especially in Germany. Instead, he concentrated his efforts on drafting memoranda, on preparing speeches, interviews, books for others; on giving advice which others accepted or rejected. He had great confidence in himself, and this self-confidence was justified, for his political insight was excellent. But he never chose to be in the limelight; in the early days the opportunity did not present itself and later he had become accustomed to working indirectly.

It is often possible to recognize his influence in the political writings of his friends, though not always with certainty; for his friends were no doubt liable to imitate him unconsciously, to employ the expressions, the quotations, the parables so well known to anyone familiar with Hahn's style.

So Hahn as a politician is a strong, impulsive personality, passionately interested in politics but aloof from and sometimes decidedly rejected by the professional politicians; one who was for decades on the periphery of active political life—sometimes close, sometimes remote.

His aims changed—or, rather, evolved—throughout a long life covering a span of turbulent history and subject to personal ill-fortune. In the years 1910–30 Hahn thought of the 'common cause' as Germany—indeed, 'Greater Germany'—and that in serving it each man would have done his duty and found happiness. It seems that this north German who settled in the south-west never attached great importance to the regions, ethnic groups or federal states of Germany. In his eyes the nation was an historical product and an historical task, a task concerned with its internal peace, its internal and external freedom, and its greatness too. These views he shared with Meinecke, Hans Delbrück, Friedrich Naumann and Max Weber, and they were realistic enough and in accord with the spirit of the time.

When the Third Reich had emerged, Hahn's feelings for the fatherland and for the nation altered, but even when an exile in Britain he could never forget that he was a German. He was not clear as to where his duty lay. Then technically he became a British subject in 1938; but his love, based on deep knowledge, for British civilization made this acquired citizenship more than a formality. And then again since 1945 'Europe' and the 'Atlantic Community' have helped to reconcile his two loyalties.

Hahn's political activities during the First World War were not really directed against Britain and his heart during the Second was not really against Germany. What he wanted during the First World War was simply peace, and peace with Britain in particular, because there he saw the best chance for peace-making and because it was the field of his special knowledge. What he hoped for during the Third Reich, both before the war and later, was peace with Germany after destruction of the Hitler régime. '*Our* armed forces', '*our* statesmen' were German in 1917 and British in 1943. For the biographer, this is undoubtedly a radical change, but it was not a complete break. Hahn's way of thinking was always humanitarian, not nationalistic, even when the nation still sufficed him as a vehicle for the human good. His thinking was always in terms of order. Nations—yes, even hostile nations—but nations that even in their antagonism might enhance one another and produce a kind of harmony. So too he saw parties in domestic politics; each working in its place for the good of the whole. One is almost tempted to speak of a belief in the pre-established harmony of Leibnitz. An episode that occurred when Prince Max of Baden was Chancellor may serve to illustrate this. Hahn's original draft of the Prince's policy statement contained a passage rejecting the idea of a grand coalition of right, left and centre; the majority parties should form the Government, and the opposition's function was to provide sharp, patriotic criticism. The members of the new Cabinet objected. It was, they said, quite wrong to appeal for criticism in Parliament and patriotic opposition at home at a time when everything depended on the solidarity of the entire nation. This criticism was both banal and insincere; inside or outside the Reichstag, the solidarity of the nation was non-existent. On one point, however, the regular politicians were probably right: the conception of a harmonious, quasi-constitutional interplay between government and opposition, one in which even the venomous and slanderous protests of the *Vaterlands-partei* would play a useful part, was too ingenuous; it was unrealistic at that time.

One must speak with caution of the philosophical principles of a man who never really expressed his aims theoretically. However, I should venture to say that for most of his life Hahn did not believe in the reality of evil, and it took a long time for Adolf Hitler to convince him to the contrary. To Socrates evil was lack of knowledge, lack of clarity, a deficiency; and so it was for Hahn, too, more or less. The purpose of his system was to free the impulses, even the seemingly evil ones, for doing good, to release them so that they could achieve what they unconsciously wanted. His politics were similarly conceived.

In every group, he believed, and in every strong individual there was something potentially good, something useful or capable of being made useful. This explains his ambivalent attitude towards National Socialism before 1933. The moralist in him could not accept compromise. After the Beuthen murder and Hitler's telegram in praise of his murderer-comrades, Hahn called upon the members of the Salem former pupils' association to choose to break either with the school or with the party. A few months later—it must have been at Göttingen in December 1932—I heard him say during the course of a lecture that no doubt Hitler already regretted his telegram. That was an error. Hitler regretted nothing, and far worse things were to come that he would not regret either. But Hahn's humanist calendar simply did not include double-dyed villains and vile monsters in human shape.

Not believing in the reality of evil, Hahn did not believe in what Carl Schmitt, our notorious political philosopher, called the 'friend-enemy relation'. There he was right; such absolute enmity can only derive from misunderstanding and obstinacy. In both wars Hahn worked for a negotiated peace: in the First World War a peace leaving the Powers more or less as they were; in the Second World War between the allies and a Germany freed of Hitler. Knowing how closely related the national civilizations of Europe were, he was contemptuous of the talk of struggle between 'British materialism' and 'German idealism' or, again, of 'inevitable economic wars'. But he did acknowledge that war sets free human potentialities, instincts and longings, such as courage, adventure, imagination and service, sacrifice for a common cause, which otherwise are often fettered and remain unused. It is part of his educational doctrine to replace the opportunities provided by war with comparable tasks in peacetime, without the killing. This concept goes back to William James, the ethically-inspired pragmatist, with whom Hahn shared the conviction that you cannot say that people just are what they are, but rather that they are or become what they do.

Since he regarded politics as a part of the humanities, as a form of self-realization and self-liberation, rather like that which man finds in art or in sports, Hahn loved the dramatic element in politics: the great leaders, classical parliamentary speeches, destiny mastered or missed on some stirring occasion. Democracy—certainly; but democracy with a distinctly aristocratic accent. The *Memoirs* of Prince Max, in the writing of which Hahn had a considerable hand, take on a dramatic shape, particularly in the last section. The portrayal of the various characters is distinct and fair, but nevertheless they are *dramatis personae*. Nor is there any lack of crises that break out 'with incredibly dramatic force', of deathly pale messengers bringing the most terrible of news at dead of night, and recipients of this news who stagger in horror or imperturbably weigh up the information. Frequently the little word 'now' is used for dramatic effect—*now* there appeared, *now* there happened, *now* there occurred.

Politics needs clarity of thought and quality of mind, although it should not be 'intellectual' in the German sense of the word. Hahn accused the intellectuals of an inability to take action when once they had an insight into a problem. After he had returned from the war and set about turning his war-time experiences to account by founding the Salem schools, one of the abilities he hoped to develop in his pupils was an ability to 'put into practice what has been seen to be right'.

Hahn's political activities began in 1914, and reached their peak during the First World War. What later became an occasional sideline was at first a continuous, full-time occupation. When the war began he was a young man, only twenty-eight, without office or title and almost without any achievement to show. What he did have was a profound knowledge of Britain, the adversary, acquired in the course of several years spent over there. What he developed during the war may well be described as political intuition, but it was more than the German State and party bureaucracy could do to recognize this in such a young outsider. Hahn's knowledge of Britain, however, was respected to some extent. As a result, he was made English reader at Paul Rohrbach's *Zentralstelle fur Auslandsdienst*, which was connected with the Foreign Office. There he was entrusted with the task of analysing the Press and thus the mood prevailing in enemy countries. Hahn was by far the ablest member of the group. Never before—and probably never since—has a government at war been supplied with such reports on internal affairs in the enemy camp.

The 'English monitor' was both arrogant and modest, with complete confidence in his own judgment, but unwilling to push himself forward in any way. He had the self-control to be objective. The quality of his work, a combination of care for the smallest detail with the imagination to draw far-reaching conclusions, was bound to attract attention—the attention of privy councillors, deputies and ministers. War has both a restricting and a liberating effect on life: people whose paths would never have crossed otherwise meet, talk, combine, conspire. In war-time Berlin, with its atmosphere of excitement, suspicion, and alternating *hubris* and despondency, there were all kinds of opportunities for such a talented mind to form contacts with journalists, with politically-minded bankers, professors and officers, and with professional politicians. One of the centres of activity was the *Deutsche Gesellschaft von 1914*, to which Hahn gave a memorable lecture on the psychology of British warfare. We find him in more or less close touch with Conrad Haussmann, a liberal from Württemberg, with Eduard David, a right-wing Social Democrat and with Friedrich Naumann; with Hans Delbrück, Alfred Weber, Friedrich Meinecke; with Max Warburg and Carl Melchior; with Solf, the Secretary of State for the Colonies, and Rosen, Minister at The Hague. In February 1917 he made the acquaintance which was to be so fruitful and fateful for both—with Prince Max of Baden. In August 1917 he stayed for the first time near Salem Castle, where he still lives.

He travelled to the neutral countries of Holland and Denmark in the modest role of interpreter, just as later, at the Versailles Peace negotiations, he was merely private secretary to one of the German delegates. The acuteness of his judgment, the sheer force of his personality, the literary mastery of his reports made such journeys into something more than his superiors had intended.

The *Zentralstelle fur Auslandsdienst*, which had become politically unruly and critical of official policy, was dissolved in the spring of 1917. Hahn then transferred to the service of the (later General) von Haeften, who was the Supreme Command's liaison officer with the German Foreign Office. Haeften was political adviser to Ludendorff, and Hahn to Haeften. There were not so very many links in the chain between the young man from Wannsee and the General-Dictator. Hahn was never quite close enough to make his influence really effective, but on a few occasions he came near to it. On one occasion Hahn was allowed to report directly to Ludendorff, and he by no means confined himself to what was supposed to be his subject, America's war potential. In his *Dokumente der Obersten Heeresleitung* (Supreme Command Documents) Ludendorff included a memorandum signed by Haeften, and he passed another on to the Reich Chancellor marked 'strongly supported'. At that time Hahn took the view—a view that he also maintained in retrospect—that Ludendorff 'wanted to get out of the war' in 1917 and that, in spite of his limitations and the violent obstinacy of his nature, he was not impervious to good advice, or would not have been if the civilian politicians, whose duty it was, had shown the necessary energy in advising him. In 1917 the Supreme Command was, in Hahn's opinion, 'ready to be stormed', but no statesman dared face the protests which a declaration of the complete restoration of Belgium (the *sine qua non* of a negotiated peace) would have raised. In January 1918 Hahn wrote to Prince Max:

> The favourable moment will, however, pass fruitlessly once more. . . . On one side we have a strong, passionate will, often possessed by demonic impatience, but receptive to all honest advice and with great power of self-control. On the other, a Cabinet policy working with petty little methods, afraid of its natural allies, incapable of facing others in open conflict. . . .

The two sides were Ludendorff and the central Government.

Anyone who knew Colonel von Haeften knows that he would never have put his name to anything that he had not understood and approved. Anyone who knew both Haeften and Hahn also knows that the younger man had by far the more powerful and inventive mind. One can detect Hahn's hand in the style of Haeften's papers, for it is characteristic enough. Haeften held his assistant in the highest esteem and allowed him the greatest freedom of speech. Only once, on a truly dramatic occasion, did he allow Hahn to feel his subordinate position. At any rate, he claims to remember saying: 'Silence! Remember you are Private Hahn of the Reserve, and have no concern with such a serious affair of state!' In fact, however, he not only let him have a say, but even a decisive say, as far as his own memoranda were concerned.

Hahn also tried to impress a wider audience with his judgments of the situation in 1917 and 1918 through Max of Baden. In spite of the military, wartime pseudo-democratic Caesarism, a German federal prince could still wield influence if he wanted to. The heir to the Grand Duchy of Baden could get through to the Imperial Chancellors, the Hindenburg-Ludendorff partnership or the Kaiser's Chief of Cabinet at any time and be certain of a polite hearing. He could also make speeches that would attract attention all over the Reich and beyond its bounds. But that was all. The system of influence which Hahn had built up, through the Prince on the one hand and the Colonel on the other, and through certain diplomats and members of the Reichstag, did reach those who wielded—or failed to wield—power in Germany. He bombarded them with one memorandum after the other. It was remarkable and astonishing that such a system of influence could have been built up by this young 'private politician'.

But, as even Hahn and the Prince suspected, it was not enough. In his *Memoirs* Prince Max writes 'It was hard to know the truth and yet not be able to proclaim it publicly. What use in the end were all our memoranda and our confidential means of persuasion?' But even though there was something rather quixotic about the efforts the two men made—or so certain professional politicians such as Philipp Scheidemann thought—one might very well ask what else they should have done, since they did not and could not control the levers of power. One might add that the committees and such-like on which the parliamentarians sat, more comprehensive, more legitimate and closer to the seat of power though they were, were no more successful in doing anything about the mismanaged war than the princely amateur and his adviser; and, furthermore, they, although it was their business, did not even try.

What were Hahn's aims during those four years, his varying theses?

The war was not inevitable; it could have been prevented, so it ought at least to be ended in a manner compatible with the honour of all the warring powers. It ought not to be allowed to escalate, to degenerate, as seemed to be the case; it should be brought under control and dealt with politically. This was a matter of policy, not diplomacy, still less secret diplomacy, least of all was it the concern of the military.

The English-speaking nations understood the power of public opinion at home, in enemy territory and in neutral countries. The

Germans failed to understand it; they had to be taught. Hahn tried to do so in his memoranda and conversations; occasionally also at public meetings, where, however, he proceeded cautiously. His lecture of November 1916, for instance, is strewn with 'veiled appeals' to his own fellow-countrymen, with quotations from British speeches, with reflections on what had once been the strong points of British policy.

> Part of the battle and a very important part of it [said
> Macdonald not long ago] is the ability to make the enemy see
> what our intentions are, so that he cannot misuse or distort our
> declarations in order to increase his own strength. One must
> work on the enemy's psychology as well as on his armed forces.

Salut à bon entendeur! Germany should do the same—should inform the world of her war aims instead of talking about them as something dark and unpleasant, while boasting uselessly of her own strength.

In any definition of war aims, clarity about the future of Belgium was a necessity. Hahn worked in vain for four solid years for a 'Belgian Declaration', for the absolute, completely unqualified restoration of her sovereignty and integrity. In it he saw a means to divide public opinion in Britain, to reinforce the group of those who were ready for peace—Grey, Asquith, Balfour and Lansdowne, not to mention the left-wing rebels. He never missed an opportunity of bringing up the Belgian question, although, as far as the public was concerned, it had to be in the form prescribed by his censors. In the lecture to the *Deutsche Gesellschaft* he quoted: 'The God who gave us iron for swords, He cannot want us slaves.' 'Gentlemen, no German, no Polish, and no Belgian slaves!' Hans Delbrück, who printed the lecture, omitted the word 'Belgian'.

Of course, Hahn well knew that for the British leaders who had been in power since 1916, Belgium was only an excuse and perhaps not even that. He wanted to present them with a 'Belgian Declaration', not as a self-humiliation, but as a profound challenge. That was an idea characteristic of his political tact and sense of style, but too subtle for those to whom it was addressed in Germany. The same was true of his vision that the German annexationists, the Pan-Germans, later renamed *Vaterlandspartei*—he calls them the 'Angry Patriots'—would always fulfil a useful function. His idea was that, although they were not to get their way, they were to talk loudly so that a negotiated peace would not be prevented by the enemy's hoping that Germany was so weakened that she would have to sue for peace. It was a good idea, but only if Germany had a government that knew what it wanted. In reality, the effect of the annexationists' activities were quite different.

Propaganda was necessary to influence opinion—a new art little understood in Berlin. When Max of Baden once considered placing himself at the head of a new 'Ministry of Propaganda', we may assume that Hahn was behind this idea. With a desperate insistence, he argued an emphatic and convincing contradiction of the thesis of Germany's sole guilt; refutation of the Entente's 'atrocity propaganda', and their confrontation with evidence of their own troops' excesses. When Sir Edward Grey made it known that he was prepared to have an impartial tribunal examine Germany's two assertions that Russian mobilization was an aggressive act and that other nations, too, had threatened Belgian neutrality, the *Zentralstelle* (which ordinarily means Hahn) tried to persuade the Government to accept precisely this proposal. In Max of Baden's *Memoirs* this episode is preceded by the following characteristic sentence: 'At that time it seemed to provide a good opportunity of creating a precedent for compromise; for we should have gained the one point and lost the other.' Truth leading to compromise; truth and compromise leading to peace; such was the third course between victory and defeat.

The Propaganda Ministry, as Prince Max and Hahn proposed it, was diametrically opposed in spirit to the Ministry later set up. To Hahn propaganda always meant a struggle for truth. He thought the German cause was good; or, to be more accurate, he thought it *could* be good or be made good. Chivalrous warfare, Christian warfare, warfare that spared as far as possible civilians, women and children, and defenceless prisoners was not merely an unconditional duty; it was also a possible way of unsettling enemy public opinion; whereas German 'frightfulness', whatever short-term success it might have, was bound to have precisely the opposite effect in the long run. From the British Press Hahn was able to gather a wealth of evidence for this thesis. In his 1916 lecture he said: 'The torch of the world's conscience is dying out in England today. If it illuminates Germany's warfare all the brighter, then the spiritual powers that England invoked against us will be on our side. . . .'

According to their leaders and spokesmen, the Germans were

fighting either for mere self-preservation or else simply to increase their power and wealth at the expense of others. These two interpretations remained vaguely and dishonestly linked; neither, Hahn realized, was enough to bring the imponderable but mighty 'spiritual powers' over to the German side. 'If tremendous power, such as we have developed in this war, is to be tolerated, it must make itself ethically justified in the eyes of the world. For that reason we must incorporate universal human aims in our national design.' The paper in which Hahn, together with Max of Baden, systematically developed this idea was handed in to the Reich Chancellery at the height of Ludendorff's spring offensive in March 1918. There it suffered the same fate as earlier memoranda. The somewhat unfortunate title, 'Ethical Imperialism', is understandable in the light of the situation at the time. In view of the Russian collapse and the Brest–Litovsk negotiations, Germany certainly became involved in an imperialist adventure of dizzy proportions. The Bolshevist atrocities in Russia's border territories gave the German Army and German policy the chance to manifest an 'imperialism' that was to be creative and liberating and would bring administrative order. But that would have required a genuine liberation of the peoples on the borders of the shattered Czarist empire, not the dishonest or semi-honest liberation decided on at Brest-Litovsk. The assertion that Germany might be an unselfish liberator and protector in Eastern Europe; that the freedoms on land and sea that she sought in the west need not come into conflict with the vital necessities of the community of nations or any of its individual members; that the only power claim that conflicted flagrantly with international law—namely, the claim to dominate Belgium—arose from complete misunderstanding, a sort of hallucination—these assertions could well be true, even though, in accordance with the mood of the moment, they were couched in rather more imperialistic language than suits our taste today. But they did not reflect the German mind. The Social Democrats took up a purely defensive attitude, while those close to the seats of power took a straight imperialistic line without any 'ethical' tinge. That is probably why no attention was paid to the memorandum.

One might perhaps sum up Hahn's work through those four fateful years as follows: the need for politics is greater in war-time than in peace-time. Policy must prepare and control what diplomacy will execute. Policy there must be. Complete honesty, precision, clarity

21 His Royal Highness chats to a girl who is taking archery as her interest for the Award

22 A group of young people on their expedition for the Duke of Edinburgh Award, stop to consult the map

23   The delivery of coal to elderly people started as a practical
Community Service for the Gold Award and is still continued as
a regular activity by youth club members

about aims must be combined with a realism which continually
adapts to changing conditions. This realism must be based on a
knowledge of enemy psychology, that of the big parties and groups
as well as the personalities of the individual leaders. One must also
know how to persuade and influence them. Without this victories are
useless. In a report to Max of Baden at the beginning of 1917 he
wrote:

> The gentlemen [from the German Foreign Office] cannot get
> out of their diplomatic attitude. They believe that the develop-
> ment of the war will one day lead to a situation in which
> negotiations will begin automatically; when that comes, they
> intend to go to work with all possible conscientiousness and
> skill to do their best for Germany. In the meantime, however,
> they wait with folded arms and do not realize that their
> passivity postpones the day of negotiations and that, to secure
> success, timing is more important than skill. . . . The reasons are
> deep-seated: they misjudge human nature. The gentlemen are
> unaware that the outcome of the war depends on the nation's
> 'morale'. They are insensitive to the trend of public opinion;
> insufficient use is made of the invaluable diagnostic material
> contained in the foreign Press, whereas the importance of
> agents and confidential informants is exaggerated; the more
> secret their messages the better.

A year later, in an article inspired by Hahn, the *vieux jeu* of mere
diplomacy is contrasted with statesmanship: 'One declares one's
readiness to negotiate and then expects to meet somewhere a go-
between sent by the enemy, possibly someone whom one already
knew, and so in a friendly conversation to solve the problem of the
world war. . . .' Secretary Kühlmann never achieved anything by
this method. By contrast, true statesmanship:

> Negotiations are prepared in a public discussion which, to a
> certain extent, finds a basis of agreement and makes this so
> clear to public opinion in the warring nations that they urge
> that an attempt should be made to overcome the remaining
> differences by diplomacy.

It was this principle that Hahn preached in vain for four years. A few examples may serve to illustrate how he tried to apply it in various crises.

With the earnestness of despair, he protested against the proclamation of unrestricted submarine warfare. The military situation did not demand it, he said; the Navy's promises were unjustified, and so was the politicians' passive pessimism. To break off the peace talks with Wilson and to force America to join in the war was just an act of mad self-destruction. After the ill-starred decision had been taken, he submitted a memorandum to the German Foreign Office containing the following passage:

> The British Government not merely desired the decision
> Germany has taken, but actually used all its journalistic and
> diplomatic resources to promote it. The Entente's policy may
> well have seemed mad to us . . . but there was method in this
> madness—namely, the method of the *agent provocateur*.

The arrow, as we can see today, hit the bull; unrestricted submarine warfare, and that alone, would bring America into the war; without America the Entente could never win; so that the decision of January 1917 literally saved Britain. . . . The young 'specialist's' criticism was too much for the Foreign Office gentlemen; it was the reason why he was transferred to Haeften's office in spite of the protests of his erstwhile superiors.

What affected him most deeply during those January days was the attitude of the civilian politicians—indeed, of the influential persons in Berlin in general. They knew that the admirals' calculations were deceptive, they knew what American intervention would mean, and yet they did not do anything even to postpone disaster—just as if Ludendorff's will were a law of Nature. Similar gloomy reflections at this lack of policy occurred to another man, Max Weber.

The decision to enter on unrestricted submarine warfare, the American declaration of war, the Russian Revolution, disappointment with unrestricted submarine warfare, which once again failed to bring in what the Admiralty had promised—all this resulted in the July crisis, the Reichstag's peace resolution and the overthrow of Bethmann Hollweg. Hahn's view of this chain of events again was similar to that of Max Weber, who described Bethmann's overthrow as a 'slaves' insurrection' by Parliament. In incongruous alliance with the General, the Reichstag could overthrow the Chancellor, but not replace him; its actions were negative and fruitless. The substance of the peace resolution, Hahn was bound to approve. War for the acquisition of territory had always seemed to him absurd; a negotiated peace to end a war that was basically due to misunderstanding was in his opinion the only desirable thing. But at this point his sensitivity to events once more raised a wall between him and the cruder routine politicians. He accused them of dishonesty, and with full justification: Erzberger, the father of the resolution, had not merely been formerly a vociferous annexationist, but he actually now said to Prince Max: 'What more do you want, Your Highness? This resolution will give me Briey and Longwy by negotiation.' He also accused them of a lack of feeling for the proper moment, of a lack of pride; it was sensible to speak of understanding to the peoples, and even to certain political groups in the enemy camp, but not to a man like Lloyd George, who boasted of knocking out Germany, just as if she were a gangster. So once more we have almost quixotic efforts of Hahn and his new ally, Max of Baden, vainly attempting to inject their own slant on official policy.

The year 1917 presented several opportunities for peace. Two events of very different scale happened in the late autumn: one was Lenin's *coup d'état* and the other Lord Lansdowne's letter to the *Daily Telegraph*. It was no great feat to recognize the opportunities offered by the collapse of Russia. To assess the importance of the Lansdowne letter, on the other hand, required knowledge such as Hahn and practically no one else in Germany possessed. It was more than a case of one man's judgment when one of the strongest, most conservative and most out-and-out imperialist of British statesmen was imploring his own Government to see reason and make peace before the war was perhaps won, but at the price of destroying European civilization. So we find Hahn moving heaven and earth to ensure that Lansdowne should receive a fittingly solemn and public reply that would strengthen his position, a reply which this time must contain an unequivocal 'Declaration on Belgium'. The struggle to bring about a dialogue with Lansdowne grew more intense in the New Year while Ludendorff was preparing his great offensive in the west that was to bring victory or, as he himself said, 'a holocaust'. The political negotiations, Hahn pleaded, must come before the military offensive; the blow could still be struck after political means had failed. Then it would be clear where the responsibility lay and the British would be burdened with the guilt of being to blame for the frightful new bloodshed. Memoranda flew from Hahn to Ludendorff's political adviser, Colonel von Haeften; from Hahn and Alfred Weber to Ludendorff, endorsed with the most impressive of signatures; speeches were made by Prince Max; inadequate replies were sent to Lansdowne for lack of any reply from the central Government, which would not reply; Prince Max visited Ludendorff, then Chancellor Hertling. Ludendorff listened with interest; was against the political offensive, of which he understood nothing; was not in favour of the 'Declaration on Belgium', but was not so rigidly opposed to it that it would have been impossible to convince him. It was the proper authorities, the civilian politicians, who failed. Hertling relied on Hindenberg and Ludendorff, on the god of battles. Ludendorff did what his strong and narrow will drove him to do, because the proper authorities did not suggest anything better. The Vice-Chancellor, Herr von Payer, said to Prince Max: 'Well, now we have decided on an offensive.' (This is the same *Geheimrat* von Payer, a worthy and respectable politician, who in the previous year had said to Hahn: 'My young friend, why should I concern myself with the enemy countries? I am a German and my concern is with my fatherland.')

Since no one had the will to halt Destiny or since those who had the will did not have the power, the storm of the spring offensive, the victories that were once again indecisive, the *hubris* that accompanied them took their course. 'A wave of chauvinism is sweeping the country just now', wrote Hahn to Prince Max at the end of March. 'Close friends of mine are being carried away. . . . May God save Germany's leaders from overweening pride.' And then came the stagnation of the offensives; the first serious setbacks in July, the more serious, decisive reverses in August. And still the 'German leaders' were out of touch with reality: there was still no change of programme, still no change of leadership. In August the head of the Reich Chancellery turned to Colonel von Haeften: he must now take over entire charge of propaganda as Under-Secretary of State. Here is the relevant passage from Prince Max's *Memoirs*:

> Indeed, when even the Imperial Government called for . . . the psychological method, they really must have been at the end of their tether. A pity that this realization came too late, for the

political offensive we recommended was intended to pave the
way for and accompany victory, but not to be a substitute for it.

The attempt of outsiders to inspire and re-direct the stubborn,
clumsy, often blind, pitifully uninspired body of German policy had
failed. How might this have been avoided?

It could be shown that Hahn actually originated the suggestion
that Prince Max of Baden should become Chancellor. It was rather
an odd idea, though not quite as odd as it might appear to later
generations; the Imperial Chancellors were appointed in queer ways,
and Prince Max was certainly at least as well qualified politically as
Dr Michaelis. And yet the whole process remains astonishing: a
young private individual wanted to put a south German prince, who
himself admitted that he was no politician, at the head of the Government of the German Reich, and actually succeeded in carrying out
his wish. Of course, he was not alone. He was clever at finding allies,
at first a few members of the Reichstag and later a whole group with
many ramifications. When the hour came, Ludendorff and the
Bavarian Government and Hertling, the departing Chancellor, and
others were all for the Prince. It was late in the day. The proper
time would have been after the resignation of the unsuitable
Michaelis the year before; and indeed Hahn and Conrad Haussmann had worked hard then to push their candidate. But instead the
choice fell on old Hertling. Prince Max wrote, resignedly: 'I have
no idea whether my time will come, whether it must come; should
Fate call me, it will no doubt knock at my door far more imperiously
than now.' Hahn replied: 'I believe necessity will knock again, but
then it will be too late.'

The Prince had not made things easy for his friends because he
considered it beneath his dignity to canvass for himself. He was
concerned for the fate of the nation and was well-endowed with
insight and goodwill, but lacked the instinct to struggle for power.
He tried to exert the influence that the combination of a high-ranking
aristocrat and respected character gave him; but this did not enable
him to save the situation. There is something to be said for Hahn's
conviction that Prince Max would have been the right man in 1917;
when he was called to office on 1 October 1918, it was no longer true.
It was too late for him to negotiate peace with Germany's power
intact. And although he had some of the gifts of a statesman, and

also something few statesmen have, a deep-seated love of the good and noble, he lacked the strong nerves needed to stand up to the avalanche of catastrophes that now poured down on him. Though bitterly opposed to the request for an armistice demanded by Ludendorff, he nevertheless yielded and allowed the offer that broke his policy to go forward to Washington with his signature. When he forced Ludendorff's dismissal four weeks later, the act was not merely valueless: it gave Ludendorff the chance to shift all responsibility from his own shoulders to those of the parliamentarians.

Prince Max thoroughly understood Hahn's ideas, and he did all he could to realize them whenever he thought them right; but that was not always the case. The ability to identify himself with the subtle ideas of an unknown young man from quite a different milieu would imply the possession of special qualities of his own, but Max was in any case too proud to become completely dependent. He had long been trying to take an active part in politics, had made special efforts to bring about peace with Russia, making use of his family connections with the Tsar's Court. During the early years of the war he had been responsible for the welfare of prisoners, and had carried out his duties in a spirit that made him an ally of Hahn's before they knew each other. In his relationship with the Prince, Hahn contributed the bulk of the ideas, and even more the style.

This special relationship became difficult once their goal was at last achieved and the Prince became Chancellor of the Reich. Hahn could advise without hindrance the princely amateur who sent out memoranda from Lake Constance. It was quite a different matter with the head of the Government in the witches' cauldron of the capital, under the Argus eye of pedantic privy councillors and case-hardened politicians. The Prince's official assistants, the members of the Cabinet, particularly the newly-appointed parliamentary Secretaries of State, Erzberger and Scheidemann, soon began to ask who the young man was who was always hanging about in the Chancellor's residence and what his business there was. In the minutes of a Cabinet meeting that took place without the Prince, who was ill, we read:

Scheidemann: Who advises the Chancellor—Hahn? . . . You can see Herr Hahn all day in the house.

State-Secretary Wahnschaffe: Hahn is an old friend of the Prince's, but has no particular influence on him. . . .

Erzberger: The fellow boasts that he is. . . .

Wahnschaffe: He must be integrated. . . .

Erzberger: Hahn said that he was opposed to the Note . . .

State-Secretary Solf: Hahn had also been sending him reports for years; a reliable man . . .

Of the members of the October Government, two, Solf and Haussmann, were old friends of Hahn's; to the rest he remained an annoying puzzle. The Prince, according to Vice-Chancellor von Payer's memoirs, had brought a confidential secretary with him, a young man with pacifist tendencies, political knowledge and literary talents, but without the experience and control of his nerves that a politician needs, a man who was 'a dark horse to all of us'. Scheidemann in his memoirs is more malicious—for this reason: that Hahn had wanted to treat Ebert rather than him as the representative of the Social Democrats, and he may have had good grounds for believing this. This was one of the first differences between the 'young man' and the old politicians. Hahn's idea of how a Cabinet should be formed was the traditional English idea: a strong prime minister chooses from the majority party those whom he considers the best, and they then do what they think right under his leadership, without worrying much about criticism. Neither the Prince nor his 'private secretary' knew enough about the machinery of a democratic mass-party, the channels through which its will is formed and the workings of its discipline.

The fate of the Government's first policy statement showed how difficult or even impossible it was for the Chancellor's adviser to impose his ideas upon a Government on which the prestige of the big parties depended. Hahn drafted the statement together with *Geheimrat* Simons, later President of the Reich Supreme Court. The latter was probably responsible for the legal subtleties; the drive, the will to master the situation was Hahn's. The speech as it was intended to be made was bold, almost a masterpiece. It was nothing less than an attempt to modify or even eventually to retract the request for an armistice which Ludendorff had forced through, and for which the Chancellor now nobly took responsibility. The means was an interpretation of the American peace programme referred to in the armistice offer. The interpretation showed both self-respect and adroitness in construing the Fourteen Points in Germany's favour. The point of this was clear: Germany would not accept Wilson's programme blindly, but offered to negotiate about its meaning on a basis of equality. The call to 'Retreat' was to become a call to 'Rally'—at last. But it was just this that roused the opposition of the ministers as well as of the representatives of the High Command; the military situation, they said, did not now permit such a proud line of policy; nor did they approve of the language used by the Chancellor, who thought he could conduct the Reichstag, majority and opposition, as if they were an orchestra and he their conductor. Hahn desperately resisted such blind submission to the Fourteen Points. He 'fought like a lion' says a note of Conrad Haussmann's, but in the end he had to be told to keep his mouth shut.

After this defeat, the second and final defeat of the policy he stood for, we rather lose sight of him. The reason for this is that he lived in the same place as the Prince and that there were therefore no letters to write and no memoranda to draw up; furthermore, the Prince was now the prisoner of a gigantic machine which he could not control. The 'Job's Messengers' that came in hourly from Turkey, Bulgaria, Austria, the Western Front and finally from the 'home front' forced on him a retreat that had largely to be improvised. Hahn's thought-out plans, his idealistic realism were no longer relevant. The achievement of Prince Max's Government, the reform of the framework of the German Constitution in spite of the darkening clouds of military and political collapse—a reform that would have been quite adequate for the needs of the next decades—has never been properly appreciated. It would in any case be impossible to estimate Hahn's share in it. Occasionally his touch can still be recognized, as in the Declaration that the Chancellor—at what cost to himself!—read over the telephone to the Kaiser on 8 November, in which he demanded the abdication of the monarch in order to save the monarchy. 'If the sacrifice is only made after blood has been shed, it will have no healing effect.' Hahn always wanted to 'heal'. The situation deteriorated rapidly with Wilhelm II's delusions, his failure to abdicate voluntarily and in time, the distressingly slow correspondence with the professor-President in Washington and, finally, the listless rebellion of the masses, on whom too great a strain had been placed for four years. The nervous breakdown of the old order—all this reduced what might have been a 'healing' new start, to an episode of hopelessness.

During the bloody, crazy twilight period between the cease-fire and the conclusion of peace Prince Max and Hahn did not completely give up. In February they and Max Weber, whose acquaintance they now made for the first time, founded the 'Heidelberg Association for a Policy of Justice'. The Association was to supply Germany with arguments during the negotiations; about who was to blame for the war and for its excesses, and on the Law to the protection of which even the vanquished had a claim. The lecture with which Prince Max inaugurated the association at Max Weber's house in the Ziegelhäuser Landstrasse is a wise distillation of four years of experience. Germany's errors, Germany's crimes are freely admitted.

> I by no means take the moral weight of these charges lightly. We who are present here felt oppressed by them during the war and opposed unjust acts by Germany wherever we could. I cannot think without bitterness of the political delusions on which this war-time policy was based. Had we upheld our good name in the world, we should have been the victors. As it was, however, we were never able to harvest the fruits of our great victories politically, so as to achieve a peace based on justice and understanding, because at the psychologically fruitful moment we employed methods which whipped up again the enemy's flagging enthusiasm for the war, and once again turned the Entente's war into a people's war, while imperialism lurked in the background.

Against these German methods he weighed up the compatible excesses of the enemy, who certainly had no right to set themselves up as censors of morals—beginning with the Russian mobilization and ending with the continuation of the hunger-blockade with its murderous consequences. He demanded a fresh start, in line with the principles of the growing sense of international law and of the incipient League of Nations. It was a choice between this and a hegemony of the Entente through dictatorial decrees, which could never give birth to a new, healing respect for Law.

As is known, Max Weber went to Versailles in person in order to argue the case for shared responsibility for the outbreak of the war. Hahn went too, disguised once more as 'private secretary', this time of Melchior the banker, who was an economic expert with the German delegation. By then the essential provisions of the treaty that the victors had cooked up were already known. The mood the Germans encountered there, the speech with which Clemenceau received them, caused Brockdorf-Rantzau, the German Minister, to adopt the sharpest of the draft replies with which he had been furnished, the one for which Hahn, together with Simons, was largely responsible. We can recognize his style: 'We are required to confess that we alone are guilty. On my lips a confession of this kind would be a lie.' Looking back, we recognize his vocabulary too: 'Russian mobilization robbed the statesmen of the chance to heal the breach and turned the decision over to the military.' And we recognize his dialectic: Germany was ready to admit any wrongs she had committed and to make reparations for them, but Germany was not the only country to have committed wrongs, and the coldly calculated wrong of the blockade continued after the armistice, with its killing of non-combatants, was less justifiable than crimes committed in the heat of war. 'Think of that when you speak of guilt and expiation.' Hahn was a man who clung tenaciously to his ideas. In 1917, after unrestricted submarine warfare had been decided on, he had wanted to justify this step in a manifesto which would pillory the murderous effect of the blockade. He was then told that this was impossible, because the Reich's Ministry of Health had just been proving the *favourable* effects of the war-time diet. He now had the opportunity of bringing up the old argument in a new guise; and it is said that Lloyd George did not like it at all.

The address displeased the allied peace-makers. But it is ridiculous to believe that humble words would have done any more for Germany; and now, after so many years, one cannot help finding some satisfaction, noting how, although the cause was lost, the words of the German delegation sounded true and undaunted.

Sounded quite true? 'On my lips'—namely, perhaps on the lips of the man who had drafted much of the speech. He, for his part, could carry his head high. Historically, it is a matter of dispute whether Germany still came under the protection of Wilson's Fourteen Points in the summer of 1919. It is true that the German Chancellor, in his offer of an armistice, had accepted Wilson's programme as 'a basis for negotiations' and that later the other side did the same. But no one knew better than Hahn how vague Wilson's principles were, or how easily manipulated. No one knew better than he how much depended, in the interpretation of the Fourteen Points, upon the strength of the positions in which the interpreters on either side found themselves. The Fourteen Points date back to January 1918. Had Germany accepted them 'as a basis' then, how different the interpretation of them would have been, how much closer to the original goodwill of their author. But at the time Germany was at the height of her power or pseudo-power, and had other ideas. When Ludendorff decided to accept Wilson's programme nine months later, he did not do so because he approved of it—it is said he had never read it—but because he thought his army was lost without an armistice, which is tantamount to saying that he thought his army was lost in any case. Why on earth should the Allies grant him the kind of cease-fire that would save his army? In October 1918 Ludendorff would have asked for a cease-fire even had there been no Fourteen Points. The all-important element of free will was absent. Vague as it was, the American peace programme was just, if properly interpreted. But one only has a claim to justice in war—that is, in a lawless environment—as long as one is still in a position to do wrong oneself, but refrains. Germany did not refrain from wrong until she herself was no longer in a position to do wrong. Thereby she lost, if one wants to be precise in such matters, all moral claim to justice at the hands of the victors; and indeed all practical claim as well, for she now no longer had anything to threaten with. Is it any wonder, then, that the interpretation of the Fourteen Points was distorted and malicious, and in some respects at variance with the text?

Prince Max of Baden and his adviser had some share in covering up this real state of things, although they of all people should have known better. They took great pains to prove where and how Wilson's peace programme had been betrayed at Versailles. Of course it had been betrayed; but as against someone who had accepted it under duress, not willingly, and who therefore had to accept the betrayal of the programme too.

The power and the goodwill of the United States, to prevent or mitigate was completely overlooked. Today we know that as a just peace the Treaty of Versailles was certainly not good, but, considered as a peace of power and revenge following a war of hitherto unparalleled savagery, it was much better than it might have been. Such interesting details as France's non-insistence on a separate Rhine state, Poland's waiving her claim to Danzig, the plebiscites in Upper Silesia and East Prussia, resulted from the American attitude.

A quarter of a century later Hahn modified his verdict on the Treaty of Versailles—one of the few examples showing that even he could change his mind:

> The whole problem is distorted by the complaints and lies which the Germans have showered upon the Treaty. In many respects it is an excellent treaty; compared with Hitler's treaties at any rate it was well-intentioned and humane. Nevertheless, Smuts was right when he said that Wilson's promises were broken at Versailles [1944].

Prince Max and Hahn worked on the bulky volume of the *Memoirs*. Sometimes their war-time allies, von Haeften, Rohrbach, Solf and Hans Delbrück, would appear at the Schloss and lecture to the grey-uniformed pupils. Speeches were made on special occasions, letters written to British newspapers and British politicians and sometimes an article in a German paper. The object of this was to achieve after all the peace of understanding missed in 1917, to see the misused Fourteen Points interpreted after all, according to the declarations of 4 October 1918, as the result of a peaceful revision. About this Germany would have to be and indeed would be extremely patient, but not without limit. This was a time not indeed to rattle one's sword, but to sharpen it. If all else was of no avail, then the German sword, which must be kept unsullied, would have to speak once again. Among the conditions from which Germany had to free herself one way or the other there were some which were indeed unbearable in the long run. There were others, such as the 'Polish Corridor', our 'bleeding eastern borders'. Such was the style of the 1920s—Gustav Stresemann's style. At Salem it had an additional colouring of 'ethical imperialism'.

Kurt Hahn's attitude towards the Weimar Republic was ambivalent, but on the whole tended towards rejection. A distant echo of 1848 was certainly alive in him. 1848—that meant a German national state instead of a federation of dynasties, and finally a national republic. On the other hand, Hahn was a monarchist, if not originally at least as the faithful servant of a German prince for whom monarchy was a matter of course. The two of them had wanted to pursue their policy under a reformed monarchy—a policy of parliamentary, yet not pure parliamentary government, of government backed by a majority in parliament, but not driven nor constrained by it. The military collapse, together with the nervous breakdown on the home front, the revolution of 9 November had upset this plan. Like so many others, Hahn too tended to connect the second event with the first more directly and one-sidedly than an objective outside observer was bound to do. He would never, it is true, have spoken of 'November criminals'; he knew only too well how hard the Social Democrat leaders had worked at first to prevent the revolution and then to get it under control. He never wanted to aggravate hatred, but always to conciliate, to counteract poisons, to heal. But whatever psychologically mitigating circumstances we may allow for it, the 'bloody carnival of the revolution'—an expression of Max Weber's that he was fond of quoting—should never have taken place. Consequently, its product, the Republic, could not inspire respect, at least in its early stages.

Did it gain respect in the course of time? Not overmuch in Hahn's eyes. He thought that it divided rather than integrated the nation, and this, unfortunately, was true; the style of the lower- to middle-class citizens who in quick succession tried their hands at guiding Germany's fortunes did not attract him. His attitude towards the Social Democrats had always been a little condescending, in the manner of the enlightened upper-middle class: some of the Social Democrats, such as Ebert, Noske, David and Severing, were, after all, very decent people, who unfortunately were often unable to effect what they wanted. During the war Hahn had, it is true, been in favour of introducing parliamentary government more definitely than Prince Max, who had had vague ideas about constitutional institutions of a specifically German character. But it should be the function of parliament, he held, to produce a strong government, not to be constantly interfering with government. In 1917 he had correctly analysed the Reichstag's gains in power: it was the Bethmann and Michaelis governments, unused to parliament, conservative and weak, which had had to make concessions to the Reichstag that went beyond the principles of sound parliamentary government. The parliamentary system was now complete; but it did not produce strong governments. To the critic at Salem, they did not look self-respecting, dignified or patriotic. It could be shown that such catchwords as 'party state' or 'democratic corruption' were not entirely strange to Hahn; after all, they were not wholly without a basis of fact. However, one needs to distinguish more clearly than Hahn did between what should have been otherwise and need not have been as it was, and what was an inseparable feature of the politics of an industrial society: as if 'horse-trading' or 'misuse of privilege for sordid profit' had been unknown in the Kaiser's Germany; as if the worst case by far of corruption under the Republic had not implicated that very East-Elbian aristocracy whom Hahn held in such high esteem.

Kurt Hahn wanted to educate young people to master modern life without damage to their souls, and, similarly, he wanted strong governments to give spiritual leadership. But, this aesthetic moralizing after the manner of Plato failed to take into consideration basic characteristic features of our civilization: the lack of seriousness, the dubious pleasures, the greed for passing sensations; the egoism of individuals and classes, the thoughtlessness of life—in fact, the life of the big city. In his pupils he wanted to develop ability to concentrate, inner composure, serious imagination; love for objectivity; *mens sana in corpore sano*; practical Christianity, obedience, 'soldierly virtues'—worthwhile aims. It is only false prophets, of whom there was no lack then as now, who deny that one cannot simply let matters take their course, that it is the responsibility of the teacher as of the statesman to keep things in check, to guide, to look for counterweights. In practice, however, the repudiation of certain very strong, very widespread tendencies of the age could become arrogance—not, indeed, in the master, but in immature pupils. At least in practice, the ambition to approach and master life as a person who has enjoyed a different and superior education could lead to escapism. It is no accident that an unusually large proportion of old Salem boys withdrew into that particular outlet for innocence and chivalry, the *Reichswehr* (the German Army).

We see Hahn praising the direct election of the President of the Reich by the people, the constitutionally very strong position of the head of state, as a 'great deed of Max Weber's'. We see him rejoicing at the election of Hindenburg, expecting his taking office to have a 'healing' effect. We see him in contact with Chancellor Brüning, and seeking contact with Chancellor von Papen, in whom he had confidence. Finally, we see him adopting an attitude towards Hitler before the latter's seizure of power and in the first few months thereafter, which one must try to understand even if a residue of astonishment and regret remains.

The fact was that it was not the real Hitler, but an imaginary one, that had a place in Hahn's political thought, rather as the *Vaterlandspartei* had once had. Germany needed 'angry patriots'. Hitler's energy had organized the power of the people, which, had it been present in November 1918 or May 1919, might have saved Germany the worst humiliations. He was the protest incarnate against the betrayal of the Fourteen Points.

> Since the day on which he, despairing of the fate of our state, began to be a voice crying in the wilderness, the force of his personality and the national revival for which he appealed spread like wildfire through the hearts of millions. [Letter from the Margrave of Baden to the *Manchester Guardian* in October 1932.]

To that extent he was good. Unfortunately, however, he associated with most undesirable elements. A memorandum of Hahn's (of summer 1933) says that the Nazi movement was compounded of contradictory elements; on the one hand, 'the best of the country gentry, workers, farmers, young people who do not want war, but are determined to revise the eastern frontiers'; on the other, 'gangsters, adventurers, former convicts'. One question remained: how had it been possible for two so utterly different groups to combine, or for the leader of the one not to disdain being the leader of the other too?

At first, in 1932, it was a question of separating Hitler from the evil characters whose prisoner he seemed likely to become. He was not to come to power, but he was to be used; once purged, perhaps he might be allowed to participate in power. Hindenburg would see to both of these points. Hahn's Hindenburg was imaginary too; he was not the real, obtuse, selfish and corrupt old man we know of. The struggle as he saw it was between what was bad in those round Hitler, what was 'reckless' in Hitler himself, and the distinguished old soldier and aristocrat whose simple intuition gave him a sure judgment of good and evil. These were the only two elements that mattered. In all the statements made or influenced by Hahn during the year of crisis there is no mention of the 'other Germany' that was to be found among the decent, loyal people—millions of them—who voted socialist to the end in spite of the mediocrity of their leaders.

After Hitler's Beuthen telegram he took up a stand—a very clear, very courageous stand. A struggle had broken out that was more than just political. 'Germany is at stake, her Christian civilization, her reputation, her military honour. . . .' But even now he refused to see in the praise that Hitler lavished on bestial murder the expression of his innermost being but rather the promptings of the evil minds around him. If only the party leader had extricated himself from them! According to a brochure of Paul Rohrbach's that appeared in September 1932 and in which Hahn's style and thought are unmistakable, Hitler could certainly have become Chancellor in August if he had wired the Beuthen murderers something like the following: 'Your deed has shown you unworthy to wear my uniform. If I do all that I can to secure a pardon for you, it is because you acted out of rage and delusion. . . . As soon as I come to power I will be no less strict than the courts at Beuthen in punishing such foul crimes; but I shall be able to prevent them better than Herr von Papen can, thanks to the strict discipline which I shall enforce on my comrades. . . .' Should this draft be from Hahn's pen—but we are not certain of this—it would be almost a parody of one of his old habits of mind: that of putting his own words into the mouth of another and expecting him to do what he simply could not do, because he was just not made that way. Only too often Hahn saw a man's function as he would wish it to be, not his substance as it really was.

This criticism of Hahn's political judgment during the crisis years 1932–4 must not be misunderstood. His detestation of what Hitler actually did was from the beginning strong, clear, and outspoken, and he openly expressed it, not without danger to himself. None the less, he *wanted* to hope that in the end a 'better Hitler' would break away from the bad Hitler, and from the even worse characters surrounding him. That hope was simply a residue of his lifelong faith in humanity, now doubtless reinforced by an unquenchable desire to get back to his homeland and his work. This hope and this desire he finally gave up after the murders of 30 June 1934 (Roehm Purge). From then until the end he had no more illusions.

In later years he spoke of his organized efforts—indeed, of a

24   St Donat's Castle, on the Welsh coast of the Bristol Channel, which is the home of the United World College of the Atlantic

25   The library at Atlantic College

26 Robert Blackburn holds a seminar with students from the U.S.A., Norway, Germany, Turkey and Guyana

27 A German and a British student play *Murder in the Cathedral*, by T. S. Eliot, at Atlantic College

28 The Cliff Rescue Unit training. The rescuer is being winched
to the top of the cliff to safety, with the casualty in a specially
designed stretcher

29 Stowing of sailing boats and canoes at the end of an afternoon's sailing activities. An inflatable rubber dinghy used by the College's Coast Guard Rescue Service, in which many new techniques have been pioneered, is on the right

30 Prince Constantin as a pupil in his study at Anavryta

conspiracy—to prevent Hitler from seizing power. Let us grant him the word. But the aim of the 'conspiracy' he had in mind was too near to Hitler's to achieve its object. It was not to profit the 'laughing Left'—as if that were the danger in the autumn of 1932!—but the 'decent folk' among Hitler's supporters whom one hoped to entice away from him and rally to the Right's slogan of 'Presidential Government'. Yet it was this very Right that made Hitler's seizure of power possible four months later. Subsequently, in May 1933, the writer of these lines saw Kurt Hahn once more in Berlin. Hahn was deeply depressed at the time, for he now realized that the cause he personally represented was lost. But he would not see that the policy dreamed of by him and his friends had been mistaken. All might have gone well, he thought, only on 30 January 1933 one set of points had been switched wrongly.

We shall be brief about this stage, which was decidedly not the happiest in Hahn's political life. It is no reproach to say that he was mistaken in Hitler; other, very excellent people were too. Nor that he saw 'decent elements' in the Nazi movement. For a time he failed to see the predominant power of evil in the whole thing. We must leave it at that.

He still failed to see it even when he was arrested in 1933 after the March elections and after a time in prison exiled from his beloved creation, the Salem schools. Already in 1918 this notorious Freemason and arch-Jew, as a Nazi newspaper put it, had, 'in a highly political mission to Headquarters', carried through the acceptance of Wilson's Fourteen Points against Ludendorff's will. . . . What moves us, even saddens us, is that Hahn still fought against such infamies, that he seriously disputed the lies put out against him. It was his tragedy, and not only his. This man of pure motives, this patriot, this peace-maker could not understand why he should be treated in such a way after all that he had done and tried to do. That is why he corresponded and exchanged pamphlets with 'wolves, swine and dirty dogs'—to quote a poet he dislikes.

The parting from Salem was followed by the parting from Germany. His urge for action, his optimism in the original Leibnizian sense of the word did not allow Hahn to sink into a bitterness that would have been quite understandable. He was an educator and must remain one. His extensive contacts in Britain, turned to profit by a tough, clever will, made the impossible possible for him: the foundation of an originally German school in Scotland, Gordonstoun, which today rivals the old public schools of England. This was an even more exacting task than the building up of the Salem schools.

He could not, of course, give up his sense of responsibility for, his burning interest in, events in Germany and in Anglo-German relations. What he did in this field during the next twelve years was a somewhat paler repetition of what he had done during the First World War in Germany—only facing the other way round this time. Then he had been a German and at the same time an expert on and saddened admirer of Britain. Now he was an Englishman and at the same time an even greater expert on and an even more saddened admirer of Germany. That he should take a direct hand in politics was even more obviously impossible to him than in 1917. Once more he had a network of acquaintances through whom he tried to act: professors, bishops, aristocrats with political interests. He was probably unconscious of the strangeness and melancholy of this repetition. By temperament he looks outwards; he has never looked inwards. He certainly did not consciously quote himself when, during Hitler's war, he often repeated, word for word, what he had said or written during the First World War.

He, who had lived through so much history in the making, now saw events threatening to repeat themselves. He had experienced the birth, growth and catastrophe of one great war. He hoped not to experience this again unless it came about through evident necessity and not, as in 1914, through misunderstanding and bungling.

So in 1938, before and during the Czech crisis, he once more took up his pen. He had no secret sources of information. But he knew his old home, country and people; he knew or divined how the generals, the conservative bureaucrats and the Churches would react. He felt that something was in train, that German public opinion was becoming important again for the first time, that there was a chance of separating Hitler from a large section of the nation. Always both a moralist and a logician of power politics, he wanted to see Britain manœuvre in such a way that there would either be no war or, if there were, that the British would be clearly seen to be in the right. Britain, therefore, must avoid committing herself too soon, as she had in 1914, but must act as the situation might require. Hitler must not be allowed to feel certain of Britain's neutrality;

otherwise he would start a war. The Czechs must not be allowed to feel certain of her non-neutrality either (as Russia had been in 1914); otherwise they might provoke war. For these reasons, offers must be made to Germany that would be clearly acceptable to the 'good elements', but not to Hitler. No Czech should be turned over to the Reich. 'It was undoubtedly very wrong to force the Sudetan Germans into the Czech state, but it would be a crime to turn a Czech minority over to the Nazis.'

> I see a way out that would be honourable and that Czecho-slovakia could accept: not a plebiscite now in the feverish atmosphere of civil war, but in a year's time when things have calmed down. In the meantime the area should be governed by an international commission backed by an international police force. . . .

If Hitler accepted the proposal, good; if he did not accept, then all his supporters would see clearly that he was the guilty party. . . . One more idea of Hahn's—how many had there been before?—that held to the right course, a subtle middle course, but was never tried out!

'Munich' made him despair because there the evil-doer got un-reserved approbation and all his opponents, and his German opponents in particular, the reverse. After the 'Night of Glass', Hahn wrote:

> It was honourable to try the policy of appeasement. It would be dishonest to continue it now. Hitler must learn that the conscience of the British will not allow them to be cordial towards the organizer of pogroms. Cordiality towards Hitler is not friendship for the German people. . . .

That had been his view for thirty years. Atrocities in any country are the concern of all nations and of all rulers. Not power politics, but moral issues are primary. But things are so ordained that moral interests and power interests may and indeed must coincide in the long run; power without morality destroys itself.

Six months before Hitler's war was unleashed, Hahn began to speak of the 'German home front' as he had once spoken to Luden-dorff of the 'English home front'. Psychological warfare to damage the enemy: in July he used this expression, meaning to damage Hitler, not Germany. He no more intended to trick Germany now than he had intended to trick Britain in 1917. Germany was to realize that she could have a fair deal if she prevented Hitler from making war or if she overthrew Hitler on the outbreak of war. And once more we have advice on how to set about doing such things, how to speak to those concerned without addressing them directly, how to help the German 'Government of tomorrow' as one ought to have helped the British 'Government of tomorrow' in 1917.

Repetition, reversal, double reversal; not only in the life of Kurt Hahn, but also in the interplay of the states. In 1917 and 1918 Britain and America had waged psychological war skilfully, Germany not at all, in spite of Hahn's efforts. Hitler understood it well until 1938 or even 1940 and later: psychological weapons played an important part in the campaign against France. At the same moment the British practically gave up all attempts to influence the German home front. The gentlemen from the BBC continued to reach hearers in Germany, but they had nothing to offer except unconditional surrender. This time the Germans were not to be able to say that they had been deceived; Britain was fighting the devil and a nation given over to the devil—whose guilt was unlimited. No more nuances, no more diplomacy, no more distinctions. The evil must be attacked at the root; the root must be severed for all time. . . . The arguments in favour of this decision, this attitude, were many, were overwhelming. Winston Churchill was convinced. Hahn, who knew better, who knew that Germany was, or could be, inwardly divided, could make no headway against them. Even less attention was paid to his advice now than in Germany twenty-five years before; he was ignored in particular by those from whom he had learned the art of psychological warfare twenty-five years before. 'If you had ten minutes with the Prime Minister,' an English friend remarked at the end of 1940, 'he would at once see the military significance of splitting German morale from top to bottom. It is so much in his line.' The interview between Churchill and Hahn was almost achieved.

He sensed the arising of the German resistance movement, leading up to the Bomb Plot on Hitler's life of 20 July 1944. Fundamentally, he was part of it. The resemblance between his thinking and planning in the 1920s and that of Moltke, Beck and Goerdeler later on is striking. The scorn for the 'party state', the somewhat vague ideas

of a form of government in Germany that should both be democratic
and authoritarian, the friendly but slightly condescending attitude
towards the 'sensible' wing of the Social Democrats, the striving for
a just revision of the Treaty of Versailles, the hopes staked on
Hindenburg, the hope—at first—for a chastened Hitler who might
after all have just intentions and be better than the criminals around
him, then the disgusted disillusion—disillusion not of power politicians, but of Christians, the faith in morality as the final, decisive
authority—all this characterized Salem as well as the 20 July conspiracy, in which several former pupils of Salem took part. If in his
memoranda Hahn was correct in his analysis of the plans and feelings
of the resistance groups long before 20 July, he was at the same time
analysing his own feelings too.

He had had to leave Germany. Since 1933 he had been educating
not German but British soldiers. He was a British subject and took
his oath of allegiance seriously. Consequently, he could not participate in any way. He regarded the German Resistance, technically
speaking, simply as a chance of splitting the 'German home front'.
His ties with Britain made it impossible for him to accept the political
aims of the German Resistance: at first, a 'greater Germany', though
with revised frontiers; later, avoidance of utter defeat. Not only his
loyalty, but his own judgment prevented him; he approved the policy
of unconditional surrender. The German army must indeed be
thoroughly vanquished, as the Allies wanted, the German state must
be rendered completely powerless, and the criminal with all his
accomplices punished. But nevertheless, he could not hide his
sympathy for the men of the Resistance. It would have been possible,
Hahn thought, to help them all the same; not by refraining from
unconditional surrender, but by promising the vanquished a fair
deal. Germany should certainly be rendered completely powerless,
but should be administered justly by the victors and not unjustly
curtailed; under the supervision of the victors, the vanquished
should have a chance to cleanse their land themselves, to dispense
justice themselves; this task the Resistance could fulfil.

The moral obliquity of Churchill and his manner of warfare during the final years brought fresh disillusionment to Hahn. His life
had indeed been rich in disillusionments, from which he forced
himself to react with fresh hope. During the First World War Hahn
had tried in vain to teach the Germans that a great nation must not

merely fight for its own preservation, but must serve a 'cause' greater than itself. This time the cause was far clearer to both sides than in 1917: the liberation of Europe from domination by National Socialism. But one must fight even the Devil, or, rather, especially the Devil, with clean weapons; one must not in the very least descend to his level either. Allied policy and strategy diverged strikingly from this principle. 'Obliteration bombing' might—possibly—be justified as a reaction to Hitler's air attacks. But why try to gloss over what was being done by pretending that its purpose was strictly military; or actually rejoice at such barbarity? Why tell the truth about the hell of the German concentration camps and keep silent about the Katyn murders? Why talk about the Soviet Union as if it were a second Commonwealth? Lethargy of soul and credulity were here at work, and the 'callousness which goes with success'. Power politics was also involved. The Coalition must be kept together; Russia was the great ally and therefore nothing derogatory must be said about her. Hahn disputed this argument; illusions are not a good basis even for power politics. Agreements about future democratic government in East Europe made with someone who meant something quite different or nothing at all by 'democracy' could not secure those areas even from the point of view of power politics.

Hahn confided his concern not merely to his diary. There is a lay sermon which he preached at Liverpool Cathedral in 1943 containing the following passage: 'No peace with the murderers, no peace with the connivers who know what is right and yet never risk their lives to save hostages from being shot, prisoners from being tortured and Jews from being exterminated.' And yet:

> Let us heed the voice of great compassion, not only compassion
> for the victims of the Nazis outside Germany, but also for
> millions of Germans who are suffering under Hitler today. . . .
> We want to know whether our forces have ever encountered a
> better Germany that deserves to be saved. And we wait
> impatiently for our statesmen of today to pledge tomorrow's
> Britain to dispense a strict and discriminating justice which a
> purged and liberated Germany has no reason to fear. . . . The
> decision will rest with one man. Whether that great soldier
> Winston Churchill will again become the far-sighted statesman

he once was is a fateful question, not just for Britain, but for all Europe. I remember how Winston Churchill in the hour of victory in November 1918 pressed and implored the governments of France and Britain to send food at once to the starving enemy. . . .

It was no small matter for a naturalized citizen of German origin to preach such things in the middle of the war. From an entry in Hahn's diary dated 'May 1945' one may deduce that some of his colleagues at Gordonstoun School attributed to him pro-German sympathies in spite of all.

You are wrong [he wrote]. I do not gloat, but I jubilate at the sound of the breaking chains. Without unconditional surrender there was no security for Britain, no liberation for Europe, no forgiveness for the German people. . . . My colleagues have longed for and prayed for the collapse of the Nazis for six years; I for twelve.

He returned immediately at the end of the twelve years. He saw his beloved Salem again and those of his friends there that remained. He helped, collected money, collected food. To help, and never mind too many subtleties of thought, had always been his strongest instinct.

His joy at reunion was not uncritical. A report on 'the state of the youth in Germany' (1946) shows touches of pessimism. He had, he said, met many unrepentant Nazis, seen many hard and angry faces; deluded people who still believed the lies they had been told for twelve years; others who did not believe anything any more, unwilling to see any difference between propaganda and truth, particularly when the truth went against them or their country; much moral apathy, and total indifference to all the suffering which Germany had caused, but not to their own. Here were new yet old dangers which would revive as vitality returned. Hahn would not have been himself, or the pragmatist, the devoted, unshakeable believer in humanity that he was if he had not seen chances of better things and thought out advice to further them. Mere observation was never his line. One must 'take stock of the facts'—an expression he loved—and that as accurately as possible, but in order to alter the facts to accord with one's will. Here too, as in 1917, as in 1940, a campaign must be fought 'to weaken our enemies and strengthen our friends'.

Precise proposals followed. For instance, one must differentiate between the real National Socialists and the simple patriots; between the guilty Nazis and those who had done nothing bad, and indeed had at times done something demonstrably good. One must prefer them to others whom happy accident had prevented from becoming party members but who were covered with dishonour nevertheless. One must differentiate, differentiate and once again differentiate. The men of goodwill or, more precisely, those in whom goodwill could be aroused must be given active responsibility, which would educate them while they educated others. A historical commission consisting of Germans of proven character should investigate German war crimes; the same commission should have the right to prove that 'a large number of soldiers and officers, mainly of lower rank, refused to obey orders that conflicted with their Christian consciences'.

> I can hear the argument: Why duplicate Nuremberg?
> 'Nuremberg' is a contaminated source of truth. The Allies
> missed their unique opportunity to engrave the Nazis' crimes on
> the pillars of history so deeply that neither time nor legend
> could obliterate them. All that was needed was a truly
> international court of justice with impartial judges. . . . But at
> Nuremberg the aggressor against Finland, Lithuania, Estonia,
> Latvia and Poland—I name only those countries taken by storm
> and not by force of subversion—sits in judgment on the crimes
> of Nazi aggression.

Convince instead of forcing. Convince by practising truth, justice and help. Suppress no truth, not even the most embarrassing. Call upon the convinced to take action themselves. Do not forgive the unforgivable; pardon human weakness; honour goodness. Regard people not as if they were dead lumps of wood, unchangeable, but as living creatures, living on many different levels, in whom there is good waiting to be released. Old ideas of Hahn's applied to the miseries of Germany in 1946.

We cannot guarantee that they had any effect. It is possible that they may have had a very indirect effect on the gradually changing policy of the occupying powers, at least on that of Britain. One might regard the setting up of the *Institut für Zeitgeschichte* (Institute for Contemporary History) later on as a realization of Hahn's proposal. It is immaterial whether there was any causal connection between the two—Kurt Hahn would not care at all whether there was or not.

Since then twenty years have passed. Kurt Hahn is still with us. He has done a great deal since 1945; more perhaps than ever before. His ideas on national education—first German and then English—the ethical content of which had always been broadly human and supranational, grew into something truly international: exchanges between Salem and Gordonstoun, Atlantic College, the Outward Bound schools. Politics receded into the background, except in the sense that Hahn's educational ideas are, and always have been, eminently political.

He could not, it is true, refrain from occasionally expressing his opinion on world politics. How could he, a convinced humanist, remain unconcerned by the atom-bomb question: he thought Hiroshima was a crime, and, what was worse, an avoidable crime. Since then he has been one of those who hold it the most urgent duty of our time, not to be glossed over, to bring under man's control the danger that man invented for the annihilation of mankind. During the war he was one of the few who raised their voices in warning against Stalin's mischief. But Russian society was not a dead, unchanging block of wood either. It can scarcely surprise us to find Kurt Hahn urging the necessity to recognize and support the changes as far as possible, here too to differentiate, to use psychological methods of warfare or rather of pacification and to seize the opportunity offered by the fundamentally peace-loving Khrushchev—for he had been doing this kind of thing for fifty years.

He has lived through many epochs: the decay of the Hohenzollern Empire, the First World War, which more than anything else moulded his way of thinking and brought out his talents, the first German Republic, the appeasement era, Hitler's war and the two decades following it, which can no longer be described as 'post-war'. He is more or less familiar with the history that went before his time, but he is not really historically minded. He is subject to the requirements of the moment. What history gives him is what his own life has also given him in such abundance: experiences, exemplary events, golden words, good and bad deeds. He is capable of quoting Lord Palmerston as if he flourished at the present day; the historical conditions under which Palmerston operated and under which alone he could operate do not interest him particularly. In just the same way, he quotes Plato, who was probably the least historic-ally-minded of political philosophers. Indeed, he is very fond of quoting. 'Oh, you and your quotations!', Simons, President of the Reich Supreme Court, once said to him disparagingly when he had been pressing him on a politico-moral matter. People and deeds interest him, not developments; not even his own development. But he has always wanted to comprehend what is, and what is today is not what was yesterday; but his comprehending mind has always remained fundamentally the same.

Active, possessed by an urge to help, always seeking allies, he has crossed the path of many important people. He would probably name Max Weber as the one who made the deepest impression on him. This experience and verdict links him with Naumann, whom he knew, and with Karl Jaspers, whom he does not know. But note that it was Weber's striking personality and certain topical judgments of his, which attracted Hahn, not his theoretical writings. These, if ever he looked through them, can have awakened little response. Weber's heroic, tragic dualism was quite strange to him; his own 'ethical imperialism' had nothing to do with Weber's 'Darwinist imperial-ism'; he would have completely rejected such distinctions as that between the ethics of disposition and the ethics of responsibility. In this he was closer to Friedrich Naumann, whose journal was called *Die Hilfe* (Help); this would be an apt description of Hahn's whole life's work. Naumann's ideas of a democratic monarchy, of over-coming class warfare by means of active goodness, appealed to him; Naumann's imperialism had an 'ethical' note. In their passage through time, Weber and Naumann were left far behind; they were born earlier and died young.

Hahn did learn a little from the men of action and the thinkers whom he met, the national-liberal historians, the free-thinking politicians. But not a great deal. Rather than learn from them, he wanted to employ them for his purposes, to use them. He was certainly capable of—indeed, naturally inclined to—admiration of others; but he could form his own ideas.

His letters, memoranda and speeches, of which only selections are available, would make a remarkable book, a commentary on half a century of history. It would be distantly comparable to Max Weber's political writings, but more humane, more enthusiastic, cleverer, but less penetrating. Hahn always sought solutions and bridges where Weber saw grim alternatives. What, he might have asked Weber, is the benefit of deep thought if it does not actually help anyone? His style was splendid. But he did not employ fine language for a bad end. What he tried to do was to clarify events and raise them to a higher moral level by giving them style; his stylistic and practical efforts coincided.

His effort to subordinate war to politics failed twice. His belief in the possibility of reconciling war and Samaritan-like conduct, war and the spirit of the Sermon on the Mount, failed in the main. This was probably inevitable in our time. He has drawn his conclusions. In 1918 he was not 'the young man with pacifist tendencies' that Vice-Chancellor von Payer saw in him. In 1965 one could call him an old man with pacifist tendencies, if the word 'pacifism' itself were not now obsolete, like so many other words of the sort.

As a politician he never acknowledged any 'absolute', not even—indeed, by no means—the nation; whereas Max Weber forced himself to accept that as an absolute, even though it went against his nature. For him only one thing was real—man, whose vehicle to virtue might at times be the nation or nation-state. But only a vehicle. He was not a metaphysical thinker. But this much he knew and practised: belief in man as an *ens reale* requires belief in an *ens realissimum*, without which the former has no firm basis.

He wanted to see man in the saddle, not things. Not war, or technology, or economics; not blind Fate. He equally abhorred fatalism and its brother, cynicism. His simple philosophy of history was one of freedom and responsibility in spite of the power of given events: 'that is unfortunately the way it happened, but it might have been different'. 'The decision whether there was to be peace or war', he wrote in 1916, 'was arrived at in Britain after the sharpest political struggle; and where there is a struggle human strength decides.' In these days of computers, 'planning games' and 'big science', Hahn's view of man is not without present significance.

Nigeria: an analysis of short-term school techniques

Hilary Tunstall-Behrens

In 1953 an Outward Bound type school was started in the British Cameroons by Alec Dickson. It was situated near Victoria on the cliffs of Man o' War Bay, where British fighting ships had watered and replenished supplies when England was leading the anti-slave trade campaign 150 and more years ago. With the open sea before and the 13,000-foot Cameroon Mountain towering behind as a back-cloth, there was an ideal environment for an adventurous training course, and there was this advantage in serving the three regions of Nigeria: that the Cameroons was considered to be on neutral ground, where the pressures of the *Heimat* were not imminent and familiar taboos could be experimentally laid aside for a month.

Young men travelled as much as a 1,000 miles on foot, by canoe, lorry and train, or a combination, involving a journey of perhaps a fortnight in order to reach Man o' War Bay.

The varied tribes and races met to live and work together in an experience in co-operation and toleration. Moslem with Christian, Catholic with Seventh Day Adventists, Yoruba, Hausa, Ibo, Fulani mixed together in a common routine, sharing the same food and purpose and facing the same strenuous and, to them, very strange activities.

Man o' War Bay was, in contrast to other Outward Bound schools overseas, never affiliated to the Trust in England, although help and many of the staff were provided by them on request. The Federal Government of Nigeria voted the funds and appointed the board and ran the school, on which the local chamber of Commerce had representation. In 1961 the Southern Cameroons opted by plebiscite to leave Nigeria and unite with the former French Cameroons, and so the Man o' War Bay Centre had to move into Nigerian territory at Kurra Falls on Jos Plateau. Its name became then the Citizenship and Leadership Training Centre. A further school was opened on Badagry Creek, Lagos, in 1964, and by 1965 there was also a mobile training unit, so that the numbers of students experiencing training numbered around 1,000 a year.

The nature and purpose of the courses changed very little after the school moved, although, in contrast to the schools mentioned in the chapter on Outward Bound in The Commonwealth (see p. 192), a definite emphasis has always been given to community development. This was a policy of self-help which was fostered by the Nigerian Government to encourage initiative in villages, so that, with some central or local government finance, bridges, roads, markets, wells, schools were often built by voluntary community labour. In many cases whole communities turned out at one time to move volumes of earth or transport logs and materials.

Community development is a direct way in which the living standard and health of the country can be raised, and is one immediate task and responsibility among many others which the literate class might well be encouraged to undertake in Africa.

Nigeria is an example of a 'plural society' and a 'developing country' where the impact of European manufactured goods and European ideas and civilization have brought about a situation of rapid change and instability. The influences which Europe brought to bear on West Africa were only in part intentional. The secondary effects of the introduction of British justice, for instance, and the powerful white district officer as referee, was to alter the structure of the country, and change the roles, the system of values, leadership, hopes and ambitions of the people. And this process was continued after independence when Africans representing central and regional authorities took over power.

In a developing society very often progress in one direction does not fit in with adjustment in another. For example, it was unfortunate that much of the schooling which the new literate class received under the British tended, in common with many of the modern social forces, to stress solely the commercializing of possessions and the right of the individual to the fruits of his own efforts, and encouraged resistance to the claims that were formerly respected, while largely failing to put anything in their place, let alone meet the need for developing acceptance of the much wider responsibilities which self-government requires.

There has probably never been a society in a condition of static equilibrium. Changes in population, of food-production, climatic changes, diseases and tribal migration and wars have altered environment. But changes in relationships and in the roles which members play in society have not always been so rapid that parents were unable to impart to their children what would be relevant for them. It can be said that a crisis has come in such societies, where the whole structure has changed and where new values and source of authority, incompatible with the old pattern, are being integrated into the system causing strain and dissatisfaction.[1]

Education has a part to play in teaching new roles and imparting sound principles which will help a nation hold together in this situation.[2] The traditional tribal culture is needed only in so far as it is compatible with the much larger society, the new nation to which the community must now be orientated. There is the training to fill the numerous government and business posts and to take the responsibilities of leadership in administering the territory and initiating further development. It can be argued that the only assurance that the illiterate masses shall not be exploited by the politicians is for native leadership to be definitely rooted in the needs of the mass of the people.

The short-term training course proves itself to be a useful adjunct to the conventional form of education in helping to further these aims and attempting to instil amongst the privileged literate classes a respect and concern for the welfare of the mass of the population.

Whereas Dr Hahn and Mr Lawrence Holt believed that in the short period of one month seeds of important ideas could be sown in a group of adolescents, and a marked self-confidence engendered for use in emergencies and even in a more general way by a transference of training, this principle has been extended experimentally in Nigeria and has proved itself effective, not only with the immediately post-adolescents, but also with a much older age-group.

From the beginning, the Nigerian short-term courses emphasized the obligation upon educated men of participation and leadership in work of sound service. Partly in order to achieve results and to have an immediate impact by training men who were already bearing responsibility for leadership in Nigeria, the students tend to be between eighteen and forty, with the average around twenty-five years of age, although there were special schoolboy courses.

The Nigerian adaptation of the short-term course was to set itself the task of training leaders for the new roles in a society of rapid change. The aims were to encourage the young men to fight useless prejudice, fetish and ignorance, callousness and fear, and to give them experience of a physical and mental energy to combat the lethargy so insidious in a hot climate four degrees north of the Equator, and in the more remote areas to stir village and town communities from a stagnant situation in which many of them had been sunk for a generation or more.

Students were to be encouraged in the conception of Nigerian citizenship and to experience working with men of all tribes and religions in close comradeship and common endeavour. Their initiative was directed to improve themselves and to lead the way in social work amongst groups and organizations with which they would be in close contact when returning to their homes. It was an ideal of responsible citizenship for the educated class in the new Nigeria.

There is a precedent for education for citizenship in pre-literate societies in Africa and elsewhere before the advent of Western civilization. In some tribal groups all adolescent boys were trained in citizenship, and it happened suddenly, usually at puberty. The education and freedom of home and family were up till that moment the main educational forces in a boy's life. As an adult, a man had to have a wider horizon and a tolerant attitude to other kinship groups than his own. New attitudes more commensurate with the interests of the tribe as a whole were put across in what was virtually a short-term course school. The techniques of this education were 'initiation ceremonies', serving the purpose of *Rites de Passage* from boyhood to manhood, from irresponsible child to citizen. The wresting of the youth from kinship groups by force in some cases and subsequent relations of restraint between son and mother emphasized the break with the family and the assumption by the young man of duties to the community at large. There was often much hardship to be borne, and this schooling included beating and the accomplishments of tasks requiring courage and endurance.[3]

In many ceremonies there was a shock-and-trauma effect in the training. The aim appears to have been a disruption, a sharp break with the past and a violent projection out of the known into the unknown. Everything that happened to the initiate during initiation had to be as different as it could be made by human ingenuity from things that happened to him before the initiation. A writer on these ordeals has commented: 'Whether training for citizenship can ever be a warm, friendly, loving, cosy and undisturbed process is a question I leave to the educators.'

The Nigeria short-term school's answer to this question is certainly 'No'. The courses follow much that is similar in these tribal ceremonies. Where they wrested boys so suddenly from a small kinship, a family group, and orientated them to a tribal loyalty there is a parallel on a much larger scale in the emergent nations in Africa.

The political climate has altered so swiftly that there has been no time to educate for independence. Education has developed at a very great speed, at the last moment virtually, and many men and women have had to take responsibility without a background schooling geared to the second half of the twentieth century. The short course set out to bridge tribal division rather than kinship, and to give a sense of national responsibility and service. A student attends a course but once, like the traditional puberty rites. Similarly, the educational strength of the experience appears to be in the challenge of surprise and strangeness. To claim that there is a shock element and trauma would perhaps be an exaggeration. But it can be said that no student ever forgets the course; it remains a landmark in his life.

In the main the courses emphasize the same techniques and training as the Outward Bound in England, only the element of strangeness is much greater. Few Englishmen will never have seen the sea before, but in Nigeria the sea is a new element and the ascent of a mountain is a unique experience.

The grouping of the students into watches, with election of captain and quartermaster, is familiar, and all activities are undertaken in this framework. Emphasis is given to physical fitness, not only through athletics, but gymnastics, swimming, canoeing and trekking in the bush. Group co-operation is most patently observed over the

31 The 'Guardians' of Salem (left), Anavryta (middle), and
Gordonstoun (right), at the holiday work-camp at Cephalonia,
Greece, after the earthquakes in 1954. One hundred boys of
seven different nations volunteered for this work. (The 'Guardian'
of Gordonstoun here is a sheik.)

32 The Headmaster of Salem, Prince George of Hanover (dark
shirt), and the Founder-Headmaster of Anavryta, Jocelin
Winthrop-Young, who organized the work-camp in 1954, to
rebuild an old people's home

33 Kurt Hahn

obstacle course and twelve-foot wall and various initiative tests of a practical kind in which the watch competition is introduced.

In the Cameroons sailing and seamanship were part of the training, and the expeditions were often partly at sea, involving camping on islands or otherwise inaccessible coastlines. Land expeditions in Africa are often in the real sense exploratory, maps being nonexistent. From single-day hikes to two-day expeditions the degree of difficulty was upgraded towards the final ascent of the 13,000-foot Cameroon Mountain, which for many was a severe ordeal, due to the relatively rarefied air, coming up so swiftly from sea-level. This expedition gave a real sense of achievement.

The sense of unity in the course was achieved naturally through everyone going through the same programme and sharing the same experiences. But an important part of the build-up of morale was the meeting together in the evenings for community activities— sometimes discussions, talks, debates, but often social activities. There rarely passed a day without some singing and dancing or improvised mime and plays about Nigeria.

About one-quarter of the training is directed towards social service. Life-saving and first aid is part of the curriculum, as in Britain, and many more varied aspects of how help can be given are suggested in discussion or in practice. On occasion, the whole course was faced with a surprise emergency: that a nearby village needed help, or a vessel had been wrecked nearby. Sometimes it was prearranged, sometimes it was a genuine incident; the students had no idea until afterwards whether it was mock or real. Afterwards there was discussion of the bearing which such situations might have in connection with district administration. A transfer of training is assumed to take place from the positive attitude which is taught at the centre. It is intended that the students will feel it their duty to take action for the prevention of accidents or, in the event of emergencies, to assist the victims.

In contrast with England, the Outward Bound badges have never had the same importance. The impetus on the course is group endeavour rather than a personal one. In the early courses at Man o' War Bay it was well understood that it was the student's example when he returned to his home which was to be the badge of membership.

Adventure certainly has its place in the courses, but in the first

ones some very surprising attitudes came to light. Camping out for
the African may seem to be a tedious chore, whereas for the European it is an adventure. For the African the typewriter spells adventure rather than a trek through the uninhabited bush. The journey
to Man o' War Bay when the school was in the Cameroons was quite
definitely an excitement and a stimulation, and the ascent of the
Mount Cameroon became in the end one of the few activities
accepted and undertaken unquestioningly. The commonly accepted
Outward Bound adventures are European, and have been trans-
planted to Africa, where no yachtsmen existed and no mountaineers,
no walking clubs or tradition of exploration for its own sake. It is
significant that Mr Dickson first saw a spirit of adventure among his
students when they were undertaking constructive work with a
purpose—that of helping a community.

It follows that everything has to be explained more carefully and
time given for discussion. Nothing can be taken for granted, for the
programme is so utterly different to anything most students have
done before and, quite apart from a certain hesitancy and caution,
there is no Spartanism evident. The reason for each activity has to
be explained. Again, this is understandable in Africa, where every
aspect of the course is on a great scale. The height of Mount
Cameroon, 13,000 feet, Kilimanjaro 18,000 feet (Gilman's Point),
the inaccessibility and anonymity of the bush, and the distances are
awe-inspiring. There are dangerous wild animals, no lifeboats,
large stretches of uninhabited coastline, there is bilharzia in the
water, filaria, malaria, sickle anaemia, which can make rarefied air
fatal, and there is superstition. The students, too, communicate in
English, which is the *lingua franca*, but a foreign tongue to them all.
In England the mixture of our countrymen, town with country,
Irish with Scots, Welsh, English and Cornish, Geordie with Cock-
ney, grammar school with secondary, is a salutary and testing part of
the training. The make-up of the course is an education in itself.
But in Nigeria this is even more striking, because, although we might
call every member Nigerian, this implies actually different races,
Negro, Bantu, Hamitic, and a myriad different tribes. The Moslem
Fulani from Sokoto and the Ibo from Afikpo have only one thing in
common—they are not white.

It was found that the use of parade-ground techniques had a
limited use; morale was more important. In maintaining discipline,

it was far more likely that a show of goodwill and humour, even a dance or participation by the staff in the hardship, would be more successful at a time of strain than the logic of a sharp order. Africa has its own way of doing things. For instance, the characteristic of a group of villagers bent on moving a large boulder out of the path is to engage in lengthy argument and discussion, shouting and exclaiming, and finally by working up to a kind of mass resolution of strength and power to move the object without apparent organization and with a cry or two peculiar to the people, which kept these individualists together.

From five to seven days of each course were taken up on a community development project. This is the main work of service in the Outward Bound sense, and it often involved the whole course moving a distance of several hundred miles. One example of this was the building of a school for a fishing community fifty miles along the coast who had no connections by road with the outside world, and virtually little with justice or police protection. Another was to help an island village remove to the mainland and to build houses and markets for them or, rather, with them; such projects are community efforts, and the experience of negotiating with the 'elders', village heads or chiefs and persuading people to work is a valuable one for the student, who has never seen it as his business to mix cement and carry head-pans with simple country people.

It remains to be mentioned that on the courses for older age-groups (and this is verified from other countries as well) the course runs with very little alteration. The techniques appear to bridge the same divisions in outside society, and result in a similar degree of participation and effort as with the adolescent.

ASSESSMENT

The Nigerian short course is not a vocational training and it is not an academic education. It claims to be character-training and, unless it is for the physical fitness, what are the governments and businesses paying out for? Physical fitness wears off, anyway, and no one pretends to afford what is virtually half a man's yearly income in these developing countries unless they are getting a return for their money.

Businesses must see an improved energy and maturity in their candidates, and, in the case of local government and Government department sponsors, we can be sure that if Outward Bound did not have results they would not be willing to spare a valuable employee for a month of his working time. The successful establishment of these schools and their steady supply of material spells in general a positive answer to the claims of Outward Bound. It must be so in the long run.

A record was kept at Man o' War Bay from the Courses 3–11, which enables figures to be given of the number of students who carried out practical works of social service after returning to their homes. This does not include those who were professional road overseers or engineers, and, although some students attempted more than one project, they have only been counted once. Of 439 students, of whom only 75 per cent were subsequently contacted, 37 per cent carried out some tangible work of service. They varied from the young man who founded a union whose activities were to support and encourage the twin-born, free education for orphans, town-cleaning every Saturday and social activities, to those who built bridges and roads with voluntary labour.

Some young men realize their personal failings—whether drink, bad temper, inconsiderateness. A letter came back: 'I was encouraged in good behaviour.'

> I owe gratitude to Man o' War Bay for helping me to become a better young man and forget my 'don't care attitude'. What surprises me most is not that we are taught these things, but that the Centre has a peculiar way of making the students accept her doctrine unquestionably, and consequently they become a part and parcel of the men, even though they are taught to accept them in a little over three weeks.

Another reports: 'Students now in the Centre must know, sir, that it is not the going in but the coming out that matters much.'

There was one case when, by means of persuasion, a student quelled a riot of 500 women who stormed a local government station. Sunday Dunkaro rescued two people buried alive when a house collapsed and other people ran away in a panic. Umaru Mora was mentioned by a provincial education officer for his bravery in starting a school among the children of a pagan community who one generation back had been cannibals. His life was threatened at times. A final example of brave action taken in spite of public opinion is that of Ehihia Oyeh, from Igbo, near Afikpo, in the Eastern Region:

> My first active work happened when I was returning from Ediba, my station. When I reached Ediba beach, suddenly I heard a terrible noise and also people crying for help. I ran to the river, despite my heavy shoes and trousers, to rescue someone from drowning. People ran away because their belief is that when anyone is found in that particular river and if anyone happens to go for his rescue both will perish. People cried and told me not to venture, but my very simple reply was that as a Man o' War Bay student I must go. So I dived inside the river and swam to the place of the drowning person. At first I thought it to be a boy; not until I rescued her did I know her to be a girl. When I rescued her, her people greeted me very much.

'Man o' War Bay puts together what the politicians have split apart,' writes one Lagos clerk, referring to the comradeship between the students of all regions. What is possible on the course is not always practicable in the outside world because of social pressures and hostile or unsympathetic public opinion. Some of the determination to put the course into practice is so strong in the individual, and the interior rewards sufficiently lasting, as to ride over callous public opinion. But for any education to be effective, the education of the community and the student must move on together. Recognition by the public is probably sufficient even if there is no tangible reward to act as a stimulus to encourage students to play their new roles. From the beginning, an energetic policy towards public relations by the principals transformed the attitude of students, and indeed sponsors, towards the course. This took the form of films, newspaper articles, mention by African Ministers of State and the foundation of old student bodies in the large towns. Not to be forgotten is the massive correspondence with old students. I believe these associations and links play a vital part in supporting the character changes which the course initiates.

It is so often thought that character is fixed at a very early age in man's life, according to the Ruth Benedict School of Psychology during breast-feeding and toilet-training, but Newcomb has observed groups where the individual's perception of himself has changed much later in life amongst Europeans;[4] and in certain primitive societies Nadel[5] has evidence of a marked change in the adult men when custom dictates they shall retire from an active life to a vicarious one. Both on the subject of transfer of training and change of attitude in character training much field-work has still to be done. It may be valuable to define character as an attitude towards taking up new roles. So little has been written about the training of character, while a great deal has been written about teaching techniques. The Nigerian course aims to train a positive, ethical attitude to taking up new roles in a developing country. It would seem that there is a transfer of training here, because the lessons taught are learned in participation on the course, and this application will be a different social situation to elsewhere in the country, in another community. Quite a body of knowledge has been assembled to demonstrate a transfer of training in mathematical teaching and in logic, but virtually nothing so far in the field in which Outward Bound is concerned.

Comparing the Nigerian version of the Outward Bound theme with the British, the Nigerian seems to have returned to the sources in two senses. Baden Powell was inspired by the tribal customs of youth age-groups in South Africa originally. When seeking the source of the Outward Bound idea, one has to accept that nothing is quite new. Only when the Outward Bound returns to Africa does it seem strange because tribal customs in this regard have now very largely disappeared, while on the other hand, with a world or at least a national view developing, it is more than ever relevant to their society and to the literate classes, the leaders of the new emergent country, to reintroduce these age-old techniques with a new slant.

In another sense the Nigerian courses are more akin to the first Outward Bound School at Aberdovey in Wales than to the schools as they have since evolved in Britain. Outward Bound was born of a marriage between the genius of an educationist and the practical business sense of a shipping-owner. There are the two elements in the Nigerian version of the Outward Bound theme: the idealist, more leisurely aim to provide an experience which can mature in a thousand ways to enrich an individual's life over the years, and the more urgent practical needs of the rapidly developing society and the pressing need for responsible and energetic leaders under African independence.

Beside the general educational value for the students, government, sponsors and staff hope for results. This is evident in the title of the courses, Citizenship Training, and in the syllabus, which includes a week of community development. Dr Hahn always believed that practical experience and habit are the real educational forces. Alec Dickson too was eager to reinforce the all too easily spoken word, with practical evidence from students they were prepared to carry out their high principles in practice.

This concern with results in Nigeria is reminiscent of the original purpose of the Outward Bound in Great Britain during the Second World War. In a very real sense it was born of the emergency in the Merchant Navy, where so many lives were lost at sea after crews had taken to the lifeboats, having abandoned their torpedoed ships. In these crises men who knew very well their duty as professionals in the big ships lacked confidence and power of command in sailing a lifeboat loaded with shock-stricken people to safety. Outward Bound courses proved a great resource in remedying this situation, so vital at that time to our own national survival.

NOTES

1 Batten, T. R., *Communities and Their Development*, London, 1957, pp. 5f.
2 Hodgkin, R. A., *Education and Change*, London, 1957, p. 283.
3 Hart, C. W. M., 'Contrasts between Pre-pubertal and Post-pubertal Education', in *Education and Anthropology*, ed. G. D. Spindler, California, 1955.
4 Newcomb, T. M., *Social Psychology*, Dryden, 1950, pp. 472–5. See L. K. Frank, *Education and Anthropology*, ed. G. D. Spindler, California, 1955, p. 148.
5 Nadel, S. F., *A Black Byzantium*, London, 1942, p. 401.

Outward Bound in the Commonwealth

E. W. Dawson

Before 1953 Outward Bound consisted of three schools in the United Kingdom, which were by no means working to capacity. Since then a steady expansion has taken place, and today eighteen Outward Bound schools exist in no less than ten countries; three more have been opened in Great Britain, of which one is a full-time school for girls.

The Outward Bound Trust has always followed the principle that overseas schools should be started and maintained by local people. This rule has been faithfully followed, and it is interesting to consider the varying motives that have prompted those concerned to ask us for help. Permission to use the name is granted when the Trust is satisfied that a sufficient number of responsible citizens are behind the project, that financial backing is forthcoming, and that all essential features of Outward Bound are applied when carrying out the training. These features are fundamental to all schools, but the reasons for establishing these centres varies according to the need of the country. We thus find in Britain that the training helps to create a bridge between the classes and religious denominations; in Africa, a bridge between races, tribal divisions and various religions.

Having recently visited a number of schools in many parts of the world, I was fascinated to observe how Outward Bound proved suitable to all these differing conditions and had been adapted to the need of the various countries.

To Australians and New Zealanders the need for this type of

training did not seem obvious at first. It was frequently said: 'Our young people already go on expeditions, sail and climb mountains, surf and undertake outdoor activities.' It was not difficult to explain that there is a world of difference between embarking on an expedition voluntarily from your own home, with everything provided, and the comforting knowledge that one is able to return there at will, and undertaking the same activity in an organized group, for a specific purpose, as a member of a closely-knit community. It is, of course, an obvious fact that those who partake in such activities are only a small proportion of the population, and that each country has many people lacking both initiative and a sense of responsibility who desperately need the experience of Outward Bound. The challenge which Outward Bound presents is both mental and physical. This was appreciated by many influential people in Australia and New Zealand, with the result that each country has a successful school which has been running for a number of years. The size and character of New Zealand greatly simplifies recruiting, but Australia, on the other hand, with their vast distances, has great problems in recruiting and in conveying students to the school in New South Wales. This will, however, be simplified when their new school in Victoria is established.

Trusts have been formed in Tanzania and Uganda, each with an African chairman, in the hope that one day they will have their own school. At present they send students to the Kenya school at Loitokitok, on the slopes of Kilimanjaro.

In 1955 the Malayan school began its first course. Situated on the West Coast near Lumut, sixty miles north of Ipoh, the school uses the challenge of both sea and jungle for young Malayans, Chinese, Indians and an occasional European boy. When Malaya became self-governing and the future of the country was so uncertain, a number of leaders in the country urged that an Outward Bound school be established. They were greatly encouraged by Field-Marshal Sir Gerald Templer, at that time High Commissioner for Malaya. The school was operated successfully under English wardens from 1955, and now has its first Malayan warden. The chief problems which confront those responsible for the running of the school are those of recruiting and finance. Strenuous efforts are being made to increase the numbers of students, and should these prove successful the financial problems will be largely overcome.

Africa, with its multi-racial problems, has enthusiastically embraced the concept of Outward Bound, and in consequence Kenya, Rhodesia and Zambia all possess well-established schools. These are run by well-known local people, both African and European. Each school is situated in wild and spectacular country, and it is a thrilling experience to visit them and to appreciate the dedicated work of the staffs in so many parts of the world.

The Kenya school, with the giant, snow-capped Kilimanjaro as its background, is in a unique position overlooking the African plains teeming with big game. The Rhodesian school is tucked under the beautiful Chimammami Mountains near Melsetter, and presents an exciting challenge to the varied members of the Outward Bound courses. A youngster cannot fail to be deeply impressed after living for a month in these spectacular surroundings. The Zambian school offers a comparable but different challenge, situated as it is in the dense bush and within easy reach of Lake Tanganyika and mountainous country. Kenya, though the longest established, still needs to increase the number of students; and voluntary help, both practical and financial, is hard to come by. Rhodesia has always lacked a sufficient number of students. The position is slowly improving, even in the present difficult time, because of the variety of courses which the committee and wardens are prepared to undertake. The school is beautifully maintained and the buildings are as good as any to be found in other Outward Bound establishments. Unlike other schools, they find little difficulty in obtaining qualified staff. The reverse is true of Zambia, where there is strong support from companies in the copper belt. They do not suffer from a shortage of students, but qualified instructors are extremely difficult to find. They have to rely very much upon young men doing Voluntary Service Overseas, who are enthusiastic but usually lacking the experience necessary for the work. The inaccessibility of the school makes supplies difficult to obtain, particularly in the rainy season, and occasionally courses have to start two or three days late when the school bus is stranded on the flooded road. There is probably a greater need for the challenge of Outward Bound in Africa, with all its emergent countries, than in any other part of the world.

In 1967 we were surprised to receive a request from the Ministry of Commonwealth Relations that we should supply a fully trained warden and two instructors to run Outward Bound training in

Singapore. This was the first that any of us at home had heard of such an undertaking, and it caused us some concern. However, we were more than comforted when we heard that New Zealand had taken them under her wing and was sending them their ex-warden, who had recently retired from the New Zealand school, together with their chief instructor, so that they might become properly established. Further doubts about the limited areas in which they could operate were dispelled when I saw for myself the jungle-covered islands and the well-protected sea which they would use for their training. I feel confident that Singapore will have a successful school, with members of the Government determined that it shall succeed and with the support of the Outward Bound Trust of New Zealand. One of the reasons for the urgency with which the authorities wish to establish a school is that half the population is under twenty-one, and therefore receptive to Outward Bound training.

I cannot leave the subject of Outward Bound overseas without mentioning the efforts of a number of keenly interested people in South Africa to create an organization on the same lines as that of Great Britain. Some years ago we were approached by educationists in South Africa for permission to use our name and form an Outward Bound Trust. The name could not possibly be used while *apartheid* continues, and they are unable to carry out one of the essential principles, that of integration. They therefore devised the Afrikaans title of *Velt & Vlei*, which means 'wide open spaces and watery expanses'. Committees exist in Cape Town and Port Elizabeth for the purpose of organizing two summer courses at each centre for coloured boys, and one centre between Johannesburg and Durban for white boys. It is hoped to develop this into an all-the-year-round school, with a management committee in Johannesburg. At present these three centres each run two summer courses a year exclusively for schoolboys. It is therefore impossible for them to avoid giving the impression that *Velt & Vlei* run summer holiday camps. The members of their various committees are well aware of this weakness, and are making strenuous efforts to interest industrialists and working people so as to increase the number and variety of students.

Each Outward Bound School overseas is autonomous, depending for its existence on its own efforts, but there is one important way in which the Trust in Britain can, and does, help. Frequently a school sends a prospective warden, and in some cases a chief instructor, for training at two and sometimes more of our schools. Or, alternatively, instructors have been sent out from the United Kingdom on two-year contracts. This has been done twice for New Zealand, who have sent us their wardens-elect. Three wardens have been sent to Australia and one Australian trainee has visited the British schools. Both wardens in Malaya have worked with us before taking up their appointments, and similarly in Kenya they have had three wardens and a number of instructors who were trained in Britain. The latest overseas school in Singapore sent their warden and chief instructor, both Singaporeans, to the United Kingdom, and two young prospective instructors went to New Zealand for training. A further school has been formed in Hong Kong and has the English warden of the Malayan school as its warden, whose place has been taken over by a Malayan. He has also visited our schools in the U.K. As wardens change and overseas schools appoint their own local staff, so the demand for home-trained British staff is diminishing, while the importance of the training of staff in fact increases. I stress this aspect of our work in order to demonstrate that, in spite of the vast distances between the various independent members of our Outward Bound family, there exists the closest co-operation, and the United Kingdom Trust has an important part to play in maintaining communications and furthering the world-wide cause of Outward Bound.

Outward Bound in the USA

Joshua L. Miner

The United States of America is a nation peopled by men from other lands, with diverse customs, speaking different languages. It is a land settled by hard men with calloused hands who drove wooden wagons through misty mountain passes, across dusty plains, to frontier homesteads on which they could raise their families in freedom and prosperity. It is the nation in which children born in the squalor of the ghetto frequently become presidents of banks. The mystique of America is one of youth, the glowing horizon, the untamed frontier.

The physical frontier of the United States is all but gone. The modern frontier is the mental and moral crisis of meeting the complex challenges of a shrinking globe amid nuclear proliferation. The young American watches the political lines of the world map change daily. He watches the strife of national pride opposing the facts of economic and social life. He observes the anomaly of greater production by fewer men working shorter hours. He is faced with the enormous decision of being 'trained' in a world facing the greatest moral and metaphysical problems in history, or being 'educated' in a nation in which the 'trained' are easily employed.

It is increasingly easy for the urbanized American youth to avoid confronting responsibility and challenge. He may climb mountains or be a skilled surgeon simply by watching the images on his television screen. He may consider that his responsibility to himself is *not* becoming involved in the trial and error of the world-wide search for peace and reason. He looks about him and often believes that the whole overwhelms the parts. The young person in the United States must examine himself and then look to the frontiers of life in his world. It is the responsibility of his elders to provide a framework within which he has the opportunity to explore his own potential.

Through a belief in the validity and appropriateness of Dr Kurt Hahn's philosophy and educational approaches for American society, a group of concerned men and women came together to help meet the needs of the nation's youth. The beginnings of Outward Bound in the United States of America took many of these individuals to adventurous personal frontiers. During the First World War, Dr Hahn had formed strong friendships with several key Americans. Not the least important was Mr Christian Herter, who was later to become Governor of Massachusetts and Secretary of State for the United States. Shortly after the Second World War these friends formed the American–British Foundation for European Education to help Dr Hahn with his work in Europe and to plant his ideas in the United States. In 1962 the foundation's name was changed to the Atlantic Foundation for the Education of the Free, Inc.

In 1950, however, Mrs Lewis Douglas, the wife of the former US Ambassador to the Court of St James, approached Mr John P. Stevens, Jr, for his help with Dr Hahn's work overseas. Mr Stevens was very interested, and suggested that I, then a young teacher, visit Great Britain and Germany to see Dr Hahn's ideas in action. I spent six weeks abroad in 1950 visiting Gordonstoun, Luisenlund, and Salem, as well as the British Outward Bound schools at Aberdovey, Eskdale and Burghead. After reporting enthusiastically on the trip to the American–British Foundation and to Mr Stevens, I returned to Gordonstoun in February 1951 with my family to be Director of Activities, housemaster, and instructor in mathematics and science. After remaining there for eighteen months, I returned to America to accept an appointment to the faculty of Phillips Academy in Andover, Massachusetts, Mr John Kemper, Headmaster of Phillips Academy, was interested in applying aspects of Dr Hahn's philosophy to the life of his own school.

During the 1950s the Americans interested in Dr Hahn's ideas concentrated on supporting his work in Europe. With the formation of the Atlantic Foundation for the Education of the Free, it seemed possible that an Atlantic College might be founded in the United States. In 1960, after considerable study, it was decided initially to give form to Dr Hahn's ideas by creating an American Outward Bound school rather than by establishing a new college.

The men who reached the decision to introduce Outward Bound into America were Professor H. Wentworth Eldredge, Chairman of Sociology Department of Dartmouth College; F. Charles Froelicher, Headmaster of Colorado Academy; Christian A. Herter, Sr, former Secretary of State and Governor of Massachusetts; John Mason Kemper, Headmaster of Phillips Academy, Andover, Massachusetts; Mrs John J. McCloy; Thomas McKittrick, International banker; Joshua L. Miner III, President of Outward Bound, Inc.; John P. Stevens, Jr, Industrialist; Henry P. Van Dusen, President of Union Theological Seminary; and Eric M. Warburg, International banker.

In 1960 Gilbert Burnett, a teacher at Phillips Academy, found that Mr F. Charles Froelicher, who had been in correspondence with the Outward Bound Trust in London, was interested in starting an American Outward Bound school. We flew to Denver, Colorado, to discuss the necessary steps with Mr Froelicher. After intensive planning, fund-raising and recruiting of staff, the first American Outward Bound school, with William Chapman, writer and educator, as its director, opened for its initial course in the summer of 1961 through the combined support and efforts of the Colorado Board of Trustees and the Trustees of the Atlantic Foundation for the Education of the Free, Inc.

In 1963 the Atlantic Foundation for the Education of the Free was approached by Mr Robert J. Pieh, Headmaster of Anniston Academy, for information about the establishment of an Outward Bound school in Minnesota. Mr Pieh was encouraged to form a board of trustees and to make the plans for a new school, the Minnesota Outward Bound school, which opened during the next summer.

As the complexities of administering two schools increased, it became apparent that a national headquarters was necessary both to co-ordinate operations and to ensure control over expansion and quality of future Outward Bound activity. Consequently, Outward Bound, Incorporated, was established and rapidly began its duties in Andover, Massachusetts.

In the same year Mr Peter O. Willauer, an instructor at the

Groton School, suggested to me that an Outward Bound Sea school be opened on the coast of Maine. Mr Willauer, who is a master sailor himself, developed a Board of Trustees and began operations at the Hurricane Island Outward Bound school in the summer of 1965.

The following year a board of trustees under the chairmanship of Mr Donald H. Vetterlain was organized in Portland, Oregon, for the purpose of establishing the Northwest Outward Bound School. Shortly after the Board's formation, the group was able to enlist the services of Mr William Byrd as Director for the school. Mr Byrd, a former teacher, had worked closely with Outward Bound for several years as Director of two Peace Corps training camps in Puerto Rico.

In 1967 the fifth Outward Bound school was established in western North Carolina. Largely through the efforts of Mr Harold Howe, Head of the North Carolina Fund and later United States Secretary of Education, a Board was formed. Judge L. Richardson Preyer, Chairman, and a strong Board of North Carolina community leaders selected Mr James Hollandsworth, an experienced teacher and mountaineer, to direct its courses.

THE AMERICAN OUTWARD BOUND SCHOOLS

Colorado Outward Bound School

The primary base of the Colorado Outward Bound school is located at Marble, Colorado, some 200 miles by road west of Denver. The school lies at an altitude of 9,000 feet, and is surrounded by rocky mountains which exceed 15,000 feet.

The Colorado course, which is available to both young men and women the year round, is planned to confront the student with increasing difficulties and independence as it progresses to long expeditions. Traditional Outward Bound elements, such as the morning run and dip, the ropes course, the wall and beam, initiative tests and the final cross-country run, complement the training in map-reading, axemanship, rock-climbing, and snow and ice mountaineering technique.

Dr Hahn's philosophy of community service is applied to instruction in first aid, mountain rescue and fire-fighting. During each

34   Europeans, Asians and Africans at the Kenya Outward
Bound School, Loitokitok, ascending Mount Kilimanjaro;
snow-clad Mawenzi is in the background

35 Summer Mountain Rescue exercise at the Baad Outward
Bound School in Germany

student's course he or she will be given the opportunity to spend three days and nights totally alone in the mountains. On this solo expedition the Colorado school encourages its students to fast, to reflect upon their lives and to record their impressions in a journal.

As in all American Outward Bound schools, the final expedition is planned and executed by student groups alone, with instructors simply manning check-points along their routes.

Each Colorado course differs from the previous one, as there is little operating reliance on a fixed base camp. Whole courses have become mobile, and expeditions have rafted down the Green River through deep canyons. In 1968–9 the Colorado school established a Colorado Front Range base for courses with curricula built around skiing, winter camping and climbing. Further expanding its horizons, the school is planning a mobile course south in the mountains of Mexico.

Minnesota Outward Bound School

The Minnesota Outward Bound school, the first to include girls, is on an enormous chain of lakes which form the United States–Canadian border. The Minnesota course prepares its students with an initial training period in wilderness skills at 'the Home Place'. Drown-proofing, first aid, life-saving and fire-fighting prepare students for the emergencies they might face on their long expeditions and solos. A brief introduction to rock-climbing, extensive map and compass work, ecology study and thorough lake and white-water canoeing instruction complete the training preparation.

The 'long expedition' of two weeks, both with and without instructors, is a demanding test of all previous lessons. Minnesota Outward Bound students have paddled close to Hudson Bay on some of the journeys and canoed and portaged through country filled with wild game.

Hurricane Island Outward Bound School

The Hurricane Island Outward Bound school is ten miles offshore of the entrance to Penobscot Bay on the cold and foggy Maine coast. In the colonial era the men of these waters produced the fleet vessels of the East Indies trade and later the great clipper ships.

The fundamental element of the American sea school is the specially designed, ketch-rigged, 30-foot rowing boat. More than half of the Outward Bound programme involves training in seamanship and navigation: dinghy sailing, coastal piloting, power-boat operation, search-and-rescue techniques, first aid and extensive drown-proofing instruction.

The island base offers 800-foot granite quarry cliff faces which present all degrees of rock-climbing challenge and many islands of Maine are ideal for the teaching of ecology.

Maintaining a twenty-four-hour radio duty watch, the students have frequent opportunity to serve the local community in this area, where boats are often in distress and forest fires are common.

The final sea expedition is entirely planned and carried out by the students alone in their boats, and they may row and sail as far north as the Canadian border.

North Carolina Outward Bound School

The North Carolina Outward Bound school lies high up on the cliffs of the Linville Gorge wilderness, one of the eastern states' most rugged areas, with 1,000-foot cliffs and dense rhododendron forests filled with wild game. The first American school to run winter courses, North Carolina prepares its students for their expedition schedule through instruction in woodmanship, ecology, search and rescue, fire-fighting and first aid. Particular attention is given to night and day map and compass work, as the almost impenetrable bush presents severe testing of such skills.

Solos and unaccompanied final expeditions place considerable responsibility on the twelve-man 'crews', which have been named 'Moray', 'Anakiwa', etc., in honour of the Commonwealth Outward Bound schools.

Northwest Outward Bound School

The Northwest Outward Bound school, much like the Colorado school, operates with great flexibility from its base camp on the headwaters of Oregon's McKenzie River. The first American school to adopt the mobile course concept for its whole student body, Northwest Outward Bound ranges widely throughout the vast

Three Sister Wilderness area. The high alpine terrain offers a fine training-ground for rock-climbing and snow and ice mountaineering. The central Oregon lava flows, which resemble the surface of the moon and which are used for astronaut training, present diversity of experience. Students participate in the planting of seedlings as part of the state reforestation efforts.

OUTWARD BOUND AS AN AMERICAN INSTITUTION

Since its beginning in the United States, Outward Bound has been nurtured by the American Independent school system. The origin of most of the Outward Bound centres can be traced to one of these schools. American independent schools have given Outward Bound the school directors, the administrative system, a natural pool of students, many staff members, and, in some cases, office space. This has been very fortunate, as the support of these schools makes it clear to the public that Outward Bound is a democratic institution transcending all bounds of race, creed and financial means.

Outward Bound in the United States has been totally supported by private individuals, foundations and business corporations. This aid has allowed the schools the advantage of complete freedom in the choice of sites, programmes and staff. The American schools are also able to take students on a 'first come, first served' basis without having to be selective.

These men and women are drawn from an age-group in which about 50 per cent are enrolled in some degree of formal course of study. Of the remaining group, some are in the armed forces, some hold non-skilled (non-apprentice) jobs, and the remainder are unemployed and occasionally unemployable. The somewhat unique difficulties of the American situation are intensified by the fact that a very small percentage of the students are 'sent' by agencies or businesses. Virtually all students make the choice of participation for themselves. Despite these problems, Outward Bound Incorporated, has been able to co-ordinate and raise scholarship funds with its schools for over fifty per cent of all Outward Bound students.

Outward Bound has made a great effort to achieve the social 'mix' which makes each student confront the universality of his human nature. The schools take the Iowa farm-boy and billet him with a San Francisco lawyer's son. They take the heir to a Boston fortune and let him paddle with the son of an Arizona Indian. They take the son of a Mississippi 'poor white' and let him share a litter handle with a boy from the streets of Harlem.

THE FUTURE OF OUTWARD BOUND IN AMERICA

As Outward Bound continues to grow rapidly in America, the organization is diversifying and expanding its programmes to meet the pressing needs of diverse elements of our society. Despite their wilderness locations and the remote aspects of their activities, the American Outward Bound schools have always been able to enrol significantly large numbers of city-dwelling students. Increased recruitment through the co-operation of civic organizations, city public schools, street academies, Churches, correctional institutions, service agencies and private individuals seems to ensure future success in guaranteeing the broad sociological participation which is a unique feature of the Outward Bound experience.

Recently professional full-time staff have been employed in several of the schools, enabling Outward Bound to develop multiple courses run all the year round, conducting programmes both in the traditional wilderness setting and directly within urban centres.

The following outline is a brief description of course types that reflect the increasing degree of Outward Bound commitment to Dr Hahn's concept of community service:

1 Student Courses

a   The regular twenty-four/twenty-five-day residential course for students (male or female between the ages of sixteen and a half to twenty-three) has been the traditional course and the heart of the entire international movement. Its programme, which emphasizes the improving of self-concept through a process of stress, challenge and personal success, has been refined through the experience of almost 1,000 international courses. Opportunities for leadership, service to others, self-reliance and adventure are carefully developed facets of this model.

The Urban League's street academies and Action Bound in Trenton, New Jersey, are organizations which credit Outward Bound with providing the attitudinal reinforcement to enable the 'disadvantaged' city-dwelling youth to succeed in his high school and college.

b Junior Courses For fourteen- to sixteen-year-olds, these programmes are quite similar to the conventional student curriculum. A project for this age-group has been active in New York City throughout the summers of 1968 and 1969, and is scheduled to continue this school year for expanding numbers of children.

c Senior Courses These courses for men and women over twenty-three years of age have become increasingly important to the total American Outward Bound effort. Through the training of adults, who take their skills back to city youths, great numbers of students can be exposed to Outward Bound-type programmes. Leadership training for staff of civic organizations (Urban League) and Government projects (Peace Corps, Job Corps, etc.) has been particularly important.

Numerous teachers of diverse races and backgrounds have completed senior courses, and, as a result, find that they have a better understanding of their pupils, their roles as educators and the techniques of working outside the conventional classroom structure. A number of these teachers have come from correctional centres and admit new attitudes towards the reform of youth. In conjunction with correctional institutions, the ministry and social workers have been broadly represented with follow-up objectives of developing 'half-way-house' leadership in the large cities.

2 *Workshops and Seminars*

During the past two years Outward Bound schools have conducted short-term training sessions primarily for educators and staff of state and civic organizations. The objectives of these programmes have been to introduce men who are in positions of influence to the philosophy and techniques of Outward Bound. In some cases extensive skills training is included, but the most significant role Outward Bound activity has played is in triggering a productive exchange of educational ideas among the participants. Several two-day 'working' seminars have directly affected the curricula of public and private schools.

3 Manpower Courses

In an effort to meet the problems of the 'hard-core unemployables', Outward Bound, led by its Colorado school, has developed special programmes to assist industry with pre-vocational, attitudinal training. Previous Outward Bound work for the Job Corps provided the experience base for instruction techniques. The innovation in this course, however, is that business supervisors participate with their trainees on all Outward Bound field activities. Heightened sensitivity training and a built-in follow-up programme ensure long-range benefits for employer, employee and the community at large. The implications of this joint adult-student course-type for future Outward Bound co-operation with such organizations as OIC, Pride, Urban League, Vista, police forces, etc., may become a major thrust of American Outward Bound activity in the next few years.

4 Educational Institution Projects

Perhaps the broadest impact that Outward Bound can make on the North American scene is through its connection with public and private schools, colleges and universities. Many high schools have adopted Outward Bound training as part of their curriculum. The depth of involvement ranges from club activities, examination substitution or an entire school-within-a-school, where the total academic curriculum is built around an Outward Bound-type programme. It is encouraging to note that in a New Jersey programme the drop-outs or potential drop-outs who make up the integrated Action Bound student body have produced the best attendance record in the entire high school, and have continued classes when race riots closed the rest of the school system.

Numerous private schools have committed themselves to the Outward Bound approach in virtually every section of the United States. More educators may follow New York's Horace Mann School in establishing an 'outdoor laboratory' with resident biologists to link Outward Bound activities to formal curriculum.

At the undergraduate level, Dartmouth College, through the co-operation of its Sociology Department, anticipates awarding credit for an undergraduate Outward Bound course which involves term-time services in north-eastern urban centres and with New Hampshire high schools and their 'disadvantaged students'. Similarly, Old Westbury, the newest of New York State's campuses, expects to incorporate Outward Bound and urban service as part of their freshman school year schedule.

Already in its second year of development, the new Prescott College of Arizona envisages expanding its large Outward Bound programme to include urban undergraduate involvement and to provide a seminar centre for western educators.

A large number of other colleges have adopted the Outward Bound model, and are now weaving it into their programmes. This trend is just beginning, and it is difficult to assess the future implications of these activities on American communities.

5 Delinquency Projects

Through co-operation with courts and correctional institutions in Georgia, Colorado, Massachusetts, etc., Outward Bound has developed special programmes for urban delinquents. Urban Bound in Denver, a court-sponsored project, enables many boys in trouble to participate in an Outward Bound-type programme which leads to specific employment opportunities at the completion of their residential course.

In Massachusetts several hundred boys have participated in Outward Bound programmes, and in a two-year study of these boys sponsored by the United States Office of Juvenile Delinquency, it was determined that Outward Bound was a valuable alternative to the institutionalization of delinquents, as the test group's post-course record showed a significant reduction in recommitment to state correctional agencies.

Encouraged by these dramatic results, the staff of the Hurricane Island Outward Bound School ran an experimental course directly within a state school for boys during the winter of 1968. The results of the experiment were so dramatic that a second phase of the programme is continuing, and evidence points to an altering of the institution's basic attitudes towards reformatory techniques.

Training of institutional staff at Outward Bound senior courses has resulted in special state projects which are reshaping entire correctional institutions.

6 Related Urban Projects

Because of the Outward Bound model and direct assistance, several urban organizations are developing special projects for elementary and secondary school age youth. Two examples of these new structures are: Horizons 4, an outdoor-oriented programme sponsored by the New York Urban League for elementary school children; and the Blairstown, New Jersey, Education Centre, under the auspices of the New Jersey Department of Community Affairs.

Conclusion

At this time American Outward Bound is at a transitional stage in its development. Having established its five residential course centres and successfully run many summer courses and some exciting special projects, the organization now has the experience to move towards a year-round service. Provided that the necessary resources and staff can be assembled, Outward Bound is eager to increase its efforts in meeting the critical needs of American society.

Of particular assistance to our efforts have been the recent visits of Dr Hahn to American projects. His sound advice and his ability to inspire American Outward Bound staff continues to be of great importance to work in this country.

As the United States is a nation which has grown on its youth, its horizons, and its frontier, it is a land in which the methods of education must be equally young and outgoing in their approach to life. Probably no system of education is better suited to the American mentality than the great educational adventure of Kurt Hahn.

The German *Kurzschulen*: Their foundation and development

Gustav Richter

The history of the German *Kurzschulen* has been very largely influenced by the exceptional political, economic, and cultural conditions existing in Germany at the time when the idea was first conceived and later as it developed.

Neither the inevitable lethargy which followed the collapse in 1945, the mere desire to survive, nor the subsequent period of hectic reconstruction and its preoccupation with purely material advancement provided suitable conditions for the introduction of an educational reform.

The first German *Kurzschule* would most certainly never have been founded—to say nothing of the second one—if the man who was responsible for the creation of Britain's Outward Bound schools (formerly called short terms schools) had not forced through his ideas in Germany as well, in spite of all opposition. That man was Kurt Hahn. As early as the summer of 1945 he left his school in Gordonstoun in order to bring help and advice to his old home country, and thereafter he came over time and time again, often making several visits in one year. He was deeply disturbed by the desperate conditions and by the general feeling of despondency which was particularly noticeable among young people. The collapse of the National Socialist régime, which for twelve years had bludgeoned the brains and the souls of the people with its false doctrines, had left a vacuum which seemed to be at once devoid of all hope and fraught with danger. The Allied Military Government policy of 're-education' of the German people was unrealistic and doomed to failure. Hahn said, 'Re-education is the wrong expression. Restoration is the proper term', and he suggested that this difficult task of restoration could best be accomplished by the establishment of *Kurzschulen*. A large number of such schools could provide German youth with opportunities to prove themselves through a variety of experiences, exercises in life-saving, and in the development of an active sense of civic responsibility. They could replace the vacuum with purposeful activity, convert despondency and lethargy into something positive and lead young people back to become valuable members of the community of free nations. 'Active citizenship is not a matter of party. It is a matter of human strength.' Hahn put his plans to the American Military Governor in Germany. To expect a favourable and enlightened reaction to such proposals so soon after the defeat of the hated Nazi régime was perhaps to expect too much. During 1948 and 1949 Hahn tried in vain time and again in America to obtain agreement and support for his schemes from official education representatives. In Germany as early as 1945 Kurt Hahn had met Thomas H. McKittrick, Vice-president of the American Chase National Bank. Together they tried to convince responsible statesmen in America of the necessity of winning over Europe's youth, including the young people in Germany, and, for this purpose, of utilizing the peculiar advantages offered by the *Kurzschulen*. However, the sceptics needed to be convinced by example, and so a group of private supporters of Hahn's plans—the 'American–British Foundation for European Education', was formed by Thomas McKittrick, to establish a limited number of *Kurzschulen*. He arranged for Kurt Hahn to meet the newly appointed American High Commissioner in Germany, John McCloy, who very quickly recognized the value and significance of the *Kurzschulen* for Germany. The McCloy Fund, which was at his disposal, enabled him to make a significant contribution towards the foundation of such a *Kurzschule*.

In spite of the sympathetic attitude of the American High Commissioner, it was almost three years before the first German *Kurzschule*, with the aid of the McCloy Fund, became a reality. Even with the exceptional material support from American sources there remained scepticism and a lack of initiative on the German

side. Many people, completely occupied in consolidating their newly
achieved and hard-won economic successes, were wary of new
experiments and efforts of a 'superfluous' nature, the more so as
normal living conditions had still not been completely re-established.
This new type of school called a *Kurzschule* was not essential for
teaching and examinations, and why worry about such schools
before adequate accommodation had been provided everywhere for
normal instruction? The influx of refugees and expellees increased
the strain upon the educational resources. Young people in employment were usually interested primarily in earning money as quickly
as possible, and were opposed to anything which might reduce the
time being devoted to this one objective. Kurt Hahn refused to yield.
Repeatedly he visited Germany in order to persuade people and to
overcome resistance to his plans. Even though a small group of
enthusiasts under the chairmanship of Dr Theodor Bäuerle, then
Minister of Education in Baden-Würtemberg, had agreed as early as
May 1950 to form a special society for the implementation of the
new ideas, there continued to be technical, material and educational
objections which delayed the final arrangements. Covering travelling
expenses with the aid of American funds, Hahn invited the most
important members of this German society to Gordonstoun for a
discussion of the principles at issue and for a visit to the English
short-terms schools. In the summer of 1951, as a result of this visit,
the German Society for European Education was founded, and its
programme, which had been agreed in Gordonstoun and drawn up
by Minna Specht, envisaged the creation of *Kurzschulen* in Germany.

An unexpected event triggered off decisive action in autumn of
the same year. The Hamburg ship-owner Heinz Schliewen had
acquired the two ocean-going sailing ships *Pamir* and *Passat* shortly
before they were due for demolition in Holland. It was his intention
to use these two remaining members of the famous family of the
'Flying P-Liners' as merchant-marine training-ships under sail, each
with a smaller permanent crew and fifty cadets. In this way he would
assist in the training of the rising generation for the German
Merchant Navy. Kurt Hahn recognized the dangers and the opportunities intrinsic in this plan. He succeeded in convincing Schliewen
of the necessity of providing a land-based training course for the
future mariners before their departure for Brazil. The course should
encourage the team spirit and self-discipline, and also teach technical

skills in preparation for the unexpected and unknown dangers of a long sea voyage. It was obvious that such a course should be arranged according to the principles of the *Kurzschulen*. The German Society for European Education formed a special committee to deal with nautical affairs and became the organizer of this new kind of work— the first German '*Kurzschule* course' as one might say. For this purpose the Federal State Government of Schleswig-Holstein— having obtained the approval of the owner, Graf Plessen—made available Schloss Nehmten on the Plöner See, a stately home which was normally reserved for residential courses for schoolchildren. A total of 100 potential sailors aged from sixteen to twenty-one years, with differing social backgrounds, were trained by specially appointed teachers in seamanship, sport, first aid, and elementary social and physical sciences. An old Gordonstoun boy, and member of Salem's staff, participated as instructor and subsequently sailed as a member of the crew on *Pamir*'s first trip to Rio. Twenty boys (fifteen German and five English), received their training in Gordonstoun, where a German ship's captain was specially employed. The course in Germany was in charge of Professor Dr Christiansen-Weniger, formerly Head of the Hermann Lietz Boarding Schools. He had been present at the decisive meeting in Gordonstoun when the German Society for European Education was established, and subsequently became a member of its executive committee. The response to the experiment was remarkable. Representatives of the Press and the radio and many personalities in public life visited Nehmten, reported on the course and roused considerable interest. When, at the end of the course, the *Pamir* put out into the Kieler Förde for a trial run with all the boys, the Federal President, Professor Dr Theodor Heuss, was also on board, and he spoke of the future development of Kurt Hahn's educational work for the youth of Germany.

The degree of enthusiasm with which the young 'sea-cadets' co-operated surprised even the greatest optimists. The certainty that German youth could and would react favourably when called upon to prove its ability created the foundations for further development. Preparations were intensified for the opening of the first permanent German *Kurzschule*, which was to be a naval school accommodated in Schloss Weissenhaus on the Hohwachter Bay between Lübeck and Kiel. Kurt Hahn and his friends succeeded in getting the final assurance of American financial support to the extent of D.M. 282,000 for the establishment of the new school. The owner of Weissenhaus—Graf von Platen-Hallermund and his family—made the greater part of the Schloss available for a period of twenty-five years, together with those parts of the grounds necessary for the work of the school, demanding in return only a very small sum to cover depreciation. He also expressed his willingness to become Chairman of the governing body and to supervise and support the work. Following the successful experiment in Nehmten, Professor Dr Christiansen-Weniger was the obvious choice to take charge of the new *Kurzschule*, and many of the Nehmten teaching staff came with him. Nine courses, each of twenty-eight days' duration, were to take place annually between March and November.

Although it was not at first possible to make use of experience in Germany itself, it seemed advisable to carry out a publicity campaign to make the new *Kurzschule* known to a wider public. Sir Spencer Summers, one of the chief founders of the British Outward Bound Movement, visited Germany to speak on behalf of the new educational methods and to lecture and report on the results of many years of work in English *Kurzschulen*. Press reports and personal accounts also played their part. At the same time it proved possible, with American aid, for 130 Germans interested in new teaching methods and representing the worlds of education, of industry, the Jugend-Rot-Kreuz (junior Red Cross) and many other fields of activity, to visit the school in Gordonstoun and its life-saving services, and the British short-term schools.

This project has played a decisive role in the establishment of the *Kurzschulen* in Germany. Time and time again during the years which followed and in the course of the struggle against almost insurmountable difficulties, our friends, influenced by this visit, were strengthened in their conviction of the value of Hahn's methods.

On 5 June 1952 the *Kurzschule* WEISSENHAUS was opened with sixty-five participants. With the peculiar conditions in Germany in mind, Kurt Hahn had propounded the maxim: 'Service to the community is opposed to the egocentric *ohne mich* attitude. The "respect for life and all living creatures" shown by Albert Schweitzer is opposed to the disregard of the individual as practised by National Socialism.'

In a letter to Bishop Lilje, who was later to become a member of the Executive Committee of the German Society for European Education, Hahn tells of a propitious meeting in 1949:

> Motoring through the Black Forest, we stopped uncertain of our road, when an old gentleman came towards us to put us right. He was Albert Schweitzer, for whose renewed blessing I had long hoped. He asked me into his house, and I was able to stay an hour with him, telling him of our plans. Without my asking, he wrote this letter with his own hand:

> 19.1.49.

> Dear Mr. Hahn,
>   I am glad you made use of the opportunity which offered itself, to tell me of your plans to train the young through active service in rescue work. Without my writing these lines, you would have known how much I rejoice that such undertakings are going on in our time.
>   These lines are written to tell you that I ask you to regard me as a friend of this work, which I hope may be richly blessed, as a warm friend.

> Albert Schweitzer

The principle of the Good Samaritan, the life-saving service, was to be the central feature of our work. Young people were to learn not to destroy life, but to save it—be in readiness to help, and to have the ability to put such willingness into practice whenever it was necessary. For this reason Weissenhaus (a life-saving station of the German Society for the Rescue of the Shipwrecked) was selected as the place most suitable for the first *Kurzschule* in Germany and despite occasional difficulties, this has remained the case. Graf Platen, the owner of Weissenhaus, is in charge of the station. He is head of the local fire brigade and also the elected dike-reeve. The *Kurzschule* works together with the fire brigade and takes an active part in the work of the life-boat station. Physical training is the essential pre-requisite for any serious participation in life-saving, and it should therefore occupy a correspondingly important position in the school curriculum, together with seamanship, first aid, environmental studies, social and physical sciences, and study groups dealing with the problems of general interest, political and non-political. The ability to live and to work together, in the community and for the community, is a guiding factor in every field of the school's activities. The boys are allocated to groups of ten to twelve. In accordance with maritime terminology, these groups are called 'watches', and each one includes an adult as Leader of the Watch, and a Senior Watch Member who is elected by the boys as their representative. The boys spend most of their time within the watch. The members of a watch eat together; they receive their instruction together and compete against the members of other watches.

The running of the new *Kurzschule* presented its organizing body, the German Society for European Education, with many problems. Places had to be filled for each new course and as far as possible two-thirds had to be occupied by apprentices from industrial undertakings and one-third by school pupils, including a few pupils from abroad, if possible. Teachers had to be available to take charge of the watches, and the necessary finances had to be forthcoming to cover all these requirements.

To fill all the places proved at first to be extremely difficult. Some ninety to ninety-five places were available for each course. This represented eight watches, and more than 800 boys were to participate during one year. The need for a central office responsible for recruitment and publicity soon became apparent. Industrial, trade and commercial circles had at first shown little understanding of the new venture, and some had even rejected it, but gradually it gained support from one or two convinced and enlightened industrialists who spread their enthusiasm. There were difficulties for the school pupils. Apart from the two holiday months of July and August, when some parents sent their children privately, a four weeks' absence from school seemed unjustifiable. A few courageous schools and parents were prepared to take the risk of absence. But there were nine courses a year and for each one of them the necessary number of participants had to be found.

The Head of the Secondary Schools Department in the Schleswig-Holstein Ministry of Education, *Ministerialrat* Möhlmann, who had also taken part in that memorable conference in Gordonstoun and who subsequently, until the time of his death, was Chairman of the German Society for European Education, ventured to take a step which could almost be described as revolutionary. He arranged for the secondary schools of Schleswig-Holstein to send whole classes to Weissenhaus during term-time, which meant that absence from school affected all alike. In one school there were two parallel classes, one less successful than the other. The poorer class was sent to Weissenhaus, and the amazing outcome was that this class achieved much better results at the school-leaving examination (*Abitur*) than did the other one which originally had been superior and which had not visited the *Kurzschule*. A newly acquired determination to learn, which had been developed in Weissenhaus, and a new vitality had significantly changed the class and more than compensated for the lessons which had been missed. This isolated instance created a precedent—more and more schools sent whole classes to the *Kurzschule*, not only from Schleswig-Holstein, but also from several other Federal states. In 1965 a total of more than 200 was reached. The filling of the available places thus became less difficult, although publicity was still necessary. Considerable opposition, which was in part based on the unfounded suspicion that the *Kurzschule* was encouraging para-military training, had to be overcome by a series of careful and tedious counteractions.

The appointment of suitable teachers was another important task. After two years, Professor Dr Christiansen-Weniger had the honour of being summoned to a position in the German Embassy in Ankara, and after his departure, which was much regretted, the headship of the school was held successively by teachers from Schleswig-Holstein, Hesse and Hamburg. Seven permanent members of staff are employed in Weissenhaus, teaching seamanship, fire-precautions, first aid and the biology of the local area. In addition, from three to five assistant teachers are employed on a temporary basis for each course. These are mostly young student teachers. They are given leave of absence from their parent state authorities in order to work closely with the young people in the *Kurzschule* and thus gain educational experience. Well over 200 such young teachers have been to Weissenhaus, and have been able to make use of these experiences in their subsequent school teaching. By such means the methods of the *Kurzschule* pass to the secondary schools—a process which will continue.

The financing of the work of the *Kurzschule* continued to be a difficult problem—much more difficult than, for example, in Great Britain, where the existence of a large number of public schools had

36   Rescue practice during a winter course at Baad

37 A night expedition with firebrands at Baad

38 Training in life-saving and artificial respiration at Weissenhaus, the German Outward Bound School on the Baltic

created a more widespread understanding and appreciation of group education for the common weal. A course fee to be paid by the participants was fixed, which it was hoped would be high enough to balance the school finances, provided that the majority of places were occupied. It was clear that industrial undertakings would pay these fees provided that they considered the sending of participants to be in the interests of their training schemes. It was, however, not clear how best to handle the school class-groups, where the parents might find the cost of a uniform and fairly high course-fee an impossible imposition. However, the authorities provided grants to about one-third of the total requirements of a *Kurzschule*, and this enabled partial scholarships to be paid to some 40 per cent of the participants (school classes as well as private pupils). This important scheme differs from those in other countries. Without making any demands, the *Bundesjugendplan* (Federal Youth Budget) gives certain grants to centres of youth training which it considers worthy. Even though administrative and bureaucratic points of view in the course of the years have often caused difficulty and anxieties over the allocation and distribution of grants, one should not underestimate the degree of understanding and support which responsible authorities have shown for the work of the *Kurzschule*. I remember the early days of Weissenhaus, and in particular I recall a discussion which had to be held near Bonn Railway Station at 6.30 a.m. in a somewhat grubby restaurant. The two persons involved were the seventy-year-old Dr Bäuerle, former Minister, Chairman of the German Society for European Education, and *Ministerialrat* Dr Lades, Head of Department, *Bundesjugendplan*. They met to discuss the possibility of grants for the *Kurzschule*, although no concrete results of the work of the school were then available. Both men had, however, been to Gordonstoun, and they had clearly recognized the value of Outward Bound. Summarizing, it may be said that the *Kurzschulen* in Germany receive some two-thirds of their income from participants' fees and one-third from state grants and private contributions.

The development of Weissenhaus made steady progress. Participation increased in the years 1953 to 1965 from 608 to the maximum number possible of 858 boys. Applications for places increased in some months to such an extent that many had to be rejected. To stimulate interest by all available means and then to be unable to accept all the applicants, represented, of course, a serious situation.

More serious, however, was the danger that the *Kurzschule* Weissenhaus should come to be regarded in Germany simply as an experiment.

This consideration led to the decision of the German Society for European Education to start another *Kurzschule* closely associated with mountains and mountain-climbing, just as the existing one had maritime associations. Once again it seemed scarcely possible to find the initial finance for the scheme, but again American friends came to our assistance and the understanding attitude of the *Bundesjugendplan* was a further aid. After the suitability of some sixty different locations had been considered within a period of a few months, the second German *Kurzschule* was opened on 1 August 1956 at BAAD in the Klein Walsertal Allgäuer Alps—this time a mountaineering school. Once again life-saving and service to the community was to form the central feature of the work. In Baad also, close co-operation with the local rescue services was assured from the outset. Mountain-climbing and mountain rescue work in summer and skiing and rescue exercises in winter supplanted seamanship and sea rescue, while fire service, first aid, sport, social science and local studies were included in the curriculum as at Weissenhaus. A highly-organized four-day mountain tour replaced the protracted cutter excursion on the high seas. Of the nine courses held each year, four are specifically winter courses and five are summer courses.

The distribution of places in the new school was to correspond more or less to that in Weissenhaus, but the filling of all the places seemed at first to be somewhat hazardous. Nevertheless, increasing interest led as early as 1962 to an extension of the school by the acquisition of a building which happened to become vacant, and the annual capacity was thus raised from 850 places to 1,080. The records show a total of 1,094 boys in Baad in 1964. Again applications had to be rejected and others entered on a waiting list, and in some cases all that could be done was to express the hope of a place in the following year. Inevitably another school had to be established in order to meet the increasing demand. In accordance with Kurt Hahn's educational principles, this school also will concentrate on readiness and willingness to help and it will be run in a manner consistent with the maxim of all German *Kurzschulen*, which is engraved on the ship's bell at Weissenhaus: 'Service to one's neighbour, service to peace.'

Of 26,000 who have been through the German Outward Bound schools up until the end of 1969, 14,000 have been to Weissenhaus and 12,000 to Baad, and of these the greatest numbers are aged between sixteen and eighteen, though some are as young as fourteen, and others as old as twenty-two. Two-thirds of the total number come from industry: apprentices, labourers and clerks, with a few employed in the professions; the remaining third come from the schools.

In 1965 the German Society for European Education began to extend the Outward Bound education to include girls. Two experimental courses each year—one winter and one summer course—were carried out near Baad in Hirschegg (Kl. Walsertal). Because of the limited space available, it was only possible to take four groups—about 50 participants—in the course. The programme of instruction was modified in a suitable manner for girls. Particular efforts were made to encourage the participants to take on common tasks, with a sensible distribution of the work and in a spirit of mutual respect and fairness, and to show how one can meaningfully employ one's abilities when it is a matter of helping oneself to stand by someone in need, or when one has to look after a person with whom one has been entrusted. The instruction in first aid was made more intensive. There was a stronger emphasis of the cultural. Each group had the task of performing a small play. Discussions in small groups and exercises in free speaking completed the programme. The results of these first experimental courses with girls have been successful beyond our expectations, and suggest that it is desirable to continue with them. For these reasons, the third German Outward Bound school, which it was possible to open in the spring of 1968 in BERCH-TESGADEN at the foot of the Untersberg, in magnificent countryside, will include each year three courses for girls in its programme. In addition to the courses for boys, which will be similar to those carried out in Baad, the new school will take several international courses with French or British participants. All of this is further evidence of the extent to which Kurt Hahn's educational principles encourage and, indeed, demand further expansion and development.

Bibliography

Karl Schwarz

There is no central archive for the collection of literature on the educational theories of Kurt Hahn. The present Bibliography has been compiled over many years and with constant attention to new publications. It also takes into account private material collected by individual schools. The Bibliography contains publications in books and periodicals as well as *some* privately printed works and unprinted material. Short reports in daily newspapers have been omitted.

I would like to thank Kurt Hahn and his secretary, Henriette von Arnswaldt, who both took great trouble in checking and revising part I of the Bibliography with me. Remarks in [ ] are my own comments or quotations to help the reader appreciate the main contents of an article or book and its importance in revealing Kurt Hahn's thought and action.

I HAHN'S SPEECHES AND WRITINGS

1908

'Gedanken über Erziehung', Referat im Philosophischen Seminar von Leonard Nelson in Göttingen, Winter 1908–9, ergänzt durch einen Aufsatz aus dem Jahre 1913, *Die Antike*, Berlin/Leipzig (Gruyter), Vol. 4, No. 2, 1928, 138–60. Also published in Kurt Hahn, *Erziehung zur Verantwortung*, Stuttgart, 1958, 9–27.

1909

'Gedanken über Erziehung', Studentenarbeit [not identical with the article of 1908], *Die Pädagogische Hochschule*, Bühl, 1930, 2. Jg., No. 1, 52–64.

1910

Frau Elses Verheissung, Erzählung., München (Albert Langen), 1910, 174 pp. [Interpretation by Karl Schwarz 'Kurt Hahn's educational Poem' in *Pädagogische Rundschau*, 1968, No. 9.]

1916

'Englands Kriegswille im Lichte der Englischen Presse', Vortrag gehalten am 20. November 1916 in der *Deutschen Gesellschaft* von 1914, *Preussische Jahrbücher*, ed. H. Delbrück, Berlin, Januar/März 1917, Vol. 1,967, 1–41.

1927

Co-operation, New edition by Golo Mann and Andreas Burckhardt, Stuttgart, Klett, 1968 (slightly shortened). Authorized translation by W. M. Calder and C. W. H. Sutton, under the title: *The Memoirs of Prince Max of Baden*, London, Constable, 1928, Vol. I, 389 pp.; Vol. 2, 408 pp.

1928

'Die Nationale Aufgabe der Landerziehungsheime', Referat auf einer Heimleiterbesprechung der Landerziehungsheime in Frankfurt, 1928, *Die Eiche*, ed. F. Siegmund-Schulze, Gotha (Klotz), 19. Jg., No. 3, 1931, 319–34. Also published in *Die Pädagogische Hochschule*, Bühl, 1930, 2. Jg., No. 1, 65–72 (only Parts I–V of the article). Also published in K. Hahn, *Erziehung zur Verantwortung*, Stuttgart, 1958, 28–43.
'The Problem of Citizenship in German Education' ('Die nationale Aufgabe der Landerziehungsheime', trans. into English). Salem, 2 July 1928. Stuttgart (Deutsche Verlagsanstalt), n.d., 26 pp.

1929

'Prinz Max von Baden' [Nachruf], *Schule Schloss Salem*, No. 9, Autumn 1929, 5–7.

1930

The Seven Laws of Salem (*Salem Album*) [with genuine photographs of Salem], 1930. Reprinted privately, n.d., 17 pp. [contains: 'The Seven Laws of Salem'; 'Reproduction of Kurt Hahn's Film Lecture'; 'Appeal'].

1932

'Rundschreiben an die Eltern unserer Kinder vom 9. Juli 1932'. Also included in booklet: *Salem*, Langensalza [1933], 48–50. Printed as manuscript.

'Das Programm von Salem'. Eine Entgegnung von Kurt Hahn im Berliner Tageblatt [reply to an article, 'Von Goethe zum Parademarsch', about Salem in *Berliner Tageblatt*. 30 August, 1932], *Berliner Tageblatt*, 14 October 1932. Also included in booklet: *Salem*, Langensalza [1933], 51–4. Printed as manuscript.

1933

'Benachrichtigung, Stellungnahmen und Entgegnungen Hahns in der Bodensee-Rundschau März 1933 aus Anlass seiner Verhaftung' [a particularly important article of 8 March 1933]. Privately printed, Salem, 8 March 1933, 4 pp.

'Staatsbürgerliche Erziehung'. [Speech made in Hamburg about Fascism and its impact on the young, and the consequences to be expected in Germany; typewritten], 16 February 1933 [similar speeches made in Berlin and Göttingen].

The Roots of the Nazi Movement, survey written in the summer of 1933. Privately printed, confidential, 16 pp.; only 25 copies printed. [The following preface added later: 'Written under two illusions: I thought then that Hitler was only the condoner of cruelties. I now know he is the instigator. I then believed Hitler wanted nothing more than to right the wrongs inflicted on Germany. There is no doubt the Napoleonic ambition was burning within him already then, and only became manifest before Munich.']

1934

'A German Public School', a broadcast, *The Listener*, London, 17 January 1934, 39–41.

Letter to the Editors of the paper called *Gordonstoun News* (8 October 1934), *Gordonstoun News*, No. 2, 26 October 1934. Reprinted in A. Arnold-Brown, *Unfolding Character*, London 1962, 22–3.

'The Practical Child and the Bookworm', broadcast of November 1934, *The Listener*, London, 28 November 1934. Also privately printed, Aberdeen (University Press), n.d., 14 pp.

1935

Report at Annual Meeting of British Salem Schools Ltd. in London on 17 July 1935, in *British-Salem Schools Ltd.*, London, Electric Law Press [1935], 11–19.

1936

Education and the Foundations of Peace, talk to the Elgin Rotary Club, March 1936, Inverness: Carruthers & Sons, n.d., 4 pp.
'Fitness of the Young: Procedure at Salem', to the Editor of *The Times* (written 1 November 1936), *The Times*, London, 3 November 1936.
An Appeal, Elgin, November 1936, privately printed, 8 pp. Also published in K. Hahn, *Ten Years of Gordonstoun*, Welshpool [1944], 8–9.
'The Responsibilities and Opportunities for the Training of Citizens', talk to the Association of Directors of Education in Scotland, 1936. Extracts in K. Hahn, *Ten Years of Gordonstoun*, Welshpool [1944], 6–7.

1937

'Seamanship', 1937, in K. Hahn, *Ten Years of Gordonstoun*, Welshpool [1944], Appendix II, 27–9.

1938

Education for Leisure, read to the Conference of Schoolmasters and College Tutors at Magdalen College, Oxford, 6 January 1938, London: Oxford University Press, 1938, 20 pp.
'A Badge for Fitness', letter to *The Times*. *The Times*, London, 5 April 1938. Also published in K. Hahn, *The County Badge*, Welshpool, 30 May 1940, 15.
'Fitness Leadership', a talk given by Kurt Hahn at Dunblane, 19 November 1938, to the National Fitness Council for Scotland, in K. Hahn, *The County Badge*, Welshpool, 30 May 1940, 44–6.
Copy of Report to the Chairman of the Governors of Gordonstoun School, Sir Alexander Lawrence, Bart., 9 November 1938. In K. Hahn, *The County Badge*, Welshpool, 30 May 1940, 43–4.
'From Boarding School to Training Home' [articles and letters written in 1938, with an introductory note, December 1938], in K. Hahn, *The County Badge*, Welshpool, 30 May 1940, 35–47 (Appendix).

1939

'Christian Peace Procedure', *Spectator*, London, 15 December 1939, No. 5,816, 860–1.

1940

The County Badge, 30 May 1940, Welshpool: Montgomery County Times Printers, 47 pp.
The Love of Enterprise. The Love of Aloneness. The Love of Skill (The Liverpool Address), the First Lecture in the New Portion of Liverpool Cathedral, 22 December 1940, at 3 p.m., privately printed, 12 pp.

'Gordonstoun muss Seinen Standort Wechseln', Ansprache auf einer Elternkonferenz in London für die Eltern der Schüler Gordonstouns. Die Krisis im Mai 1940. In K. Hahn, *Erziehung zur Verantwortung*, Stuttgart, 1938, 44–9.
'The Urn' [about the beginnings of Salem School, with an excellent description of the first Salem hockey team; partly reprinted in Hahn's talk on his eightieth birthday], 4 pp. [typewritten] [1940].

1941

The Badge. From an Address at the Annual Conference of the National Association of Physical Education, London, September 1941, Liverpool: A. W. Duncan, n.d., 14 pp.

1942

Pre-service Training. Compulsion? Attraction? Persuasion? A Criticism of the Conservative Sub-Committee's Report on Education, October 1942, Elgin, 1942, 11 pp.

1943

Two Sermons, 1943, Elgin 1943; reprinted 1944. Limited to 500 copies for private distribution only, 20 pp. [contains: 'Quinquagesima', 1–11, and 'Empire Youth Sunday', 12–20].
Quinquagesima, 1943. Eine Laienpredigt, gehalten in der Kathedrale von Liverpool ['Quinquagesima' trans. into German]. Privately printed, n.d., 11 pp. Also published in K. Hahn, *Erziehung zur Verantwortung*, Stuttgart, 1958, under the title 'Über das Mitleid'.

1944

Ten Years of Gordonstoun. An Account and an Appeal, Welshpool: County Times Printers [1944], 28 pp. Confidential. For private circulation only.
Evidence. 1944. Privately printed, 23 pp. Confidential [contains: 'Report of 29th October 1943'; 'Report of 17 February. Hitler's Speech. Analysis'; 'Report of 9th August 1944. The Plot'].

1945

Diary from 5th May to 16th May 1945, Plas Dinam/Montgomeryshire, 1945. For private circulation only, 18 pp.

1946

The State of the Young in Germany. Impressions gathered on a Journey through Germany in April 1946. Inverness: R. Carruthers, July 1946, 16 pp.

1947

Training for and through the Sea. Address given to the Honourable Master
  Mariners' Company in Glasgow on 20 February 1947, Elgin, 1947,
  10 pp.
Erziehung durch und für die See (*Training for and through the Sea* trans.
  into German). Ansprache gehalten bei einem Zusammentreffen der
  Honourable Master Mariners' Company in Glasgow am 20. Februar
  1947. Privately printed, n.d., Konstanz, 10 pp. Also published in K.
  Hahn, *Erziehung zur Verantwortung*, Stuttgart, 1958, 57–63.
Active Citizenship: an Address to the Elgin Rotary Club, Elgin, 1947,
  10 pp.
'Bürgersinn' (*Active Citizenship*, trans. into German by Lina Richter).
  Vortrag im Elgin Rotary Club am 15. Mai 1947. *Die Sammlung*,
  Göttingen, 2. Jg., No. 9, 1947, 497–501.

1948

The Protection of Adolescents. Reprinted from *Health Horizon* from their
  issue of October 1948. Aberdeen: University Press, n.d., 7 pp.
'Lob der Einsamkeit'. Aus einem Vortrag in Oxford. *Die Zeit*, Hamburg,
  3. Jg., No. 7, 12 February 1948, 5.
A Memorandum. New York, May 1948, 38 pp. [with documentary texts
  and illustrations].

1949

The Loyalties by which we live: address given on 13 January 1949 at a
  Conference on Rural Life at Home and Overseas, held under the
  auspices of the Church Missionary Society at High Leigh, Hoddeston,
  Herts. Aberdeen: University Press, 1949, 8 pp.
'A Letter to Bishop Lilje'. Gordonstoun School, Elgin, January 1949.
  Inverness, n.d., confidential.
Additional Memorandum. New York, May 1949, 7 pp.
'The Decline of Democracy': talk at the 60th Annual Meeting of the
  Parents' National Educational Union held on Thursday, 26 May 1949,
  at Bishop Partridge Hall, Church House, Westminster, *The Parents'*
  Review, London, Vol. LX, No. 12, December 1949, 275–83.
'Der Niedergang der Demokratie' ('The Decline of Democracy', trans.
  into German), Vortrag gehalten bei Jubiläum der 'Parents' National
  Educational Union', *Die Sammlung*, Göttingen, 10. Jg., No. 11,
  November 1955, 544–9.

1950

Aims and Obstacles, broadcast B.B.C., London, 22 October 1950.

Aberdeen: University Press, 1950, 8 pp. Also published in *The Listener*. London, 16 November 1950, under the title 'An Experiment in Education'.

1951

Gästehaus in Gordonstoun. Privately printed [1951], 1 p. 'Ein Weg zur Heilung der Jugend', Rettungsdienst und Kurzschule (written 10 May 1951), *Jugendrotkreuz Informationsdienst*, Bonn, No. 14, December 1951, 5–6.

1952

'Kurzschulen', *Neue Zürcher Zeitung*. Zürich, No. 492, 6 March 1952, 7. [The first half of this article is a reprint of 'Ein Weg zur Heilung der Jugend', 1951.] Reprinted in *Freundliches Begegnen*, Düsseldorf, 2. Jg., No. 8, 1952, 4–6 (shortened).

Short-term Schools ('Kurzschulen', trans. into English), Aberdeen: University Press, n.d., 10 pp. [with a few alterations].

1953

'Rückblick' (*Aims and Obstacles*, trans. into German): Rundfunkvortrag gehalten in London (B.B.C.) am 22 Oktober 1950 [with a new Introduction in the German version], *Die Sammlung*, Göttingen, 8. Jg., No. 12, December 1953, 573–9. Also published in K. Hahn, *Erziehung zur Verantwortung*, Stuttgart, 1958, 63–9. Also published in W. Flitner/ G. Kudritzki, *Die Deutsche Reformpädagogik*, Vol. I, Düsseldorf and München: Küpper, 1961, 93–8 (shortened).

1954

'Gordonstoun and a European Mission', in *American-British-Foundation for European Education*; privately printed, January 1954, 30–9.

'The Hydrogen Bomb: Relevance of Geneva Protocol', a letter to *The Times* (written, Salem, 7 April 1954), *The Times*, London, 10 April 1954. Reprinted in *Warnings*, Plaistow, 1959, 1–3.

'Talk at Outward Bound Conference', Ashorne Hill [2 and 3 October 1954]. 4 pp. [typewritten].

Hoffnungen und Sorgen: Vortrag vor den Salemer Lehrern, November 1954; privately printed [1955], 23 pp. [This version is not identical with *Hopes and Fears*.]

'Erziehung zur Verantwortung': Vortrag in Duisburg am 28. Oktober 1954. *Die Sammlung*, Göttingen, 11. Jg., May 1956, 246–58. Also published in *Jugendrotkreuz und Erzieher*, Karlsruhe, 9. Jg., No. 6, June 1957, 1–3, under the title 'Die Jugend und der Rettungsgedanke' (extracts). Also published in K. Hahn, *Erziehung zur Verantwortung*, Stuttgart, 1958, 70–81. Also published in K. Klinger/G. Rutz (ed.), *Die Tagesheimschule*, Frankfurt/M, 1964, 65–77.

1955

'The Development of Character': Lecture delivered on 7 October 1955 at the N.A.T.O. Defence College, Course 8 [typewritten], 23 pp. [with an Afterword by Air Marshal Darvall, 23–4].

1956

'The H-Bomb' [not identical with article 'The Hydrogen Bomb', 1954], in *News Chronicle*, London, 23 February 1956. Also published in *Warnings*, Plaistow, 1959, 14–17.

1957

Hoffnungen und Sorgen eines Landerziehungsheims: Rundfunkvortrag, gehalten im Süddeutschen Rundfunk am 30. Mai 1957, Hamburg: Gruner, 1957, 16 pp. Also published in *Die Zeit*, Hamburg, 12. Jg., No. 26, 27 June 1957, 19, under the title 'Stoff pauken genügt nicht' (extracts). Also published in *Deutsches Rotes Kreuz*, Lübeck, No. 9, September 1957, 8–11. Also published in K. Hahn, *Erziehung zur Verantwortung*, Stuttgart, 1958, 82–93 (slightly shortened). Also published in *Contact*, Köln, 2. Jg., No. 7, July 1962, 56, under the title 'Erziehung durch Erlebnistherapie' (extracts).

'Outward Bound' [history of the Outward Bound movement up to 1957], in *The Year Book of Education, 1957*, ed. G. Z. F. Bereday and J. A. Lauwerys, Yonkers-on-Hudson, N.Y. 1957, 436–62. Also published in D. James (ed.), *Outward Bound*, London, 1957, 1–17, under the title 'Origins of the Outward Bound Trust' (extracts from Part I; in particular, from 436–49).

Speech at a meeting held at Admiralty House on Thursday, 21 November 1957, sponsored by the London Committee of the Friends of Gordonstoun. Privately printed under the title, *Gordonstoun. Speeches at a Meeting*, n.d., 6–14.

'Hommage à Jean Walter' [obituary notes on Jean Walter, Founder of the Zellidja scholarships], *Espaces Zellidja*, Paris, 1957, Numéro spécial, 12–13.

1958

'Survival of Public Schools', broadcast B.B.C. Overseas Service, 3 January 1958 [typewritten], 3 pp. Also in *The Listener*, London, January 1958. *Erziehung zur Verantwortung: Reden und Aufsätze*, Stuttgart: Klett [1958,

1959, 1963], 100 pp. (Serie: *Aus den deutschen Landerziehungsheimen*, Vol. 2).

'The Atlantic Colleges', address at the Plenary Session of the Atlantic Community Conference at Bruges, September 1957, *Time and Tide*, London, 8 February 1958.

'Ein Europäischer Schulplan', Atlantik-Schulen der Nationalitäten ('The Atlantic Colleges', trans. into German). Rede auf der Plenarsitzung der Atlantischen Konferenz in Brügge im September 1957, *Der Europäische Osten*, München, 5. Jg., No. 51, January 1959, 39–43.

'Die nationale und internationale Aufgabe der Erziehung', Vortrag gehalten am 22. April 1958 vor den Mitgliedern des Industrie-Clubs Düsseldorf, *SV-Schriftenreihe zur Förderung der Wissenschaft*, Essen-Bredeney, 7. Jg., No. 5, 1958, 39 pp.

1959

Address at the Forty-eighth Annual Dinner of Old Centralians, Grocers' Hall, London, 17 November 1958, *The Central* (the Journal of Old Centralians), London, No. 119, February 1959, 3–8.

Replies to a Questionnaire prepared by a Committee on which Lord Evans serves [Hahn's first contacts with British physicians in regard to later projects], 10 April 1959 [typewritten], 5 pp.

The Respite, 8 July 1959 [Geneva Conference, June 1959]; privately printed, 12 pp.

Preface to *In Memory of Ralph Noel Pocock*, London: Curwen Press, 1959, vii–viii [edition of letters and writings by Pocock, died 1949].

1938–1959: a comparison; privately printed, 8 pp.

'Juvenile Irresponsibility', written in October 1959, *Gordonstoun Record*, Serial No. 42, Annual No. 6, 1961, 12–19. Also published in the *Sunday Telegraph*, London, 2 April 1961, under the title 'A Cure for the Lawless Young' (extracts).

'Education and Changes in Our Social Structure': speech delivered at the BACIE National Conference, September 1959. *BACIE Journal*, London, Vol. 14, No. 1, March 1960, 5–16.

Warnings, Plaistow: Curwen Press, May 1959. For private circulation. In an edition of 100 copies, 22 pp. [a collection of several articles printed and unprinted, mainly political comments].

1960

Outward Bound (the Moral Equivalent of War): address at the Annual Meeting of the Outward Bound Trust on 20 July 1960. Issued by the Outward Bound Trust, London: Watford Printers, 1960, 8 pp.

'Die List des Gewissens': Widmung an Minna Specht, in H. Becker/

W. Eichler/G. Heckmann (ed.), *Erziehung und Politik*, Minna Specht zu ihrem 80. Geburtstag, Frankfurt/M. (Öffentliches Leben), 1960, 311–316.

'The Ruse of Conscience' ('Die List des Gewissens', trans. into English; slightly shortened in the beginning), *Gordonstoun Record*, Serial No. 41, Annual No. 5, 1960, 27–9.

'Planbild einer Pädagogischen Provinz', in G. Brummer/E. Strübel (ed.), *Bodenseebuch 1960*, No. 37. Kreuzlingen: Bodan A.G., 1960, 106–24 (a slightly altered version of *Die Nationale und Internationale Aufgabe der Erziehung*, 1958).

'Saving Life', letter to the Editor. *The Times Educational Supplement*, London, 51st year, No. 2366, 23 September 1960, 363.

1961

'Wunschtraum oder Wirklichkeit?', October 1961 [typewritten], 8 pp. [the German problem and ways to its solution].

'Pipe-dream or Reality?' October 1961 ('Wunschtraum oder Wirklichkeit', trans. into English). 8 pp. [typewritten].

'The Decline of the West offers a Diagnosis and a Cure: A Challenge to Youth', talk to the Directors and Senior Staff of the Bourneville Works, in April 1961, *Bourneville Works Magazine*, Bourneville, Vol. LIX, No. 8, August 1961, 287–91. Reprinted under the title *Service by Youth*, Bourneville, 1961, 8 pp.

1962

Talk on Atlantic Colleges at the Sheffield Lunch on 12 November 1962, in *Atlantic Colleges* [1963], 8–13.

'Unnecessary Deaths', *The Listener*, London, Vol. 67, No. 1,726, 26 April 1962, 715–16.

'The Rev. A. G. Fraser' [obituary], *Gordonstoun Record*, Serial No. 43, Annual No. 7, 1962, 14.

'Der Jugend zu schützenden Gewohnheiten helfen, Brief an die Herausgeber', *Frankfurter Allgemeine Zeitung*, Frankfurt/M., No. 147, 28 June 1962, p. 8. Also published in *Die Taube*. Familienblatt für die Mitglieder der Hofrat Sackschen Stiftung, 63. Jg., No. 128, Autumn 1962.

'Erziehung und die Krise der Demokratie', Festvortrag anlässlich der Verleihung des Freiherr-vom-Stein-Preises 1962 am 11. Juli in Hamburg, in *Freiherr-vom-Stein-Preis 1962*, ed. Stiftung F. V. S. zu Hamburg, Hamburg [1963], 19–44.

'Verfall und Heilung der Jugend', Beilage zu: *Informationen für die Truppe*, Bonn, 1962, No. 4 (shortened version of 'Die nationale und internationale Aufgabe der Erziehung', 1958).

'*The Aristocracy of Service*', talk at the County Hall, Maidstone, Kent, on 17 October 1962. Konstanz: Verlag am Fischmarkt, n.d., 20 pp.

'State of the Young in England', B.B.C. talk, July 1962, *The Listener*, London, July 1962.

1963

'Schulen die Erziehen', Gespräch mit Kurt Hahn, *Der Anruf*, Mitteilungen des Brüderlichen Kreises, Hamburg, 11. Jg., No. 55, March 1963, 17–19.

1964

'Reform der Erziehung und der Schulen, in *Führung und Bildung in der heutigen Welt*, herausgegeben zum 60. Geburtstag von Minsterpräsident Georg Kiesinger, Stuttgart: Deutsche Verlagsanstalt, 1964, 381–6.

1965

The Young and the Outcome of the War, the Essex Hall Lecture, 1965, London: The Lindsay Press, 1965, 32 pp.; reprinted 1965 [lecture at the University College of Swansea during the Annual Meetings of the General Assembly of Unitarian and Free Christian Churches].

Outward Bound, address at the Conference at Harrogate on 9 May 1965, London: Watford Printers; issued by the Outward Bound Trust, 7 pp.

'Erziehung zum Helfen', Vortrag auf der Erziehertagung des Jugendrotkreuzes in Ulm (10–12 June 1965), *Jugendrotkreuz und Erzieher*, Pforzheim, 18. Jg., January 1966, No. 1, 3–5, and February 1966, No. 2, 21–3.

1966

'Erinnerungen und Ausblicke', 5. 6. 1966. Eine Rede, die zum Teil gehalten und zum Teil nicht gehalten wurde; in *80. Geburtstag Kurt Hahn*, Ravensburg [1967], 39–56.

1967

'After the War', letter to *The Times*, 8 July 1967 [comments on the war in the Near East].

1969

'Drug Addiction', letter to *The Times*, 23 September 1969.

II   BIOGRAPHICAL WRITINGS AND APPRECIATIONS

ARMYTAGE, W. H. G., *The German Influence on English Education*, London: Routledge & Kegan Paul, 1969, ch. 9.

ARNOLD-BROWN, ADAM, *Unfolding Character. The Impact of Gordonstoun*, London: Routledge & Kegan Paul, 1962, 246 pp.
—— 'Der Einfluss von Abbotsholme' [upon Kurt Hahn], in Röhrs (ed.), *Bildung als Wagnis und Bewährung*, Heidelberg, 1966, 182–8.
BAUMANN, OTTO, 'Kurt Hahns 70. Geburtstag', *Schule Schloss Salem*, No. 36, 1956–7, 1–3.
BECKER, HELLMUT, 'Kurt Hahn zwischen Kindern und Erwachsenen', *Neue Sammlung*, Göttingen, 6. Jg., No. 3, May/June 1966, 262–5. Reprinted in Röhrs (ed.), *Bildung als Wagnis und Bewährung*, Heidelberg, 1966, 98–101.
B[EER], B[RIGITTE], 'Kurt Hahn 80 Jahre', *Frankfurter Allgemeine Zeitung*, Frankfurt/M., No. 128, 4 June 1966, 2.
BERTHOLD, MARKGRAF VON BADEN, *Kurt Hahn 70 Jahre*: Festrede im Kaisersaal vor versammelter Schule und Gästen am 5. Juni 1956 in Salem, privately printed, 11 pp. [1956].
BONDY, BARBARA, 'Der Gründer von Salem wird fünfundsiebzig', *Süddeutsche Zeitung*, München, 5 June 1961.
BREZINKA, WOLFGANG, 'Hahn, Kurt', *Lexikon der Pädagogik*, ed. Deutsches Institut für wiss. Pädagogik Münster and Institut für vergleichende Erziehungswissenschaft, Salzburg, Freiburg: Herder, 1953, Vol. II, cols. 568–9.
EDINBURGH, DUKE OF, 'Kurt Hahn. Laureation Address', 4 November 1953, University of Edinburgh, Honorary Degree of Laws, privately printed, 2 pp.
FENN, ANTHONY, 'Plato's Principles of Moral Education' [and Kurt Hahn's ideas in Gordonstoun, L'Ecole des Roches, Outward Bound School Baad], *Gordonstoun Record*, Serial No. 41, Annual No. 5, 1960, 35–44.
FLITNER, WILHELM, 'Hommage à Kurt Hahn', *Pädagogische Rundschau*, Ratingen, 21. Jg., No. 7, July 1968.
HAHN, BEATE, 'Herkunft und Tradition der Familie Kurt Hahns', *Pädagogische Rundschau*, Ratingen, 20. Jg., No. 6, June 1966, 580–7.
HARBINGER, IRENE, 'Ein deutsch-englischer Pädagoge: Kurt Hahn und seine Schulen', *Englische Rundschau*, Köln, 1953, No. 35, 446.
HASSELHORN, MARTIN, *Kurt Hahn und die Salemer Erziehung*: Eine Studie über Kurt Hahn und die Salemer Pädagogik von 1920 bis 1923, Schloss Spetzgart bei Überlingen (Photoprint), 1964, 61 pp.
HECKSTALL-SMITH, HUGH, *Doubtful Schoolmaster*, London: P. Davies, 1962, 195 pp.
HEISE, HEINRICH, 'Schule und Leibeserziehung. Kurt Hahn zum 80. Geburtstag', *Westermanns Pädagogische Beiträge*, Braunschweig, 18. Jg., No. 12, December 1966, 547–59.
HENTIG, HARTMUT VON, 'Kurt Hahn und die Pädagogik', in H. Röhrs (ed.), *Bildung als Wagnis und Bewährung*, Heidelberg, 1966, 41–82.

IBALD, L., 'Der Schulmeister von Salem. Kurt Hahn, der Pädagoge, Politiker und Diplomat', *Rheinischer Merkur*, Köln, No. 40, 2 October 1953, 8. Jg., 6.

International Who's Who, 'Hahn, Kurt', London, 1968–9, 536.

KÖPPEN, WERNER, 'Kurt Hahns 80. Geburtstag', *Pädagogische Rundschau*, Ratingen, 20. Jg., No. 9, September 1966, 844–5.

KRESS, O., 'Seiner Schwächen Herr werden, Kommentar zu einem Filmbericht über Kurt Hahn, seine Schulen und Schüler', Berlin: Provobis, 1963, 28 pp. [typewritten].

LANDAU-WEGNER, LOLA, 'Familie und Tradition' [of Kurt Hahn], in H. Röhrs (ed.), *Bildung als Wagnis und Bewährung*, Heidelberg, 1966, 102–7.

LARSEN, EGON, 'Ein grosser Erzieher: Dr Kurt Hahn', *Die Weltwoche*, Zürich, 30 December 1960, No. 1,416, 5.

—— 'Die hohe Schule der Lebensretter. Der grosse Erzieher Kurt Hahn will in Westeuropa "Atlantische Kollegs" gründen', *Süddeutsche Zeitung*, München, No. 297, December 1960.

LUES, HANS, 'Vorwort', in K. Hahn, *Erziehung zur Verantwortung*. Stuttgart [1958], 5–8.

—— 'Kurt Hahn—80 Jahre', *Louisenlund*, 1966 [school magazine], No. 2, 14.

LÜHE, IRMGARD VON DER, 'Erziehung zur Verantwortung', in I. v. d. Lühe, *Elisabeth von Thadden*, Düsseldorf/Köln: Diederichs, 1966, 85–96 and 190–1 [Thadden's co-operation with Kurt Hahn at Salem 1924–26, El. v. Thadden was killed by the Nazis in Berlin in 1944].

MANN, GOLO, 'Kurt Hahn als Politiker', *Neue Rundschau*. Berlin/Frankfurt/M., 76. Jg., No. 4, 590–622. Also published in H. Röhrs (ed.), *Bildung als Wagnis und Bewärhrung*, Heidelberg, 1966, 9–40. Also published in *Die Welt*, Hamburg, No. 128, 4 June 1966, ii (extracts).

—— 'Festrede' [at Hahn's 80th anniversary], in *80. Geburtstag Kurt Hahn*, Ravensburg [1967], 5–17.

MEISSNER, ERICH, 'The Headmaster, Dr. Kurt Hahn', *Gordonstoun Record*, No. 30, Summer 1953, 4–6.

—— *The Private Sphere in Education*: an address to the Staffs of Gordonstoun, Altyre, Aberlour and Wester Elchies, November 1954, Aberdeen: University Press, 1954, 27 pp. [based on Hahn's educational ideas].

—— 'Kurt Hahn. A Tribute on the Occasion of His 70th Birthday', *Gordonstoun Record*, No. 37, 1956, 14–18.

M[ÜLLER]-M[AREIN], J[OSEF], 'Ein Pädagoge aus Leidenschaft', *Die Zeit*, Hamburg, 21. Jg., No. 24, 10 June 1966, 4.

PADBERG, RUDOLF, 'Weckung der Urteilskraft und Entscheidungsfähigkeit', in R. Padberg, *Personaler Humanismus*, Paderborn: Schöningh, 1964, 184–6 [humanistic tendencies in Hahn's educational ideas].

PAECKELMANN, WOLFGANG, 'Kurt Hahn', *Leben und Arbeit*, Fulda. 1954, No. 1, 35–7.

RICHTER, LINA, 'Politiker und Erzieher', *Die Zeit*, Hamburg, 11. Jg., No. 22, 31 May 1956, 2.

RÖHRS, HERMANN (ed.), *Bildung als Wagnis und Bewährung*: Eine Darstellung des Lebenswerkes von Kurt Hahn, Heidelberg: Quelle & Meyer, 1966, 344 pp.

—— 'Die pädagogische Provinz im Geiste Kurt Hahns', in H. Röhrs (ed.), *Bildung als Wagnis und Bewährung*, Heidelberg, 1966, 83–97.

SANDERSLEBEN, RUDOLF VON, 'Die Geschichtsinnung von Herrn Hahn' [report of a boy on the working group on history, directed by Kurt Hahn in autumn 1953 at Salem], *Schule Schloss Salem*, No. 35, 1955–6, 28–9.

SCHWARZ, KARL, 'Die Aktualität in der Pädagogik Kurt Hahns', Pädagogische Prüfungsarbeit, Studienseminar Darmstadt, January 1963, 120 pp. [typewritten].

—— 'Die Pädagogik Kurt Hahns und die Leibesübungen', *Die Leibeserziehung*, Schorndorf, 12. Jg., No. 9, September 1963, 291–7.

—— 'Bibliographie zur Pädagogik Kurt Hahns', in H. Röhrs (ed.), *Bildung als Wagnis und Bewährung*, Heidelberg, 1966, 326–38.

—— 'Kurt Hahns pädagogisches Poem. Eine Analyse des Schulromans "Frau Elses Verheissung" ', *Pädagogische Rundschau*, Ratingen, 22. Jg., No. 9, September 1968, 534–43.

SIEVERTS, RUDOLF, 'Ansprache des Rektors der Universität Hamburg anlässlich der Verleihung des Freiherr-vom-Stein-Preises 1962 an Kurt Hahn', in *Freiherr-vom-Stein-Preis 1962*, ed. Stiftung F. V. S. zu Hamburg [1963], 7–18.

STEWART, W. A. C., *The Educational Innovators*, Vol. II, *Progressive Schools*, *1881–1967*, London: Macmillan, 1968, ch. 10.

[Unsigned] 'Biographische Notiz', in K. Hahn, *Erziehung zur Verantwortung*, Stuttgart, 1958, 94–7.

—— 'The Moral Equivalent', *Time*, New York, Vol. 51, No. 23, 7 June 1948, 73 (Domestic Edition) or 26 (Atlantic Edition).

—— 'An Educational Triumph' [K. Hahn received the Honorary Degree of Laws at the University of Edinburgh, 1953], *Gordonstoun Record*, No. 31, Autumn 1953, 7–14.

—— 'Das Porträt: Kurt Hahn', *Lebendige Erziehung*, München, 5. Jg., No. 10, October 1956, 241.

—— 'Character Builder', *The Observer*, London, 13 November 1960, 13.

—— 'Ein grosser Jugenderzieher. Besuch bei Dr. Kurt Hahn' ('Character Builder', trans. into German), *Englische Rundschau*. Köln, 10. Jg., No. 25, 2 December 1960, 392–3.

—— 'Tradition in Bewegung. Das Lebenswerk des Pädagogen Dr. Kurt Hahn', *Hamburger Abendblatt*, Hamburg, 15. Jg., 11 July 1962.

[Unsigned] 'Founder of Gordonstoun' [Hahn became C.B.E.], *Glasgow Herald*, Glasgow, 13 June 1964.
—— 'Honours for Kurt Hahn' [Hahn's eightieth birthday at Salem], *The Times Educational Supplement*, London, 56th year, No. 26,664, 10 June 1966, 1,830.
—— *80. Geburtstag Kurt Hahn*, Festreden und Ansprachen, Ravensburg: Holzschuh [1967], 56 pp. [contains all the speeches and addresses at Hahn's birthday celebration in the Kaisersaal at Salem].

III SALEM SCHOOL

ASBROCK, MARIANNE, 'Selbstlos derselben Sache dienen. Salems Schulen haben einen gemeinsamen Regelkodex', *Deutsche Zeitung*, Köln, 1959.
BERNSTORFF, HARTWIG, GRAF, VON, 'Bemerkungen über Salem', *Süddeutsche Zeitung*, München, 11 January 1964. Also privately printed [1964], 8 pp.
BERTHOLD, MARKGRAF VON BADEN (ed.), *Salem*, Den Salemer Eltern, die heute zu uns stehen. Langensalza (Beltz) [1933].
—— 'Rede zur Wiedereröffnung der Schule Schloss Salem [an extract] am 12. November 1945', *Schule Schloss Salem* [*Salem School Record*], No. 28, April 1949, 18–20.
BLENDINGER, HEINRICH, *Salem*, Die neue und die alte Schule, Lindau: Thorbecke Verlag, 1948, 38 pp.
—— 'Salemer Erziehung. Versuch einer "pädagogischen Provinz" '. In: Heinrich Blendinger (ed.): *Salem*. Lindau, 1948, 7–25.
—— 'Landerziehungsheime. Pädagogische Anregungen'. *Die Sammlung*, Göttingen, 3. Jg. 1948, 95–102.
BRERETON, HENRY, 'Journey to Salem. A Personal Chronicle'. In *Gordonstoun and Salem*. Ravensburg [1947], 39–52.
DISCH, HILDEGARD: 'Die Schule Schloss Salem in den Jahren 1933–1945'. *Schule Schloss Salem*, No. 28, April 1949, 3–18.
EWALD, MARINA, 'Der Aufban und Ausbau Salems (1919–1933)', in H. Röhrs (ed.), *Bildung als Wagnis und Bewährung*, Heidelberg, 1966, 108–26.
—— and ALTROGGE, HEINRICH, 'Bericht über die Zeit vom November 1945–September 1948', *Schule Schloss Salem*, No. 28, April 1949, 21–30.
FLÖRKE, WILHELM, 'Der Lehrgang und die Wissensvermittlung in Salem', in H. Röhrs (ed.), *Bildung als Wagnis und Bewährung*, Heidelberg, 1966, 165–71.
GEORG WILHELM, PRINZ VON HANNOVER, 'Die Salemer Internats-Schule', *Schule*, Offenburg, 1. Jg., No. 2/3, 1946, 36–9.

—— Das Wesen der Mitverantwortung in den Salemer Schulen, Vortrag bei der Elterntagung in Salem am 22. Mai 1952, Überlingen [1952], 12 pp.

—— Self-government in Salem (Das Wesen der Mitverantwortung in den Salemer Schulen, trans. from German into English), privately printed, 10 pp.

—— 'Salem', American-British Foundation for European Education, January 1954, privately printed, 21–9.

—— 'Der Wiederaufbau der Salemer Schulen nach dem Kriege', in H. Röhrs (ed.), Bildung als Wagnis und Bewährung, Heidelberg, 1966, 132–53.

GERSDORFF, HORST VON, 'Salem (Schülermitverantwortung)', in W. Schäfer (ed.), Schülermitverantwortung in den deutschen Landerziehungsheimen, Stuttgart: Klett [1964], 62–6.

GLAESER, OTTO, 'Die Salemer Klosterschule', Ein Vergleich, in H. Blendinger (ed.), Salem, Lindau, 1948, 27–38.

HÜBNER, KLAUS ACHIM, Salem, Idee, Aufgabe, Weg. Eine Informationsschrift über die Schulen Salems, hrsg. Alt-Salemer Vereinigung, Heidelberg, 1965, 40 pp.

KÖPPEN, MARIA, 'Aufgabe und Probleme der Juniorenschulen', in H. Röhrs (ed.), Bildung als Wagnis und Bewährung, Heidelberg, 1966, 154–64.

KÖPPEN, WERNER, Die Schule Schloss Salem in ihrer geschichtlichen Entwicklung und gegenwärtigen Gestalt, Ratingen: A. Henn, 1967, 202 pp.

KUPFFER, GERTRUD, 'Der Hermannsberger Versuch einer Neugestaltung des Tages- und Unterrichtsplanes an einem Landerziehungsheim', Bericht aus der Schloßschule Salem, Die Sammlung, Göttingen, 15. Jg., July/August 1960, No. 7/8, 400–13.

KUPFFER, HEINRICH, 'Die Periode der Anfechtung und Gefährdung (1933–1945)', in H. Röhrs (ed.), Bildung als Wagnis und Bewährung, Heidelberg, 1966, 127–31.

LENNERT, RUDOLF, 'Salem im Rahmen der Landerziehungsheime', in H. Röhrs (ed.), Bildung als Wagnis und Bewährung, Heidelberg, 1966, 172–81.

LÜTGENHORST, MANFRED, 'Kennen Sie Salem?' (photographs by Will McBride), Twen, München, 4. Jg., No. 9, 1962, 71–87.

MANN, GOLO, 'Ein Regent in der Republik. Markgraf Berthold von Baden', Die Zeit, Hamburg, 18. Jg., No. 52, 27 December 1963, 8. Also privately printed [1964], 8 pp.

MAX, PRINZ VON BADEN, 'Rede bei der Eröffnung der Schule in Schloss Salem am 14. April 1920', privately printed, Salem, 4 pp. Also published under the title, 'Die erste Schulfeier', in Berthold Markgraf von Baden (ed.), Salem, Langensalza [1933], 19–21 (shortened version).

MEISSNER, ERICH, 'Das Salemer System', Referat am Erwachsenenabend der Schloßschule Salem, 26 October 1933 [typewritten], 8 pp.

MEISSNER, ERICH, 'Fordernde Kameradschaft und unabhängiger Sinn', Rede am 9. November 1933 vor der Schülerschaft Salems, *Schule Schloss Salem*, No. 40/41, 1962–3, 9–12.

—— 'The Struggle of Salem School against the Nazi Régime', an Address to the Gordonstoun Society, January 1942, supplement to the *Gordonstoun Record* [1942], 11 pp.

—— '36 Thesen zur Salemer Erziehung', Unsere Aufgabe, Salem, April 1960 [typewritten], 7 pp.

PERGER, EDUARD VON, 'Erziehungsmethode der Schule Schloss Salem', in L. Prohaska (ed.), *Die zwischenmenschliche Beziehung und ihre Formen*, Wien: Österr. Bundesverlag, 1958, 202–10.

SABBAN, FRANCOISE, and HERIX, EDITH, 'Schule Schloss Salem', *Stop*, Journal du Lycée de Montgeron, 1963–4, No. 4, 16–26.

Schule Schloss Salem [School Record], No. 1 (1926), Nos. 44–5 (1965–7).

SUTCLIFFE, DAVID B., 'Ein Vergleich zwischen dem pädagogischen Ansatz in Salem und Gordonstoun', in H. Röhrs (ed.), *Bildung als Wagnis und Bewährung*, Heidelberg, 1966, 213–27.

ULRICH, KEY L., 'Schule Schloss Salem', in *Baden*, Monographie einer Landschaft, Karlsruhe, 1949, 1. Jg., No. 4, 55–6.

[Unsigned] 'Verfassung des Salemer Bundes' (nach der Versammlung im März 1927), *Schule Schloss Salem*, No. 2, Spring 1927, 13–15.

—— 'Verfassung des Salemer Bundes' (neuer Entwurf März 1928), *Schule Schloss Salem*, No. 5, Summer 1928, 16–20.

—— 'Die Salemer Verfassung', *Schule Schloss Salem*, No. 7, Winter 1929, 22–6.

—— 'Die Schule Schloss Salem. Die Salemer Zweigschulen', Ein Beitrag der Schulleitung, in *Salem*, Münster, Schloss, Schule, Lindau und Konstanz (Thorbecke), 1958, 38–51.

—— 'Salem—Schule der Elite' (photographs by Stefan Moses), *Stern*, Hamburg, No. 21, 23 May 1965, 42–50.

—— 'Unser Mann in Salem' [unqualified criticism], *Underground*, Frankfurt/M., 1. Jg., No. 1, November 1968, 56–60.

VOLKMANN, WILFRIED, 'Salem im Zeichen der Zehnjahrfeier', *Schule Schloss Salem*. No. 11/12, Summer/Autumn 1930, 5–7.

VORSTAND DES VEREINS SCHULE SCHLOSS SALEM (ed.), *Der Salemer Plan*, herausgegeben am 5. Juni 1966 zum 80. Geburtstag von Kurt Hahn, Ravensburg, 1966, 19 pp.

IV   GORDONSTOUN SCHOOL

BRERETON, HENRY L., *Gordonstoun*, written January 1949, Aberdeen: University Press, 1950, 56 pp.

—— *Flag Service Address*, 14 December, 1952, privately printed, 8 pp.

—— 'Gordonstoun in the 18th century', *Gordonstoun Record*, 1957, Serial No. 38, Annual No. 2, 80–91.

—— 'Die Gründung und Entwicklung von Gordonstoun', in H. Röhrs (ed.), *Bildung als Wagnis und Bewährung*, Heidelberg, 1966, 189–97.

——'Gordonstoun und die englische pädagogische Tradition', in H. Röhrs (ed.), *Bildung als Wagnis und Bewährung*, Heidelberg, 1966, 198–204.

—— *Gordonstoun. Ancient Estate and Modern School*, Edinburgh: Chambers, Ltd, 1968.

BRITISH SALEM SCHOOLS, LTD, *Report on the Progress of Gordonstoun School, 1934–1935*, London: Electric Law Press, 19 pp.

BRYANT, ARTHUR, 'Developing Character and Self-confidence. Gordonstoun School, which is now of Age', *The Illustrated London News*, 21 January 1956, 78–9.

CHEW, F. R. G., *Gordonstoun*, Aberdeen: University Press, July 1962, 30 pp. (1st edition, Aberdeen, June 1960, 26 pp.).

DÖNHOFF, MARION, GRÄFIN, 'Eine Schule der Selbstbewährung. Besuch bei dem Pädagogen Kurt Hahn in Schottland', *Die Zeit*, Hamburg, 3. Jg., No. 3, 15 January 1948, 2.

FRANKL, WILHELM, 'Pflichtfach in Gordonstoun: Nächstenhilfe. Fürstensöhne und Arbeiterkinder lernen Menschen retten und Brände löschen', *Ziviler Bevölkerungsschutz*, München, 7. Jg., No. 1, January 1962, 22–6.

Gordonstoun News [school record], No. 1 (1934)-No. 8 (1936).

Gordonstoun Record [school record], No. 1 (December 1936)-No. 49 (1968).

HOBHOUSE, JOHN, *10 October 1951*. Address at the Service held at Altyre on Sunday, 21 October 1951. Privately printed, 8 pp.

—— 'Ansprache bei der Gedenkfeier für Mark Hobhouse' (10 October 1951, trans. into German), *Schule Schloss Salem*, No. 33, 1953–4, 9–12.

KANNEWURFF, FRIWI, 'Salemer in Gordonstoun' [6 Salem boys at Gordonstoun in the autumn term 1948], *Schule Schloss Salem*, No. 29, 1948–50, 45–50.

MACKENZIE, CAMERON, 'Gordonstoun at Altyre, 1951–1960', *Gordonstoun Record*, 1960, Serial No. 41, Annual No. 5, 20–2.

MEISSNER, ERICH, *Gordonstoun and Salem*, Elgin, 2nd edition, 1948, 32 pp.

—— 'The Coronation of the Queen', an address given to Gordonstoun School on 2 June 1953, supplement to *Gordonstoun Record*, No. 29, 12 pp.

—— 'The Weakness of the Good', address to the colour-bearers of Gordonstoun and Altyre, *Gordonstoun Record*, 1958, Serial No. 39, Annual No. 3, 14–15.

PEASE, JOSEPH, 'Early Days at Gordonstoun: First Term', *Gordonstoun Record*, 1958, Serial No. 39, Annual No. 3, 92–8.

SWIRE, J., *Gordonstoun 1934–1955*, a survey upon the occasion of the School's Coming of Age, Colchester: Benham [1955], 40 pp.

SWIRE. J., *A Brief Introduction to Gordonstoun*, Elgin, 1962, 7 pp.

—— *Commentary of the Gordonstoun Film*, Elgin, 1960, 12 pp.

—— *Going to Sea in the Merchant Navy*, a note upon the Merchant Navy as a career, with an account of the training facilities available at Gordonstoun School, including practical seamanship and nautical course, Elgin, 1957, 16 pp.

TENNANT, IAIN, address (Gordonstoun), in *Speeches* at a meeting held at Admiralty House on Thursday, 21 November 1957, sponsored by the London Committee of the Friends of Gordonstoun, privately printed, 15–16.

TRELEAVEN, PHILIP, 'Gordonstoun—eine charakterbildende Schule', *British Features*, Bonn 1965, 5 pp. [typewritten].

[Unsigned] *Gordonstoun and Salem*, Ravensburg (Filkentscher) [1947], 65 pp. [Contents: Meissner, 'Gordonstoun and Salem'—'The Christening of the Garibaldi'; Brereton, 'Journey to Salem'; 'Philip Mountbatten. Record of His School Career'].

—— 'School for Spirit', *Time*, New York, Vol. 76, No. 20, 14 November 1960.

—— 'Spreading Network of Kurt Hahn Schools', *The Observer*. London, 28 January 1962.

—— 'Prinz Charles geht nach Gordonstoun', *Englische Rundschau*, Köln, 12. Jg., No. 3, 2 February 1962, 40.

—— 'So kommt ein König zu Verstand', *Stern*, Hamburg, 18 March 1962, 18–25, 122–3.

WILKINSON, ENDYMION, 'Gordonstoun and la Grande Passion', *Spectator*, London, No. 7,017, 21 December 1962, 959–60.

YOUNG, JOCELIN WINTHROP, 'Early Days at Gordonstoun: Seamanship', *Gordonstoun Record*, 1957, Serial No. 38, Annual No. 2, 48–9.

V ANAVRYTA

Anavryta [school record], No. 1 (October/December 1955).

JEFFERIES, 'Anavryta. Griechische Nationalschule', *Schule Schloss Salem*, No. 30, 1950–1, 43–5.

YOUNG, JOCELIN WINTHROP, 'Anavryta—the First Ten Years', *Gordonstoun Record*, 1958, Serial No. 39, Annual No. 3, 63–5.

—— 'Anavryta', in H. Röhrs (ed.), *Bildung als Wagnis und Bewährung*, Heidelberg, 1966, 228–34.

VI OUTWARD BOUND SCHOOLS

International and General

BECKER, HELLMUT, 'Die Aufgaben der Kurzschulen in unserer Zeit', *Deutsche Jugend*, München, 15. Jg., No. 1, January 1967, 13–20.

BREZINKA, WOLFGANG, 'Kurt Hahn und die Kurzschulen', in W. Brezinka, *Erziehung als Lebenshilfe*, 3rd edition, Stuttgart/Wien, 1963, 237–43, 383.

CLEGG, ALEC, 'Some more Equal than Others', *Strive*, Vol. 1, No. 7, Summer 1969, 17–22.

FLEMING, WILLIAM LAUNCELOT SCOTT [= The Bishop of Portsmouth], 'Beyond His Grasp?' [the values of an Outward Bound Course], in D. James (ed.), *Outward Bound*, London, 1957, 212–19.

Fletcher Report, University Press Ltd, Autumn 1970.

GÖLLER, KARL HEINZ, 'Die Kurzschul-Bewegung Outward Bound', *Der Lehrerrundbrief*, Frankfurt/M., 7. Jg., No. 10, October 1952, 462–6.

HOGAN, JIM, 'The Contributions of Outdoor Activities to Education', address given to the Annual Conference of the British Association of Organizers and Lecturers in Physical Education [with special references to the Outward Bound Movement], *Strive*. London, Vol. 1, No. 6, January 1969, 8–13, 40.

—— *Beyond the Classroom*, Reading: Educational Explorers, 1970.

—— *Impelled into Experiences*, London: Educational Productions Ltd, 1969.

International Bulletin of Outward Bound, London, Vol. 1, No. 1 (April 1966)–No. 4 (October 1967), continued under the title *Strive* (see below).

JAMES, DAVID (ed.), *Outward Bound*, London: Routledge & Kegan Paul, 1957, 2nd impression 1958, 3rd impression 1961; 222 pp.

KLAFKI, WOLFGANG, 'Kurzschulen', in *Pädagogisches Lexikon*, ed. Groothoff and Stallmann, Stuttgart Berlin (Kreuz), 2nd edition, 1964, cols. 807–8.

LUCY, GEOFFREY, 'Erziehung durch Härte und Abenteuer', *Das Beste aus Reader's Digest*, Stuttgart, 17. Jg., February 1964, No. 2, 154–68.

—— 'Les écoles de l'aventure', *Sélections du Reader's Digest*, Paris, 18. Jg., March 1964, 22–31 ('Erziehung durch Härte und Abenteuer' trans. into French).

MACKINTOSH, H. STEWART, 'Character training and the Contribution made by Outward Bound' in D. James (ed.), *Outward Bound*, London, 1957, 157–73.

NOLD, JOE, 'Beyond Outward Bound', *The International Bulletin of Outward Bound*, London, Vol. 1, No. 3, April 1967, 4.

PRICE, TOM, 'Some Aspects of Character Training', Edmond Rich

Memorial Lecture to the Royal Society of Arts in London on 23 March 1966, *International Bulletin of Outward Bound*, London, Vol. 1, No. 4, October 1967, 13–17.

RAAPKE, HANS-DIETRICH, 'Bewährung im Helfen (Kurt Hahn)', in H.-D. Raapke, *Das Problem des freien Raums im Jugendleben*, Weinheim [1959], 145–8.

RICHARDS, GORDON, 'Extension of Personality or . . .', *Strive*, London, Vol. 1, No. 7, Summer, 1969, 34–7.

SCHNEIDER, FRIEDRICH, 'Kurzschule', in *Lexikon der Pädagogik*, ed. Deutsches Institut für Wiss. Pädagogik, Münster, and Institut für Vergleichende Erziehungswissenschaft, Salzburg, Freiburg: Herder. Vol. III, 1954, cols. 125–6.

SCHWARZ, KARL, *Die Kurzschulen Kurt Hahns*, Ihre pädagogische Theorie und Praxis, Ratingen: Aloys Henn Verlag, 1968, 298 pp., with photographs. [International book on Outward Bound, on the ideas of Dr. Hahn and on the practical results and experiences with Outward Bound courses.]

—— 'Leistung und Bewährung der Jugend in den Kurzschulen Kurt Hahns', *Recht der Jugend*, Berlin, 12. Jg., No. 6, March 1964, 84–90.

—— 'Leistung und Bewährung der Jugend in den Kurzschulen', *Jugendrotkreuz und Erzieher*. Karlsruhe, 16. Jg., No. 6, June 1964, 81–8.

—— 'Die Ausbreitung des Kurzschulmodells von Kurt Hahn. Ein Beitrag zur Geschichte von Outward Bound', *Pädagogische Rundschau*. Ratingen, 19. Jg., February 1965, No. 2, 102–21.

—— 'Erziehung in den Kurzschulen Kurt Hahns', *Das Studienseminar*, Frankfurt/M., 10. Jg., No. 1, October 1965, 59–73.

—— 'Die Vorgeschichte der Kurzschulbewegung', *Neue Sammlung*, Göttingen, 6. Jg., May/June 1966, No. 3, 266–74.

—— 'Wagnis und Abenteuer als erzieherische Mittel in den Kurzschulen', *Zeitschrift für Pädagogik*, Weinheim, 13. Jg., October 1967, 421–35.

—— 'Die Kurzschulen Kurt Hahns', in Th. Dietrich (ed.), *Die Landererziehungsheimbewegung*, Bad-Heilbrunn: Klinkhardt, 1967, 154–60.

—— 'Neue Tendenzen in der Kurzschulerziehung' [new developments in Outward Bound in Europe and in the U.S.], *Recht der Jugend und des Bildungswesens*, Berlin Neuwied, 17. Jg., No. 4, April 1969, 97–103.

Strive [Outward Bound magazine], Vol. 1, No. 5 (June 1968)–No. 7 (Summer 1969). [No. 1–No. 4 have the title 'The International Bulletin of Outward Bound.]

SUMMERS, SPENCER, *Kurzschulen*, Outward Bound schools, Vortrag gehalten in verschiedenen deutschen Städten im Oktober 1953 [in Hamburg, Bonn, Frankfurt/M., Düsseldorf, Köln], Winsen [1953], 11 pp.

YOUNG, GEOFFREY WINTHROP, 'The Message of the Mountains', in D. James (ed.), *Outward Bound*, London, 1957, 98–107.

Great Britain

ADAMS, MICHAEL, *On the Inside* (33 minutes' colour film on British Outward Bound Schools), produced and delivered by Town and Country Productions, Ltd, London.

BEAUMAN, E. BENTLEY, 'High Adventure at the Outward Bound Schools', *The Field*, London, 7 August 1958, 228–9.

BEHR, ALFRED VON, 'Kurzschulen' [with special reference to Eskdale], *Schule Schloss Salem*, No. 30, 1950–1, 41–3.

BLAIN, RALPH, 'Exposure', Notes on Recognition of Symptoms, and on Treatment [results of a Working Party in Scotland], *The Climber*, Castle Douglas, October 1963.

BOLAND, BILLY, 'The Boy Who Got Away' [a boy from Easterhouse Estate, Glasgow, reports with enthusiasm on his Outward Bound course at Moray], *Strive*, London, Vol. 1, No. 7, Summer 1969, 2–3.

CARPENTER, PETER, 'Outward Bound', *Modern English*, Cambridge, Vol. 1, No. 13, December 1962.

CLARK, VICTOR, 'Sail Training in Outward Bound', reprinted from *Motor Boat and Yachting* [1964], London, 4 pp.

CLEGG, ALEC B., *Outward Bound in Education*, address at the Conference at Harrogate on 9 May 1965, issued by the Outward Bound Trust, London [1965], 8 pp.

COLLINS, J. DEREK, 'Outward Bound', dissertation, University of Durham, 1963, 35 pp. [typewritten].

DAVIES, LESTER W. (ed.), 'Outward Bound Mountain School, Ullswater', Instructor's Handbook, 13 pp. and 14 chapters Appendix [typewritten].

—— 'The Fell Bounder. Aid to Modern Rescue', *Strive*, London, Vol. 1, No. 6, January 1969, 16–17.

—— 'The Fourth Pillar' [article on 'project work' as the fourth pillar in Hahn's education, with special reference to Ullswater Outward Bound School], *Strive*, Vol. 1, No. 7, Summer 1969, 13–16.

DODD, JAMES, 'Ashburton—eine harte Schule für junge Mädchen'. [On the first girls' courses at Devon Outward Bound School since 1959.]

DOWLER, W. F., 'Outward Bound in Eskdale', *Gordonstoun Record*, 1957, Serial No. 38, Annual No. 2, 65–7.

EDINBURGH, DUKE OF, 'Foreword', in D. James (ed.), *Outward Bound*. London, 1957, ix.

FAIRHALL, DAVID, 'Outward Bondage', *Manchester Guardian*, Manchester, Vol. 89, No. 25, 19 December 1963, 13.

FULLER, J. FRED, 'From the Bridge' [Aberdovey], in D. James (ed.), *Outward Bound*, London, 1957, 59–74.

—— 'Drown Proofing', the new water survival technique, *Sport and Recreation*, London, Vol. 5, No. 1, January 1964, 17–19. [The new technique was developed by Fred Lanoue and became part of the time-table in Aberdovey in 1962.]

GREENBANK, ANTHONY, 'Another Kind of Finishing School' [Rhowniar], *The Times Educational Supplement*, London, 55th year, No. 2,606, 30 April 1965, 1,315.

GUNTER, RAY, speech by the Minister of Labour at the 21st Anniversary Luncheon of the Outward Bound Trust held in London on 10 May 1967, 2 pp. [typewritten].

HARDCASTLE, MARTIN, *Internal Report on Outward Bound*, issued by the Outward Bound Trust, London, 1969.

—— 'Mix Well—Do not beat' [about the first experimental mixed course in the Outward Bound School 'Rhowniar', Towyn, in 1969], *Strive*, London, Vol. 1, No. 7, 29-31.

HART, ALAN, 'Outward Bound School, Devon', *Outward Bound*, a quarterly review from the Outward Bound Mountain School, Rhodesia, No. 4, March 1964, 9-11.

HICKSON, K., 'Outward Bound Schools' [Aberdovey and Eskdale], *Journal of Education*, London, Vol. 83, May 1951, 251-2.

HOARE, DESMOND J., 'Outward Bounding', *Officer*, London, No. 5, Autumn 1961, 41-8.

HOGAN, JAMES MARTIN, 'Die Gründung der ersten Outward Bound-Schule in Aberdovey, Merionethshire', in H. Röhrs (ed.), *Bildung als Wagnis und Bewährung*, Heidelberg, 1966, 270-6.

HOLT, LAWRENCE, 'The Christening of the Garibaldi', speech on 26 June 1943 in Aberdovey, in *The Christening of the Garibaldi*, three speeches, Welshpool [1943], 3.

HUXLEY, JULIAN, 'County Badge Progress', *Spectator*, London, Vol. 169, 27 November 1942, 499. Also published in Kurt Hahn, *A Memorandum*, New York, 1948, 33-5.

JASWAL, B. S., 'Visit to Outward Bound Mountain School [Ullswater]', *The Himalayan Mountaineering Institute Darjeeling Newsletter*, No. 10, 1 January 1964, 63-70.

KEOWN, ERIC, 'Adventure Story', *Punch*, London, 24 October 1951, Vol. CCXXI, No. 5,791, 468-9.

KRETZSCHMAR, WINNI, 'Die Aberdovey Seeschule', *Schule Schloss Salem*, No. 32, 1952-3, 26-30.

LAVERS, G. R., 'Outward Bound', reprinted from *The Seeker*, the Organ of the Industrial and Social Order Council of the Society of Friends, 2 pp. Also published in Kurt Hahn, *A Memorandum*, New York, 1948, 36-8.

LESLIE, J. A. C., *Moray Sea School, Burghead, Morayshire*, Dundee and London: Valentine & Sons, October 1949, 20 pp.

LESLIE, M. E., 'The Moray Sea School. Beginnings', *Gordonstoun Record*, 1960, Serial No. 41, Annual No. 5, 44-8.

LINDSAY, LORD, letter to *The Times*, *The Times*, London, 7 December 1940. Also published in Kurt Hahn, 'Outward Bound', in *The Year Book of Education*, Yonkers-on-Hudson, 1957, 441.

LONGLAND, JACK, 'Outward Bound Junior Courses', in D. James (ed.), *Outward Bound*, London, 1957, 174–87.

LUNNON, V. M., 'Outward Bound', *Physical Education*, Vol. 50, July 1958, 55–60.

MOFFAT, GWEN, 'Outward Guide', *Manchester Guardian*, Manchester, 24 April 1963.

MONTGOMERY OF ALAMEIN, FIELD-MARSHAL THE VISCOUNT, 'Leadership of Youth' [the importance of character-training through Outward Bound], in Field-Marshal the Viscount Montgomery of Alamein, *The Path to Leadership*, London: Collins, 1961, 173–5. Reprinted in *The Sunday Times*, London, 12 February 1961, 23.

OUTWARD BOUND TRUST, *Bulletin*, No. 1 (June 1952)–No. 12 (November 1960). [No more numbers published; contains general news and reports from the British Outward Bound schools.]

—— *Report of the Council for the Year*, London, No. 1 (1948)–No. 21 (1968).

—— *Health and Safety Regulations at Outward Bound Schools*, London, January 1957, 8 pp.

—— *Junior Courses at the Outward Bound Schools*, London, n.d., 8 pp.

—— *Outward Bound Senior Courses*, for young men between nineteen and twenty-six years of age, London, September 1961, 4 pp.

—— *Outward Bound in the 60s and 70s*, a report of the Conference held at Harrogate on 8 and 9 May 1965, London [1965], 20 pp.

—— *Character Training Through Adventure*, the Outward Bound Schools, London, n.d., 20 pp.

—— *21st Anniversary Appeal, 1967*, London, 1967, 12 pp.

PARSONS, J., *Outward Bound in Industry*, address at the Conference at Harrogate on 8 May 1965, London [1965], 3 pp.

PUTNAM, ROGER, 'Mountain Rescue' [in Eskdale and Ullswater], *Strive*, London, Vol. 1, No. 7, 13–16.

READER HARRIS, DIANA, 'Outward Bound Training for Girls', in D. James (ed.), *Outward Bound*, London, 1957, 188–99.

RICHARDS, GORDON, 'Special Courses. The Case for Diversification', *Strive*, No. 5, June 1968, 4–8.

SHARP, DON, *The Blue Peter* [film of the British Film Company in Eastman Colour, taken in Aberdovey in June 1954, directed by Wolf Rilla].

STIVENS, DAL, 'Schulfach Charakterbildung. Ein englisches Experiment macht Schule', *Freie Bildung und Erziehung*, Darmstadt, 32. Jg., April 1956, No. 4, 97–100.

[SUMMERS, SPENCER] 'Religion at Outward Bound', memorandum on religious instruction in Outward Bound schools as approved by the Council on 19 June 1952, in A. Arnold-Brown, *Unfolding Character*, London, 1962, Appendix 1, 232–5.

—— 'Outward Bound To What? To Life!', reprinted from *London News Letter*, London, Spring 1953, 8 pp.

—— 'The History of the Trust', in D. James (ed.), *Outward Bound*, London, 1957, 18–58.

—— 'Die Frühzeit', in H. Röhrs (ed.), *Bildung als Wagnis und Bewährung*, Heidelberg, 1966, 259–69.

—— and TEDDER, LORD, 'Outward Bound', *The Times Educational Supplement*, London, 52nd year, No. 2,460, 13 July 1962, 55.

THOMAS, D. R. O., 'The Outward Bound Schools and Industry', in D. James (ed.), *Outward Bound*, London, 1957, 137–56.

TOMLINSON, GEORGE, 'Message from the Minister of Education on the Celebration of the Hundredth Course at the Outward Bound Sea School' [Aberdovey], privately printed.

—— 'Abridged Address by the Minister of Education at the Opening of the Outward Bound Mountain School' [Eskdale], 18 June 1950, privately printed, 2 pp.

TREVELYAN, GEORGE, 'The Christening of the Garibaldi', Speech on 26 June 1943 in Aberdovey, in *The Christening of the Garibaldi*, three speeches, Welshpool [1943], 4–7.

[Unsigned] *Moray Badge. Book of Progress*, n.d.

—— *Fitness from the First*, 'A Plan for Youth', 'The Gap in Physical Education', articles and correspondence reprinted from *The Times* and *The Times Educational Supplement*, May 1939, privately printed, 11 pp.

—— *The County Badge or the Fourfold Achievement*, London: Oxford University Press, 1942, 32 pp.

—— 'Training under Sail for Fitness' [Aberdovey], *The Times Educational Supplement*, London, No. 1,455, 20 March 1943, 135.

—— *The Christening of the Garibaldi*, three speeches, 26 June 1943, Welshpool: *County Times*, 1943, 8 pp.

—— *Memorandum* on the Physical 'Standard' Tests submitted by the Secretary of the County Badge Experimental Committee to the Central Council of Recreative Physical Training, January 1944, privately printed, 17 pp.

—— 'Outward Bound at Aberdovey', *The Times Educational Supplement*, London, No. 1,513, 2 September 1944, 423.

—— 'The Short Term Training School. Lessons from the Aberdovey Experiment', *The Times Educational Supplement*, London, No. 1,553, 35th year, 3 February 1945, 53.

—— 'An Opportunity for Adventure. Sea School for Youth', *The Times*

Educational Supplement, London, 39th year, No. 1,774, 30 April 1949, 276.

—— 'Character and Friendship through Hardship. A New Outward Bound Mountain School' [Eskdale], *The Times Educational Supplement*, London, 40th year, No. 1,833, 16 June 1950, 474.

—— 'Outward Bound Mountain School. Photographs' [Eskdale], *The Illustrated London News*, London, Vol. 217, 1 July 1950, 13.

—— 'Moray Sea School. A Real Service', *The Times Educational Supplement*, London, 42nd year, No. 1,948, 29 August 1952, 721.

—— 'Outward Bound' [Moray Sea School], *Scottish Field*, Glasgow, Vol. CV, No. 656, August 1957, 34–5.

—— 'Outward Bound Meeting. Future Tasks', *The Times Educational Supplement*, London, 47th year, No. 2,202, 2 August 1957, 1,073.

—— 'From the Half-deck', reports by some boys who have been on courses, in D. James (ed.), *Outward Bound*, London, 1957, 75–83.

—— 'Outward Bound Girls' Training Scheme', *The Times Educational Supplement*, London, No. 2,314, 25 September 1959, 320–1.

—— 'The Outward Bounders', *The Sunday Times*, London, 24 February 1963.

—— 'Outward Bound to better the Boys', *The Times Educational Supplement*, London, 54th year, No. 2,526, 18 October 1963, 534.

—— 'Outward Bound in Smog' [City Challenge in Leeds, July 1967], *The Times Educational Supplement*, London, 57th year, No. 2,719, 30 June 1967, 2,181.

—— 'Germany—exchange—Britain', *Strive*, Vol. 1, No. 1, January 1969, 34–6.

VILLIERS, ALAN, *And not to Yield*, a story of Outward Bound, London: Hodder & Stoughton, 1953, 160 pp. [This book is not a history of Outward Bound, but 'an imaginary adventure story of a course at the Sea School, Aberdovey'.]

—— 'The Impact of the Sea', in D. James (ed.), *Outward Bound*, London, 1957, 84–97.

YOUNG, GEOFFREY WINTHROP, 'The Christening of the Garibaldi', speech on 26 June 1943 in Aberdovey, in *The Christening of the Garibaldi*, Welshpool [1943], 7–8.

—— 'Address at the Official Opening of the Outward Bound Mountain School, Eskdale, June 1950', in A. Arnold-Brown, *Unfolding Character*, London, 1962, 165–6.

Germany

BONDY, BARBARA, 'Schule als ein grosses Abenteuer. Ein neues

Schulexperiment im Walsertal', broadcast, Bayrischer Rundfunk, 16 August 1957, 1st programme [typewritten], 12 pp.

—— 'Die Leidenschaft des Rettens. Zu einem pädagogischen Jubiläum', *Süddeutsche Zeitung*, München, No. 46, 22 February 1962.

—— 'Mädchen in der pädagogischen Provinz' [the first German Girls' Course at Hirschegg], *Süddeutsche Zeitung*, München, No. 128, 28 May 1965, 78.

—— 'Outward Bound. Zehn Jahre Kurzschule Baad', *Süddeutsche Zeitung*, München, No. 253, 22–3 October 1966.

BRÜCKNER, GUSTAV HEINRICH, 'Beispiel Weissenhaus', *Der Anruf*, Hamburg, 11. Jg., No. 55, March 1963, 24–30.

BRÜLL, HEINZ, 'Landschaftskunde in Weissenhaus', *Waldjugenddienst*, Frankfurt/M., 5. Jg., No. 3, September 1957, 5–6.

CHRISTIANSEN-WENIGER, FRITZ, 'Kurzschule Nehmten', *Die Sammlung*, Göttingen, 7. Jg., No. 7/8, July/August 1952, 326–36.

—— 'Dienst am Nächsten. Die Kurzschule Weissenhaus', *Westermanns Monatshefte*, Braunschweig, 95. Jg., No. 2, 1954, 64–6.

—— 'Eine neue Form der Jugendarbeit. Die Kurzschule', A New Form of Youth Work: The Short Term School. Une Nouvelle Forme de 'Education de la Jeunesse: L'Ecole Réduite' (in German, English and French), *Europa-Journal*, Koblenz, December 1954, 23–32.

[DENT, H. C.] 'Training for Citizenship. Adventure in Service at Germany's Outward Bound School', *The Times*, London, 4 October 1955.

—— 'Outward Bound in Germany', *The Times Educational Supplement*, London, No. 2,108, 14 October 1955, 1,054.

DÖNHOFF, MARION GRÄFIN, 'Weissenhaus', in *American-British Foundation for European Education*, privately printed, January 1954, 40–8.

—— 'Jugend will sich bewähren. Die Kurzschule Weissenhaus', *Merian*, Holsteinische Schweiz und die Küsten Ostholsteins, Hamburg, 9. Jg., No. 8, 1956, 58–64.

—— 'Kurzschule Weissenhaus', Broadcast Hessischer Rundfunk, 15 November 1959 [typewritten], 4 pp.

GEORG WILHELM, PRINZ VON HANNOVER, 'Grundsätzliche Gedanken zur Kurzschule', *Jugendrotkreuz Informationsdienst*, Bonn, No. 14, December 1951, 7.

GRONEFELD, GERHARD, 'Urlaub ohne Freizeit. Kurzschule Haus Bergengruen' [Girls' Courses at Hirschegg], *Westermanns Monatshefte*, Braunschweig, 108. Jg., July 1967, 52–9.

GUNDELAH, KLAUS, 'Wandlung durch Weissenhaus', *Waldjugenddienst*, Frankfurt/M., 5. Jg., No. 3, September 1957, 3–4.

HEUSS, THEODOR, 'Erwiderung des Bundespräsidenten anlässlich der Probefahrt des Fracht-Segelschulschiffes "Pamir" in Kiel am 15. Dezember 1951', in *Ansprachen*, privately printed, 16–20.

—— 'Ansprache beim Besuch der Kurzschule Weissenhaus bei Kiel am 24. Juni 1955', privately printed, 2 pp.

JACOBSEN, CORNELIA, 'Der jüngste Lehrer ist 21 Jahre. Dritte Kurzschule der "Deutschen Gesellschaft für Europäische Erziehung" '[*Kurzschule Berchtesgaden* opened], *Die Zeit*, No. 27, 5 July 1968, 41.

[JAMES, WALTER] 'On Watch in the Mountains', *The Times Educational Supplement*, London, 48. Jg., 29 August 1958, No. 2,258, 1,304.

KESSELHUT, ERNST, 'DLRG besucht die Deutsche Gesellschaft für Europäische Erziehung' [Weissenhaus], *Der Lebensretter*, No. 9, September 1955, 175, 186–7.

KIPPHOFF, PETRA, 'Erziehung durch die See. Zum 10. Geburtstag eines Experimentes, das schon lange ein Erfolg ist', *Die Zeit*, Hamburg, 17. Jg., No. 23, 8 June 1962, 13.

LÖDING, WALTER, 'Die Kurzschule Weissenhaus', *Hamburger Lehrerzeitung*, Hamburg, 10. Jg., 1957, No. 5, 1–9.

LOSCHEW, PETER, 'Kutter, Knoten und Kadetten. Das Experiment von Ohmten', *Die Zeit*, Hamburg, 6. Jg., No. 49, 6 December 1951, 2.

LÜBBEN, HEINRICH, 'Die Kurzschule Weissenhaus', *Freundliches Begegnen*, Düsseldorf, 3. Jg., No. 6, 1953, 6–9.

LÜBCKE, F. W., ' "Ansprache" gehalten anlässlich der Probefahrt des Fracht-Segelschulschiffes "Pamir" in Kiel am 15. Dezember 1951', in *Ansprachen*, privately printed, 4–6.

LÜDERS, PETER-JÜRGEN, 'Auch das sind Abenteuer. Warum schickt die Industrie junge Arbeiter in die Outward-Bound-Schools?', *Süddeutsche Zeitung*, München, No. 270, 1968.

LUTTIZ, ASTRID VON, 'Sie wollen hoch hinauf' [photographs of Baad Outward Bound School], *Feuerreiter*, Köln, 40. Jg., 27 June 1964, 20–3.

MCKITTRICK, THOMAS H., 'A Plan is Launched', in *American-British Foundation for European Education*, privately printed, January 1954, 5–11.

MESTER, LUDWIG, 'Der freiwillige Einsatz in der Gemeinschaft', *Die Leibeserziehung*, Schorndorf, 2. Jg., No. 8 August 1953, 1–3.

MÖHLMANN, CARL, 'Die Kurzschule Weissenhaus', *Die Sammlung*, Göttingen. 10. Jg., 1955, 271–80.

MÖTTELI, CARLO, 'An Bord des Segelschulschiffes "Pamir" ', *Neue Zürcher Zeitung*, Zürich, No. 136, 20 January 1952, 4.

MÜNCH, HELMUT, 'Die Kurzschule', *Basler Schulblatt*, 28. Jg., No. 3, 1967, 70–6.

PAETZMANN, ERIKA, 'Berg und charakterfeste Erziehung. Dritte Kurzschule Deutschlands in Berchtesgaden eröffnet. Auch Mädchen sind dabei', *Süddeutsche Zeitung*, München, No. 153, 26 June 1968, 19.

PAULI, GERHARD, 'Die Kurzschule Baad', *Neues Land*, München, 12. Jg., No. 4, July 1960, 82–6.

PAULI, GERHARD, 'Schule als Abenteuer und Bewährung', *Leibesübungen*, Frankfurt/M., 11. Jg., No. 1, January 1960, 14–19.

PESSEL, DIETER, 'Die Kurzschule Baad. Die Schule als Abenteuer (Bericht, eines Ostzonenflüchtlings)', *Die Sammlung*, Göttingen, 13. Jg., No. 4, 1958, 219–22.

RICHTER, GUSTAV, 'Deutsche Gesellschaft für Europäische Erziehung' (German Association for European Education), in *American-British Foundation for European Education*, privately printed, January 1954, 12–20.

—— 'Die deutschen Kurzschulen—ihre Entstehung und Entwicklung', in H. Röhrs (ed.), *Bildung als Wagnis und Bewährung*, Heidelberg, 1966, 300–10.

—— and MÜNCH, HELMUT, *Kurzschule und Charakterbildung*, ein Bericht aus der Arbeit [Kurzschule Baad], München: Juventa, 1960, 120 pp., with photographs.

—— and LINA: 'Outward Bound in Germany', *The Times Educational Supplement*, London, No. 2,405, 23 June 1961, 1,304.

RIEDEL, JOHANNES, 'Die Kurzschule Weissenhaus', *Archiv für Berufsbildung*, Braunschweig, 5. Jg., No. 2, February 1953, 27–9.

ROHLINGER, RUDOLF, and GOLDHAMMER, GÜNTER, *Internat für vier Wochen*, eine Reportage aus deutschen Kurzschulen, broadcast by television, Westdeutscher Rundfunk, Köln, 30 June 1968.

ROSCHMANN, HANS, 'Silauf in der Kurszchule Baad', *Ski*, Stuttgart, 10. Jg., No. 7, 27 February 1958, 303.

SCHLIEWEN, HEINZ, ' "Ansprache" gehalten anlässlich der Probefahrt des Fracht-Segelschulschiffes "Pamir" in Kiel am 15. Dezember 1951', in *Ansprachen*, privately printed, 1–3.

SCHWARZ, KARL, 'Kurzschulen—ein neuer Weg', *Olympische Jugend*, Frankfurt/M., 8. Jg., No. 10, October 1963, 10–13.

—— 'Expedition und Rettungsdienst als pädagogische Zentren in den deutschen Kurzschulen', in H. Röhrs (ed.), *Bildung als Wagnis und Bewährung*, Heidelberg, 1966, 311–25.

—— 'Turnen und Sport in den Kurzschulen', *Turnen*, Celle, 112. Jg., No. 6, March 1967, 4–6.

SCHWEBSCH, MANFRED, 'Die Kurzschule', in L. Mester (ed.), *Freizeitpädagogik*, Schorndorf, 1961, 40–5. Also published in *Die neue Berufsschule*, München, 1963, No. 2.

SEEBOHM, HANS CHRISTOPH, ' "Ansprache" gehalten anlässlich der Probefahrt des Fracht-Segelschulschiffes "Pamir" in Kiel am 15. Dezember 1951', in *Ansprachen*, privately printed, 7–15.

STÄTTER, WILLI, 'Streife Sieben', *Junge Hilfe*, Karlsruhe, 13. Jg., No. 5, Mai 1961, 111–13.

STRANDDISTEL, DIE [school magazine of the Kurzschule Weissenhaus],

No. 1 (Summer 1954)–No. 3 (Autumn 1955). [No more numbers published.]

THER, OTTO M., 'Avalanches in the Alps', *The International Bulletin of Outward Bound*, London, Vol. 1, No. 3, April 1967, 20–3.

TUNSTALL-BEHRENS, HILARY, *Pamir—a Voyage to Rio in a Four-Mast Barque*, Foreword by Alan Villiers, London: Routledge & Kegan Paul, 1956, 232 pp.

—— 'Pamirs erste Reise nach ihrer Wiederinstandsetzung', *Schule Schloss Salem*, No. 31, 1951–2, 53–5.

[Unsigned] *Ansprachen*, gehalten anlässlich der Probefahrt des Fracht-Segelschulschiffes 'Pamir' in Kiel am 15. Dezember 1951, privately printed, 20 pp.

—— 'Outward Bound in Germany. Training for the Deep Sea' [the first German experimental Outward Bound course at Nehmten], *The Times Educational Supplement*, London, 42nd year, 12 January 1952, No. 1,915, 29.

—— 'Vor der Fahrt ins Leben. Kurzschule für Jungen in England und Deutschland', *Frankfurter Allgemeine Zeitung*, Frankfurt/M., No. 254, 31 October 1953, 13.

—— *American-British Foundation for European Education*, the story of an experiment, privately printed, January 1954, 48 pp.

—— 'Jugend-Schulung. Wenn Du eingezogen wirst', *Der Spiegel*, Hamburg, 8. Jg., No. 36, 1 September 1954, 12–13.

—— 'Neue Schule der Hilfsbereitschaft. Kurzschule für Bergrettung eröffnet', *Jugendrotkreuz und Erzieher*, Karlsruhe, 8. Jg., No. 10, October 1956, 14–15.

—— 'Baad—Treffpunkt europäischer Jugend. Schule für wagemutige junge Männer im Kleinen Walsertal' [photographs], *ZB-Illustrierte*, 1958, 2nd edition of September, No. 20, 4–5.

—— 'German Outward Bound. Lack of Rigour', *The Times Educational Supplement*, London, 51st year, No. 2,414, 25 August 1961, 201.

—— 'Der Geist von Weissenhaus', Dienst am Nächsten—Dienst am Frieden, *Christ und Welt*, Stuttgart, 15. Jg., No. 37, 14 September 1962, 6.

VOGGENREITER, HEINRICH, and LEESE, ROSEMARIE, 'Schule für Abenteuer und Bewährung. Kurzschule Weissenhaus in Holstein', in *Jugend in Freiheit und Verantwortung*, Bad-Godesberg: Voggenreiter Verlag, 1961, 124–43.

WILDEN, HERBERT, 'Weissenhaus—eine Kurzschule für richtige Jungen oder solche, die es werden wollen!', *Junge Hilfe*, Karlsruhe, 13. Jg., No. 11, November 1961, 231–2.

WITTIG, HANS, 'Die Kurzschulen Kurt Hahns', *Westermanns Pädagogische Beiträge*, Braunschweig, 15. Jg. No. 5, May 1963, 200–6.

WUCHER, ALBERT, 'Jugend will sich bewähren. Im kleinen Walsertal wurde die zweite deutsche Kurzschule eröffnet', *Lebendige Erziehung*, München, 5. Jg., No. 10, October 1956, 224–6.

United States of America

BERRY, J. R., 'Rugged Camps turn Boys into Men. Outward Bound Camps', *Popular Mechanics*, New York, May 1966, 116–19.

BETTIS, STAN, 'Outward Bound', *Cascades Magazine*, 1967.

BLAINE, GRAHAM B., 'Providing Challenge', in G. B. Blaine, *Youths and the Hazards of Affluence*, New York: Harper & Row, 1966.

BROWN, ALEXANDER T., and WILLIAMS, DYKE V., *Outward Bound into the Mainstream* [spreading the Outward Bound idea into public education in the U.S.], privately printed, March 1967, 8 pp.

CAESAR, GENE, 'How to Build a Man the Hard Way' [Minnesota Outward Bound School], *True Magazine*, July 1965; reprinted in *Outward Bound Schools in Print*, December 1965, 4–6.

—— 'Outward Bound' [a Girls' Course in the Minnesota Outward Bound School], *Seventeen*, September 1966, Vol. 25, 92–3.

DAY, JANE, 'Summer Camps: Blazing New, Challenging Trails', *National Observer*, December 1967.

EPPRIDGE, BILL, 'Marshmallow becomes a Man. A Rough New School makes over a Bumbling Boy', *Life*, New York. Domestic Edition, Vol. 57, No. 6, 7 August 1964, 58–65 [mainly photographs].

FERGUSON, H. N., 'Shock treatment for Teen-agers', *Today's Health*, Chicago, Vol. 45, April 1967, 28–33.

FROELICHER, CHARLES F.; 'For the Sake of the Young', *Johns Hopkins Magazine*, Baltimore, Vol. XIV, No. 2, November 1962, 10–21, 31.

GIBBONS, E., 'Outward Bound again', *Organic Gardening and Farming*, Vol. 15, April 1968, 96–103.

GOODMAN, DICK, 'Outward Bound', *NESDEC News* (New England School Development Council), 1967.

GROSSMAN, EDWARD, 'A Rough Cure for Adolescence', *Harper's Magazine*, Vol. 234, No. 1,404, May 1967, 69–80.

HATCH, M. CHARLES, 'American Outward Bound Programmes', *The International Bulletin of Outward Bound*, London, Vol. 1, No. 1, April 1966, 14–16.

HENDERSON, C., 'The Mobile' ['mobile courses' in Colorado Outward Bound School], *Strive*, London, Vol. 1, No. 7, Summer 1969, 4–8.

HOLLANDSWORTH, JAMES C., '*Warspite* bell goes to New American school' [North Carolina Outward Bound School], *The International Bulletin of Outward Bound*, London, Vol. 1, No. 4, October 1967, 30–3.

KELLY, FRANCIS J., *Juvenile Delinquency Project*. Progress Report, 28 February 1967, 7 pp. [typewritten].

LAFONTAINE, BARBARA, 'Babes in the Woods' [Girls' courses at Minnesota Outward Bound School], *Sports Illustrated*, Chicago, Vol. 25, No. 2, 11 July 1966, 60–73, and No. 3, 18 July 1966, 41–55.

LAMAR, MARTHA, 'Is Our Youth going Soft?', Princeton Portraits, Joshua L. Miner, *Princeton Alumni Weekly*, Vol. 64, No. 23, 28 April 1964.

LAWRENCE, LYDIA, 'Outward Bound. Rugged Challenge for Teen-agers', *Reader's Digest*, Pleasantville, N.Y., 42nd year, Vol. 82, No. 492, April 1963, 183–91.

LINGO, T. D., 'Dropping Back into High School. Adventure trails camp-school of mountain creativity', *Education*, Indianapolis, Vol. 86, May 1966, 557–60.

MAYNARD, A. L., 'Nature as Teacher', *Saturday Review*, Vol. 52, 17 May 1969, 76–7.

MINER, JOSHUA L., 'Die Outward-Bound-Bewegung in den USA', in H. Röhrs (ed.), *Bildung als Wagnis und Bewährung*, Heidelberg, 1966, 293–9.

—— 'Outward Bound' [with special reference to Colorado courses], *Appalachia*, December 1965, 732–40.

NOLD, JOSEPH N., 'Conservation and Social Problems', *The International Bulletin of Outward Bound*, London, Vol. 1, No. 4, October 1967, 13–17.

NORDIN, KENNETH, 'Boys find Action' [Hurricane Outward Bound School], *The Christian Science Monitor*, August 1965; reprinted in *Outward Bound Schools in Print*, December 1965, 7–8.

OETTING, RAE, 'Challenging the Wilderness', *Ford Times*, May 1966.

OUTWARD BOUND, INC., *Annual Report*, No. 1 (1966)–No. 3 (1968), 16 pp.

PELL, CLAIBORNE, 'Youth and the Challenge of Our Time', address at the 1964 Joint Conference on Children and Youth in Washington, D.C., on April 8, 1964, *Congressional Record*, Proceedings and Debates of the 88th Congress, Second Session, Washington, Vol. 110, No. 76, 20 April 1964.

—— 'Education: the Acceptance of Responsibility', speech delivered before the Select Committee on Youth of the Ontario Parliament, Toronto, Canada, 16 July 1964, *Vital Speeches of the Day*, Pelham, N.Y., Vol. 30, No. 23, 15 September 1964, 725–7.

PICKARD, H. S., 'Outward Bound is committed to helping young people achieve the will and the skill "to serve, to strive, and not to yield" ', *NEA Journal*, 'Today's Education', November 1968, Vol. 57, 20–2.

PRANGE, CONRAD, 'Stern Tests Provided in Oregon's Forest', *The Oregon Statesman*, Salem, Oregon, 17 July 1966 [Northwest Outward Bound School, Oregon].

QUEAL, CAL, 'Nature Challenges the Jobless', *Sunday Empire Magazine*, Denver, 25 August 1968.

RIGG, H. K., 'The School of Hard Knocks', *Skipper Magazine*, February 1967.

STANFORD, NEAL, 'Modern School of Hard Knocks' [opening of Hurricane Outward Bound School], *The Christian Science Monitor*, Boston, Mass., Vol. 56, No. 201, 22 July 1964, 3.

STEINMANN, RICHARD, 'As It looks from the Inside' [Colorado Outward Bound School], *American Youth*. May/June 1965, reprinted in *Outward Bound Schools in Print*, December 1965, 1–3.

[Unsigned] 'Character, the Hard Way' [Colorado Outward Bound School], *Time*, New York, Vol. 80, No. 5, August 1962, Domestic Edition, 34.

—— 'Going British in the Rockies', *The Times Educational Supplement*, London, 54th year, No. 2,571, 28 August 1964, 275.

—— 'Men of the Mountains. Colorado Outward Bound School', *The Times Educational Supplement*, London, 53rd year, No. 2,497, 29 March 1963, 659.

—— *Outward Bound Schools in Print*, privately printed, December 1965, 8 pp.

—— *Outward Bound Schools* [brochure], several editions since 1965, 40 pp.

—— 'Pitting Managers against Nature', *Business Week*, New York, 16 March 1968, 106–14.

—— 'The College of Hard Knocks', *Parade Magazine*, 1968 (photographs by Ben Ross).

—— 'Summer Camps with a Difference', *News Front*, management's news magazine, November 1967.

—— 'You don't have to be Powerless' [about the 'Doers', about 'Peace Corps' and Outward Bound], *Time*, New York, Vol. 92, No. 16, 18 October 1968, 40–1.

—— *Outward Bound into the Mainstream of Education*, privately printed [1968], 16 pp.

WILLAUER, PETER, 'To Serve, to Strive and Not to Yield', *Groton School Quarterly*, March 1966, reprinted, 16 pp.

—— 'To meet a Challenge. Hurricane Island', *Yachting*, New York, Vol. 125, March 1969, 74–5.

Australia

ELLIOT, JOAN, 'Outward Bound Observed', *Strive*, London, Vol. 1, No. 5, June 1968, 9–12.

EMONS, JOHN, 'Outward Bound School', *M.L.C. News*, the house journal of the Mutual Life and Citizens Assurance Company, Sydney (reprinted), 1964, 3 pp.

EVANS, A. H., 'The Australian Outward Bound Memorial Foundation', *The International Bulletin of Outward Bound*, London, Vol. 1, No. 1, April 1966, 29–30.

HEMPEL, PETER, '26-Day Course Builds Boys' Character' [the first Australian Outward Bound course at Narrabeen], *Camden News*, 28 December 1956.

LEWIS, J. E., 'Outward Bound in Australia', *The B.H.P. Review*, February 1965, 3–6.

OUTWARD BOUND AUSTRALIA, *Character Training Through Adventure* (Narrabeen National Fitness Camp is the site for the first Outward Bound Short-term School to be held in Australia), Sydney, n.d., 4 pp.

[Unsigned] ' "Tough" Camp for Building Boys' Character', *The Sydney Morning Herald*, Sydney, 15 December 1956.

—— 'Australian Epic', *Strive*, London, Vol. 1, No. 7, Summer 1969, 46–8.

WITHAM, DAVID, 'The Hawkesbury Bush', *The International Bulletin of Outward Bound*, London, Vol. 1, No. 2, August 1966, 32–4.

Holland

RANFT, J. H., 'Safety Precautions at the Netherlands', *The International Bulletin of Outward Bound*, London, Vol. 1, No. 2, August 1966, 30–1.

STAKENBURG, ARNOLD J. T., 'Die Outward-Bound-Schule in Holland', in H. Röhrs, *Bildung als Wagnis und Bewährung*, Heidelberg, 1966, 287–92.

—— 'The Outward Bound School in the Netherlands' ('Die Outward Bound Schule in Holland', trans. from German into English), *The International Bulletin of Outward Bound*, London, Vol. 1, No. 1, April 1966, 22–4.

STICHTING TOT OPRICHTING EN INSTANDHOUDING VAN 'OUTWARD BOUND' ZEE- EN BERGSCHOLEN IN NEDERLAND, *'Outward Bound' Scholen*, 1962, 12 pp.

Kenya

HARRISON, ROY, 'Safari by Numbers' [Loitokitok Outward Bound School], *Strive*, London, No. 5, June 1968, 30–2.

LAKE, RICHARD A., 'The Outward Bound Mountain School of East Africa' [beginnings and first experimental courses], *Overseas Education*, London, Vol. 32, No. 2, July 1960, 54–60.

MIDDLETON, GORDON, 'Loitokitok', *Gordonstoun Record*, Serial No. 42, Annual No. 6, 1961, 36–41.

PRITCHARD, DEREK, 'Outward Bound in East Africa', *The International Bulletin of Outward Bound*, London, Vol. 1, No. 1, April 1966, 31.

PRITCHARD, DEREK, 'The Greatest Safety Factor. Aspects of Safety at the Loitokitok School', *The International Bulletin of Outward Bound*, London, Vol. 1, No. 2, August 1966, 14–17.

[Unsigned] 'Climbing Kilimanjaro' [the first experimental course in Kenya], *The Times Educational Supplement*, London, 42nd year, No. 1,926, 28 March 1952, 267.

—— 'Outward Bound in Kenya', *The Times Educational Supplement*, London, No. 2,405, 23 June 1961, 1,305.

—— *The Outward Bound Mountain School of East Africa*, Nairobi: The English Press [1963], 8 pp.

Malaysia

FULLER, G. W., 'Outward Bound School—Lumut', *Gordonstoun Record*, Serial No. 43, Annual No. 7, 1962, 80–7.

—— 'News from the New Outward Bound School, Lumut, Dindings', *Gordonstoun Record*, No. 35, Spring 1955, 8–11.

HUTSON, V. M., 'Adventure in the Dindings', in *School of Self-Discovery*, The Outward Bound School, Lumut, Kuala Lumpur, 1961, 6–9.

TUCKER, JACK, W., 'Malaya', *The International Bulletin of Outward Bound*, London, Vol. 1, No. 1, April 1966, 18–19.

—— 'Jungle Training in Malaya', *The International Bulletin of Outward Bound*, London, Vol. 1, No. 2, August 1966, 25–7.

[Unsigned] *School of Self-Discovery*, The Outward Bound School, Lumut, Kuala Lumpur: The Economy Printers, 1961, 23 pp.

—— *School of Self-Discovery*, Kuala Lumpur: Than Fong [1964], 10 pp.

New Zealand

HARRISON, J. B., 'Cobham Outward Bound School in New Zealand', *The International Bulletin of Outward Bound*, London, Vol. 1, No. 1, April 1966, 5–7.

OUTWARD BOUND TRUST OF NEW ZEALAND, *Newsletter*, Wellington, No. 1 (1963), yearly publication.

[Unsigned] 'Outward Bound at Anakiwa' [opening of the school], *The Times Educational Supplement*, London, 52nd year, No. 2,467, 31 August 1962, 213.

—— 'Facilities and Site of Cobham School Second to None', *The New Zealand Herald*, Auckland, 26 April 1963.

—— 'Success of "Outward Bound" ', *The Star*, Kingston, Jamaica, 17 February 1964 [the first successful year at Cobham School].

Nigeria

AZIKIWE, NNAMDI, reply on the occasion of His Excellency's visit to the Citizenship and Leadership Training Centre, Kurra Falls on 12 March 1963 (Press release from Federal Ministry of Information, No. F. 507), Lagos, 12 March 1963, 6 pp. [typewritten].

DICKSON, ALEC G., 'Man o' War Bay', *The Geographical Magazine*, London, Vol. 26, No. 10, February 1954, 557–61 (with photogravure supplement), 8 pp.

—— and MORA, *Man o' War Bay, 1951–1954*, Edinburgh: Bishop & Sons, n.d., 76 pp.

DICKSON, MORA, *New Nigerians*, London: Dobson, 1960, 256 pp.

HOLT, JULIAN, 'Man o' War Bay', *Sea*, Liverpool: Elder Dempster Lines, Autumn 1963, 1–6.

MALAFA, P. E. N., 'Man o' War Bay assumes New Role', *Overseas Education*, London, Vol. 34, January 1963, No. 4, 157–61. [The 'old' and 'new' training centre, Man o' War Bay.]

MITCHISON, LOIS, 'Outward Bound in Africa. All Hands get Black', *The Times Educational Supplement*, London, No. 2,272, 5 December 1958, 1,749.

NICHOLSON, DAVID, 'Voluntary Service in West Africa', *Gordonstoun Record*, 1961, Serial No. 42, Annual No. 6, 56–62.

SNOWSELL, RAYMOND E., *Looking Forward towards Good Citizenship*, Man o' War Training Centre, London: Dunstan & Co., 1960, 24 pp.

—— 'Man o' War Bay Training Centre', *Gordonstoun Record*, 1961, Serial No. 42, Annual No. 6, 63–6.

—— *Touring Team*, Citizenship and Leadership Training Centre, Kurra Falls, 8 pp. [typewritten].

—— 'Man o' War Bay', *The International Bulletin of Outward Bound*, London, Vol. 1, No. 2, August 1966, 8–11.

TUNSTALL-BEHRENS, HILARY, 'Outward Bound Overseas' [Outward Bound in Nigeria, Kenya and Malaysia], in D. James (ed.), *Outward Bound*, London 1957, 108–36.

—— 'Kurzschulen im Britischen Commonwealth', in H. Röhrs (ed.), *Bildung als Wagnis und Bewährung*, Heidelberg, 1966, 277–86 [with special reference to Nigeria].

[Unsigned] 'Sea, Mountain and Wilderness. Tough Training for Nigerians', *The Times Educational Supplement*, London, 42nd year, No. 1,926, 28 March 1952, 267.

—— *Outward Bound to the New Nigeria*, Man o' War Bay Training Centre (1950–8), London: Dunstan & Co., 1958, 45 pp.

—— *New Horizons*, Citizenship and Leadership Training Centre, Kaduna: Baraka Press [1966], 32 pp.

Rhodesia

BARBANELL, DEREK C., 'Early Days of Outward Bound in Rhodesia', *Outward Bound*, a Quarterly Review from the Outward Bound Mountain School, Rhodesia, No. 11, December 1965, 5–6 and No. 12, March 1966, 6–7.

—— *Instructors' Handbook*, Outward Bound Mountain School, Melsetter, 17 pp. [typewritten].

—— 'Courses for Executives', *The International Bulletin of Outward Bound*, London, Vol. 1, No. 1, April 1966, 12–13.

COUSINS, H. M., 'Student's Viewpoint', *Outward Bound*, a Quarterly Review from the Outward Bound Mountain School, Rhodesia, No. 3, December 1963, 7–9.

GREENWAY, STELLA, 'Up Chimanimani' [the first Senior Women Course in Rhodesia's Outward Bound School], *Outward Bound*, a six-monthly review from the Outward Bound Mountain School, Rhodesia, No. 17, December 1967, 6–10, reprinted in *Strive*, London, Vol. 1, No. 6, January 1969, 29–33.

KINGDON, ALAN, 'Outward Bound. A Social Service and a Challenge to Youth', reprinted from *The Chamber of Mines Journal*, May 1963, 6 pp.

MURRAY, R. E., 'To Serve . . .', *Outward Bound*, a six-monthly review from the Outward Bound Mountain School, Rhodesia. No. 19, January 1969, 7–8.

Outward Bound, a quarterly [from No. 16, a six-monthly] review from the Outward Bound Mountain School, Rhodesia, No. 1 (June 1963)–No. 19 (January 1969).

OUTWARD BOUND ASSOCIATION OF RHODESIA, *Outward Bound—Rhodesia*, 12 pp. [1968].

ROBINSON, B., 'The Mountain Rescue Course: 1st to 10th November, 1964', *Outward Bound*, a quarterly review from the Outward Bound Mountain School, Rhodesia, No. 7, December 1964, 7.

TAYLOR, NORMAN, 'The Executives' Course: 1–9 August, 1964', *Outward Bound*, a quarterly review from the Outward Bound Mountain School, Rhodesia, No. 6, September 1964, 3–4.

[Unsigned] 'Chair-Bound are Outward Bound' [the first Executives' Course in August 1964], *The Rhodesia Herald*, Salisbury, 10 June 1964.

—— 'Outward Bound Together', *The Times Educational Supplement*, London, 52nd year, No. 2,454, 1 June 1962, 1,128.

WILSON, A. J., 'Outward Bound. A Challenge for Rhodesia's Youth' (pictures by P. Winterbach), reprinted with permission of the Rhodesian Selection Trust Ltd, 8 pp.

WITHAM, D. G., 'The First Expedition', *Outward Bound*, a quarterly review from the Outward Bound Mountain School, Rhodesia, No. 1, June 1963, 4–7.

Zambia

PAYNE, D'ARCY T., 'Safety', *The International Bulletin of Outward Bound*, London, Vol. 1, No. 2, August 1966, 21–5.
—— 'Race Relations', *The International Bulletin of Outward Bound*, London, Vol. 1, No. 3, April 1967, 29.
—— 'Running Executives' Courses in Zambia', *The International Bulletin of Outward Bound*, London, Vol. 1, No. 4, October 1967, 30–3.
ZAMBIA SUPPLEMENT [Appendix to *Outward Bound*, a quarterly review from the Outward Bound Mountain School, Rhodesia], No. 1 (March 1965)–No. 3 (September 1965) [no further numbers published].

Outward Bound in the Army and Navy

JÄGER, HEINRICH, 'Bericht über den Besuch in der 1st (British Corps), Outward Bound School in Kristiansand, Norwegen', 18 June 1964, 4 pp. [typewritten].
MOUNTBATTEN OF BURMA, EARL LOUIS, 'Outward Bound in the Royal Navy', in D. James (ed.), *Outward Bound*, London, 1957, 206–11.
TEMPLER, GERALD, 'Outward Bound in the Army', in D. James (ed.), *Outward Bound*, London, 1957, 200–5.
THE ARMY OUTWARD BOUND SCHOOL, Towyn: 'A Short Account', 8 pp. [typewritten].

VII UNITED WORLD COLLEGES

ATLANTIC COLLEGE, Half-yearly Progress Report, No. 1 (20 January 1963)–No. 11 (January 1969), 8 pp.
Atlantic College Magazine [school magazine], Bridgend, No. 1, 30 May 1964.
BOURNE, RICHARD, 'A World of Education' [the value of the Atlantic College for international education], *The Guardian*, Manchester, 24 April 1969.
BRERETON, HENRY L., 'Scholars and Seamanship', *Oversea*, New York News Bulletin, Vol. 2, 14 March 1963, 10.
COMMISSION FOR THE ATLANTIC COLLEGES, INC., *Educational Aspects of the Atlantic Colleges*, New York [1968], 16 pp.

258   Karl Schwarz

DARVALL, LAWRENCE, 'The Atlantic Schools Concept', *Gordonstoun Record*, 1958, Serial No. 39, Annual No. 3, 22–6.

—— 'The Concept of the Atlantic Colleges', *European-Atlantic Review*, London, Summer 1959, 9–10.

—— 'Schools for N.A.T.O. A Sense of Common Destiny', *The Times Educational Supplement*, London, 47th year, No. 2,163, 2 November 1956, 1,305.

—— speech at the Sheffield Lunch on Monday, 12 November 1962, in *Atlantic Colleges*, 24 pp. [1962].

EDWARDS, TUDOR, 'The First Atlantic College', *Leben und Arbeit*, Fulda, March 1963, 34–7, reprinted from *Birmingham Post*.

GOWER, J., 'Money for an Atlantic Eton', *Time and Tide*, London, Vol. 41, No. 29, 1960, 820.

GREIG, DEBORAH, 'The Most Examined Young People in the World', *Education*, official journal of the Association of Education Committees, Vol. 133, No. 10, 7 March 1969, 307, 319.

HOARE, DESMOND J., 'Correction, Mr. Vaizey', *The Teacher*, 11 January 1963, 19.

—— 'Das Atlantic College', in H. Röhrs (ed.), *Bildung als Wagnis und Bewährung*, Heidelberg, 1966, 235–47.

—— and THOMAS, MELBOURNE, *Coast Rescue Services*, Conference at the Atlantic College, St Donat's Castle, Glamorgan, 21 April 1964, report, Cowbridge: Brown & Sons, May 1964, 8 pp.

HODDER, JOHN S., 'Way to New Worlds. The Atlantic College', *N.A.T.O. Letter*, London, Vol. 10, No. 11, November 1962, 11–15.

—— 'Weg zu neuen Welten. The Atlantic College' ('Way to New Worlds', trans. into German), *N.A.T.O. Brief*, Bonn, November 1962, 13–17.

HÖPFL, HEINZ, 'Das erste Atlantic College. Musterbeispiel eines internationalen Internats', *Frankfurter Allgemeine Zeitung*, Frankfurt/M., No. 164, 18 July 1964.

KNOWLES, MELITA, 'A School for All Nations', *The Christian Science Monitor*, Boston, 13 January 1968.

LEACH, ROBERT J., *International Schools and Their Role in the Field of International Education*, Pergamon Press, 1968.

LÖFFLER, EUGEN, 'Atlantische Schulen. Eine neue Form übernationaler Schulen', *Der Deutsche Lehrer im Ausland*, München, 9. Jg., No. 4, 1962, 104–8.

MOUNTBATTEN OF BURMA, EARL LOUIS, 'Educating Internationalists' *European Review*, London, Spring 1969, Vol. 19, No. 2, 18–19.

MÜLLER-MAREIN, JOSEF, 'Ein Schloss in Südwales am Meer. Stürmische Reise zum Atlantic-College', *Die Zeit*, Hamburg, 19. Jg., No. 1, 3 January 1964, 2.

PETERSON, A. D. C., 'Sixth-form College with a Difference', *Spectator*, London, 25 June 1965.

POTTS, H. C., 'First Term at St Donat's Castle', *Gordonstoun Record*, 1962, Serial No. 43, Annual No. 7, 45–9.

ROAD, ALAN, 'Atlantic College', *Englische Rundschau*, Köln, 13. Jg., No. 3, 1 February 1963, 40–1.

SCHUSTER, GEORGE, *The Atlantic College Project*, Purposes and Progress, 1962–8, December 1968, 6 pp.

SMITH, GEORGE IVAN, 'United World College of the Atlantic', *United Nations Headquarters: Secretariat News*, Vol. 24, No. 10, New York, 29 May 1969.

SPOLTON, LEWIS, 'Sixth-form Colleges. Will Croydon regret?', *The Times Educational Supplement*, London, No. 2,439, 16 February 1962, 305.

SUTCLIFFE, DAVID B., 'Das Atlantic-College', *Neue Sammlung*, Göttingen, 3. Jg., No. 3, May/June 1963, 259–71.

—— 'New Departure', *St Martin's Review*, November 1963, 20–1.

TERTE, ROBERT H., 'A College for World Unity', *The New York Times*, New York, 9 February 1964.

UNITED WORLD COLLEGES, International Progress Report No. 1 (January 1969), 8 pp.

[Unsigned] 'Hahn's Castle', *Time and Tide*, London, Vol. 41, No. 37, 1960, 1,062–3, and No. 38, 2,093–4, 1960.

—— 'Bid for St Donat's Castle. First Atlantic College planned', *The Times Educational Supplement*, London, 50th year, No. 2,358, 29 July 1960, 141, 150.

—— 'College on the Moat', *Newsweek*, New York, Vol. 56, No. 20, 14 November 1960, 52 (International Edition).

—— 'St Donat's Makes Ready. Atlantic College Date-line', *The Times Educational Supplement*, London, No. 2,437, 2 February 1962, 194.

—— *Atlantic Colleges* [contains the talks at Sheffield Lunch on 12 November 1962], n.d., 23 pp.

—— 'College in a Castle', *Time*, New York, Vol. 80, No. 15, 12 October 1962, 70.

—— 'Fifty-five boys and a Girl. Birth of Atlantic College', *Newsweek*, New York, Vol. 60, 22 October 1962, 44.

—— *The Atlantic College in the United Kingdom* [prospectus], 1st edition, 1962, 16 pp. From 1969 on published under the title, *United World Colleges. World College of the Atlantic*.

—— 'Sixth-form International. Atlantic College's Second Year', *The Times Educational Supplement*, London, No. 2, 525, 54th year, 11 October 1963, 497.

—— 'Curriculum seasoned with Salt. A Piquant Experiment in

International Education', *Life International*, New York, Vol. 35, No. 10, 18 November 1963, E11–E16 [photographs].

—— 'Classroom in a Castle. A World-wide High School', *Junior Scholastic*, 17 April 1964.

—— 'College for *Élite* of Teenagers', *The Times*, London, 25 June 1965, 13, 18.

WEISBROD, BERND, 'Das Atlantic College', *Der Eisbrecher*, Heidenheim, No. 10, September 1965, 234–8.

Notes on authors

Hellmut Becker   Hellmut Becker is Director of the Institute of Educational Research in the Max-Plank-Gesellschaft, which he founded, and Honorary Professor for the Sociology of Education in the Freien Universität, Berlin. He is president of the *Deutschen Volkshochschulverband* (Organization for German Adult Education), Superintendent of the Study Group of the Association of private welfare schools, as well as Member of the Board of the Association of Schloss Salem Affiliates. He belongs to the Council at Atlantic College and is Director of the German Organization for European Education, the supporting institution of the German Outward Bound Schools.

Sir Robert Birley, K.C.M.G., F.S.A.   Professor and Head of Department of Social Science and Humanities, City University, London. He was formerly Headmaster of Eton College (from 1949–63).

Henry L. Brereton   After eight years at Abinger Hill, a pioneer school in Surrey, he joined Gordonstoun as Director of Studies, also acting, for the first few years, as Headmaster of the Preparatory School. Subsequently he became Second Master and, after Dr Hahn's retirement, Headmaster; he was then Warden of the school, retiring in 1968.

Peter Carpenter   He is now on the staff of an institute of education; he was an instructor at an Outward Bound School and conducted research into the effects of Outward Bound training on character. He is also an Honorary Award Liaison Officer for the Duke of Edinburgh's Award.

Anne Corbett   After working as a research assistant in the labour relations department of I.C.I., she wrote about British education for the Central Office of Information, and is now education correspondent of *New Society*.

Eddy Dawson Captained Leicestershire's cricket team in the 1920s and 30s and toured Australia and South Africa with the M.C.C. From 1953–68 he was Executive Director of the Outward Bound Trust; during this time, the number of Outward Bound Schools in Great Britain increased from two to six and the number of young people participating every year from 1,611 to 5,165. He also took a particular interest in the founding of Outward Bound Overseas (see chart on p. xxiii for the growth of O.B.).

Marina Ewald She became a friend of her brother's schoolmate, Kurt Hahn, while still at school, and both followed the development of the Lietz Country Boarding School with enthusiasm. During the First World War she served on the War Committee as a scientific adviser for oils and fats. At the close of the war she revived old school plans together with Kurt Hahn, initiating the reopening of Salem, where she still teaches.

James M. Hogan 1941–5 Secretary, County Badge Experimental Committee, and jointly Warden of Outward Bound Sea School, Aberdovey. In 1959 he became Deputy Education Officer, West Riding County Council, having been an Education Officer in Somerset and Birmingham.

Lola Landau-Wegner Has worked on newspapers and radio, and is the author of several plays and poems. Since 1936 she has lived in Jerusalem, where she writes children's programmes for Israeli radio and stories for young people.

Golo Mann The son of the author and Nobel Prize winner, Thomas Mann; he attended school at Schloss Salem from 1923–7. He was awarded his Doctorate of Philosophy in Heidelberg in 1932; in 1942 he was named Professor of History at Olivet College in Michigan, U.S.A., and from 1943 to 1946 he was a member of the American army. Between 1947 and 1960 he was successively, Professor for Modern History at Claremont, California, and guest professor at the University of Münster in Westfalen. He was active as Professor of Modern History and Political Science at the Technical University in Stuttgart from 1960 to 1964.

Donald McLachlan Worked on *The Times* in its London and Berlin offices until 1936 when he resigned to resume teaching. He returned to *The Times* in 1938 to be Editor of *The Times Educational Supplement*. From 1947 he was for seven years Foreign Editor of *The Economist* and then returned to daily journalism as Deputy Editor of the *Daily Telegraph* in 1954, and in 1961 he was founding Editor of the *Sunday Telegraph*.

Joshua L. Miner After the Second World War he became Assistant Headmaster of the Hun School, in Princetown, New Jersey, and in 1950 he became a Housemaster and instructor at Gordonstoun. He has been on the faculty of Phillips Academy in Andover, Massachusetts since 1952, and serves the Atlantic Foundation as a trustee and presently is a trustee and President of Outward Bound Inc.

Tom Price 1961–8 Warden of Outward Bound School, Eskdale, and from 1968, Inspector of Schools, West Riding. A keen mountaineer, he was also for several years bowman and signalman of Workington lifeboat.

Gustav Richter His mother was Hahn's co-worker during his political career in Berlin. She later witnessed the growth and development of the schools, Salem and Gordonstoun. Gustav Richter, therefore, has been acquainted with Kurt Hahn and his work since 1915. Beginning in 1946, he studied the English Outward School Systems and has subsequently been entrusted with a variety of tasks which furthered the realization of the Outward Bound idea in Germany. He has been a member of the German Organization for European Education, which is responsible for the management of the Outward Bound Schools in Germany, since its foundation.

Hermann Röhrs In 1957 professor at the College of Economics in Mannheim, and since 1958 Professor and Director of the Seminar for Pedagogics at the University of Heidelberg. A member of the Board of Advisers of the German Sport Athletic Association and the Trusteeship for Academic Sport; also President of the German-speaking (Germany, Austria, Switzerland) section of the World Education Fellowship.

Karl Schwarz (the late) Teaching and other educational work in Salem 1961–2; 1962–4 a teacher at the Outward Bound Schools of Weissenhaus and Ullswater. He made a residence study in Baad, Aberdovey, Devon, Eskdale and at Atlantic College, and worked in co-operation with the German Association for European Education and the Outward Bound Trust.

Sir Spencer Summers, M.P. During the war, he was Director General, Regional Organization, Ministry of Supply. He became a Member of Parliament in 1940, and was Secretary for Overseas Trade towards the end of the Coalition Government, and during the Caretaker Government in 1945. He first became associated with Dr Hahn in 1943, and under the auspices of Sir George Trevelyan, Master of Trinity College, Cambridge, convened a meeting of interested parties in 1946, which culminated in the formation of the Outward Bound Trust. He has also collaborated with Dr Hahn in other ventures, including the Trevelyan Scholarships and the Atlantic College.

Hilary Tunstall-Behrens As a boy he was on the first Outward Bound Course ever held, at the Sea School at Aberdovey, during the Second World War. He has been an instructor at Aberdovey, and at the first German Outward Course at Plön. He sailed before the mast in the Pamir to Rio, and was for four years at the Nigerian Outward Bound School at Man O' War Bay; he has also taught at Salem.

Jocelin Winthrop-Young He was educated at Salem, 1931–3, and at Gordonstoun, 1933–8; being one of the first two boys in Gordonstoun at its foundation. He was the first Headmaster of Anavryta School, Athens, from 1948 to 1959; during which time he was also tutor to King Constantine of Greece. He has been a member of the Board of Governors of Box Hill School, the first co-educational school in England to be run on Salem lines, since 1961. Since January 1964, he has also been Director of the Boarding School in Salem.

Index